THE
KATE CHOPIN
COMPANION

The Last Chopin Home in New Orleans, 1413 Louisiana Avenue.
Photograph by Judy Cooper.

THE
KATE CHOPIN
COMPANION

*With Chopin's Translations
from French Fiction*

THOMAS BONNER, JR.

GREENWOOD PRESS
NEW YORK • WESTPORT, CONNECTICUT • LONDON

Library of Congress Cataloging-in-Publication Data

Bonner, Thomas, 1942–
    The Kate Chopin Companion : with Chopin's translations from
French fiction / Thomas Bonner, Jr.
        p. cm.
    Bibliography: p.
    ISBN 0–313–25550–4 (lib. bdg. : alk. paper)
    1. Chopin, Kate, 1850–1904—Dictionaries, indexes, etc.   2. Short
stories, French—Translations into English.   3. Short stories,
English—Translations from French.   I. Title.
PS1294.C63Z459   1988
813'.4—dc 19   88-15463

British Library Cataloguing in Publication Data is available.

Library of Congress Catalog Card Number: 88–15463
ISBN: 0–313–25550–4

First published in 1988

Greenwood Press, Inc.
88 Post Road West, Westport, Connecticut   06881

Printed in the United States of America

The paper used in this book complies with the
Permanent Paper Standard issued by the National
Information Standards Organization (Z39.48–1984).

10   9   8   7   6   5   4   3   2   1

FOR JUDITH, ASHLEY, AND LAURA

Contents

Acknowledgments

I wish to acknowledge and thank the United Negro College Fund, the Andrew W. Mellon Foundation, and Xavier University of Louisiana for their complete support of *The Kate Chopin Companion* project during the academic years 1982–1983. Institutions providing major services include the Xavier University Library, the Howard-Tilton Memorial Library of Tulane University, the New Orleans Public Library, and the Missouri Historical Society. Professor Joseph Patrick Roppolo, Professor Philip Tapley, President Norman C. Francis, Sister Rosemarie Kleinhaus, S.B.S., and Dr. Alfred Guillaume assisted in seeking sponsorship for my work. My colleague Professor Thaddeo Babiiha has been most generous with his time and advice, as have Professors Emily Toth, Barbara Ewell, Jean Bardot, Colby Kullman, and Philip Kolin. Lastly there are the persons to whom this book is dedicated, my family, for so much of it infringed on their time, needs, and energy. My thanks and appreciation go to all.

Kate Chopin has a special meaning, since my first encounter with "Désirée's Baby" in the fall of 1956 when I was a freshman at Jesuit High School in New Orleans experiencing the early stages of the end of racial segregation. Thirteen years later at Tulane University in Professor Donald Pizer's seminar on the 1890s, I rediscovered Chopin, who continues to reward my reading and study.

Introduction

In the waning years of the nineteenth century and the initial years of the twentieth century, Kate Chopin contributed two novels and nearly 100 short stories to the canon of American literature. When she began writing earnestly in St. Louis during 1888, she drew much material from her years in New Orleans and Cloutierville, Louisiana. Her narratives did record a way of life considered eccentric if not archaic by readers in Boston and New York. Her early recognition as a writer came from the exotic accounts of Acadian balls, courtship rituals, and the intermingling of races and nationalities. For more than half a century she was well known by her first collection of short stories, *Bayou Folk*, the publication of which coincided with the national interest in the literature of local color.

Although many of her narratives fit neatly into this particular fashion, she was also exploring human enigmas that over the years have defied solution. Marriage and its effect on the lives of its contractors and the community are persistent themes. Chopin examines the complex nature of the maturation of young women and their early adulthood. Children and the elderly also have a special function in the development of theme and plot. The nuances of relations among racial and national groups receive delicate probing. These subjects and others coincide with the recent national interest in the roles of an individual in a democratic society. The Civil Rights Movement in general and the Women's Movement in particular have inspired reinterpretations of Chopin's fiction. As a result, her work is enriching other generations of readers who, like those in the post-Reconstruction South, have to reevaluate themselves as they adjust to and try to control the nature of change.

Since the mid-twentieth century critics Cyrille Arnavon, Kenneth Eble, and Edmund Wilson have helped shift attention from *Bayou Folk* to *The Awakening*, the novel on which Chopin's current international reputation largely rests. In 1969 Per Seyersted, a Norwegian scholar, edited her complete works and provided an up-to-date critical biography. As a consequence of these efforts, all of Chopin's fiction—the separately published, the collected, and the newly published—became available to readers and scholars. Over the past 15 years Chopin has become, according to Paul Lauter, the thirty-seventh most taught American writer on college and university campuses. Her fiction appears now in all manner of anthologies. *The Awakening* and other stories are easily available in French and German all across Europe. A new biography by Emily Toth is being prepared and a broader range of critical books are about to be issued. A distinctly new phase of interpreting Chopin's fiction has begun.

This volume comprises a dictionary of characters, places, plot briefs, poem briefs, biographical items, and selected glossary; period maps of New Orleans, Louisiana, and Missouri, including St. Louis; and a bibliographic essay on primary and secondary sources. Also featured are Chopin's translations from the French of eight Guy de Maupassant short stories, five appearing in print for the first time, and one story by Adrien Vely. The translations appear in the order of composition: Adrien Vely's "Monsieur Pierre" (1890), August 8, 1892, published in St. Louis *Post-Dispatch*; Guy de Maupassant's "A Divorce Case" ("Un Cas de Divorce"), manuscript, July 11, 1894; "Mad?" ("Fou?"), manuscript, September 4, 1894; "It?" ("Lui?"), February 4, 1895, published in *St. Louis Life*, February 23, 1895, Vol. 11, pp. 12–13; "Solitude" ("Solitude"), March 5, 1895, published in *St. Louis Life*, December 28, 1895, Vol. 13, p. 30; "Night" ("La Nuit"), manuscript, March 8, 1895; "Suicide" ("Suicides"), December 18, 1895, published in St. Louis *Republic*, June 5, 1898; "For Sale" ("A Vendre"), manuscript, October 26, 1896; "Father Amable" ("Le Père Amable"), manuscript, April 21, 1898. The manuscripts of the stories indicated and the published versions are held by the Missouri Historical Society and are published here with the society's permission.

Chopin began reading Maupassant earnestly in 1888. She records being captivated by his writing: "Here was life, not fiction" (CW 2: 700–701). From 1892–1898, she translated carefully selected stories from different editions. During these years, she wrote the *The Awakening* and the majority of the short fiction for which she is now so well known. The translations of fiction, including Vely's, all have strong psychological themes and distinct images that clearly relate to Chopin's own fiction. The titles of the translations are immediate clues to many themes and images in the narratives. For example, "Solitude" alludes to an early title of *The Awakening*. The evening walks in "Night" suggest the walking motif in that novel, but also the recurrent use of darkness in "A Respectable Woman." Chopin's style of sexual realism owes much to "A Divorce Case." In structure, there are also indications of influence with the ironic denouement and the epistolary technique. Although Chopin planned to publish the translations, she was unsuccessful. They are more important, however, for what they reveal about her own work than for what they reveal of Maupassant's.

Chopin's narratives have roots in Missouri and Louisiana, although she has several stories with foreign settings and a few with carefully undefined settings. As her characters are often closely related to place, understanding of these relations and their attendant effects are helpful for a fuller reading, especially with repeating characters and little-known locales. For example, in *The Awakening* Robert Lebrun mourns the death of Claire Duvigné, a young lady to whom he had been devoted. His vulnerabilities are better understood if one realizes that this young woman is a central figure in "At Chênière Caminada," which presents her as a romantic image to whom a young Acadian boatman is attracted. Her refusal to consider him as more than a servant and then her death explain his reticence and shyness when he appears in *The Awakening*. Both narratives are set in New Orleans and Grand Isle. Many people know the location of New Orleans, but few have an acquaintance with Grand Isle, an island on the lower southeast coast of Louisiana. When one encounters Iron Mountain (Missouri) in "A Shameful Affair," most readers will not realize that it is located southwest of St. Louis in the Ozark plateau and that its symbolic distance from St. Louis operates in much the same way as that between New Orleans and Grand Isle. Even expressions and names have their ambivalences, for Assumption in one story refers to a Roman Catholic feast day, and in another to a civil parish (county) in Louisiana.

The dictionary delineates the characters and the places in Chopin's fiction. There are more than 900 characters and well over 200 places that affect the course of the stories and the novels. A considerable number reappear in them as major and minor elements. The variety of professions and working roles indicates much about the society that Chopin knew so well. Of significance here are many unnamed characters in principal and supporting roles who contribute to the development of social themes. The places have definite influences on the characters. The French parishes draw an intense allegiance from their citizens. The plantations and the country stores, while they function in the manner of the country houses and inns of eighteenth- and nineteenth-century English novels, suggest a demeanor or attitude about those persons who dwell or do business or seek entertainment there.

The dictionary uses an alphabetical arrangement. The annotation for a character includes name, family relationship, work in which he or she appears, description in that work, appearances in subsequent works, and commentary on relating character to theme or other aspects if helpful. The annotation for a place indicates name, location, work or works in which it appears, and description of its use. A poem brief includes title, date of composition, information on variants, meaning, images, and motifs. Biographical terms may be persons, institutions, and places important in the life of Kate Chopin; the annotation describes the subject and the relation to the author. In both characters and places there are citations of works without description or comment when repetitive material would be involved or when significance is slight. The annotation for a plot brief provides the name of the story, its date of composition, and a summary of the work.

Selected localisms, terms, and expressions also are included with an explanation of meaning. Since Chopin's fiction is now widely published, it would be impractical to link these entries to specific texts, but a few, including fragments, have become available in *A Kate Chopin Miscellany*, and these are indicated with *KCM*. A few references are made to the *Complete Works* and are indicated with *CW*. Chopin's use of dialect affects some of the spellings and names and titles, but these variations are not difficult to decipher.

The maps of relevant areas in Louisiana and Missouri should help in making the connections between characters and place, story, and setting, more concrete. Cram's 1892 map of Louisiana provides views of the northern and southern parts of the state. The Plan of New Orleans (S. Augustus Mitchell, 1872) details the French Quarter (bounded by Canal Street, Rampart Street, Esplanade Avenue, and the Mississippi River), the American Quarter above Canal Street, and the Faubourg Marigny below the French Quarter. The plat of Natchitoches (Charles Everett, 1902) reflects the town as Chopin knew it. The map of Missouri (Missouri Immigration Society, 1881) has an inset of the St. Louis area and other areas of the state related to Chopin's fiction. Reproductions of the maps are made through the courtesy of the Louisiana Collection, Tulane University Library.

The bibliographic essay, "A Guide to the Literary Works by and about Kate Chopin," is designed to assist the reader in locating primary and secondary sources. The essay opens with a discussion of relevant bibliography. Primary sources include editions, manuscripts, and letters. The section on secondary sources includes biography and criticism. Biographical sources range from the standard biography by Seyersted to shorter accounts in books on American literature. Criticism divides into general estimates, special topics and themes, and sources relating to *At Fault*, *The Awakening*, and the stories. The various parts of the essay are interdependent, so that while it can be read continuously, it can also be consulted in its specific parts.

Publications that have been especially helpful on this project include Per Seyersted, *Kate Chopin: A Critical Biography* (Baton Rouge: Louisiana State University Press, 1969); Per Seyersted, ed., *The Complete Works of Kate Chopin*, 2 vols. (Baton Rouge: Louisiana State University Press, 1969); Per Seyersted, ed., and Emily Toth, asst. ed., *A Kate Chopin Miscellany* (Natchitoches and Oslo: Northwestern State University Press, 1979); Donald A. Ringe, "Cane River World: Kate Chopin's *At Fault* and Related Stories," *Studies in American Fiction*, 3 (1975): 157–166; Patricia Hopkins Lattin, "Kate Chopin's Repeating Characters," *Mississippi Quarterly*, 3 (1980): 19–37, and Jean Bardot's "L'Influence Française dans La Vie et L'Oeuvre de Kate Chopin," (Diss., University of Paris IV—Sorbonne, 1985–1986).

Chopin has become a literary figure in the national and international senses. While a reasonable command of English enables one to read and profit from her writing, there are basic questions and confusions that this volume should resolve so that readers from Bangor, Maine, or Tours, France, can concentrate on the forms, themes, and influences that dominate Chopin's fiction.

Chronology

1805	Thomas O'Flaherty born in County Galway, Ireland.
1825	O'Flaherty comes to St. Louis, Missouri.
1839	O'Flaherty marries Catherine Reilhe.
1840	George O'Flaherty born.
1844	Thomas' wife dies; O'Flaherty marries Eliza Faris (born 1828).
1848	Thomas O'Flaherty, Jr., born.
1849?	Mme. Charleville, Eliza's mother, is widowed; resides with O'Flaherty family (perhaps as early as 1844).
1850	Katherine O'Flaherty (later Kate Chopin) born on February 8.
1855	Thomas O'Flaherty dies in a rail accident. Katherine begins study at St. Louis Academy of the Sacred Heart; becomes friends with Katherine Garesché.
1861	"Kate" and "Kitty" confirmed by Archbishop Kendrick in May.
1863	George O'Flaherty captured by Union forces during the Civil War; dies of typhoid fever. Mme. Charleville dies.
1868	Kate graduates from the Academy; keeps commonplace book from 1867 to 1870.

1869	Kate visits New Orleans, Louisiana, in the spring for three weeks; writes "Emancipation: A Life Fable" afterward.
1870	Kate marries Oscar Chopin, whose family is from France and Natchitoches Parish, Louisiana (Cloutierville area); travels to Europe on a wedding trip. Oscar's mother, Julia Benoist, dies in April; his father in November. Kitty Garesché enters the Sacred Heart convent as a postulant. Oscar and Kate move to New Orleans in October.
1871	Jean Chopin born on May 22 (first of Kate's six children). Kate traveled to St. Louis frequently during her residence in New Orleans.
1873	Oscar Chopin born.
1874	Chopins move into the Garden District from a downriver neighborhood; visit Grand Isle during summers while living in New Orleans. Oscar fights in Reconstruction Battle of Liberty Place on September 14. George Chopin born.
1876	Frederick Chopin born.
1878	Felix Chopin born.
1879	Chopins move to Cloutierville, Louisiana. Lelia Chopin born.
1882	Oscar dies of swamp fever.
1884	Kate moves to St. Louis.
1885	Eliza O'Flaherty, Kate's mother, dies in June. Dr. Frederick Kohlbenheyer, her obstetrician, becomes Kate's confidant.
1887	Kate visits Natchitoches Parish (Cane River country).
1888	Kate begins literary career by writing the poem "If It Might Be" and beginning the story "Euphraisie" (unfinished).
1889	"If It Might Be" published in *America* (Chicago) on January 16—first work in print. Stories "Wiser than a God" and "A Point at Issue" published.
1890	*At Fault* (novel) published privately.
1891	"Young Dr. Gosse" (novel manuscript later destroyed) submitted unsuccessfully to publishers.
1893	"Désirée's Baby" published in *Vogue* on January 4. Kate travels to the East.
1894	*Bayou Folk* (23 stories and sketches) published. Kate visits as she often does along the Meramec River in Missouri during the summer. "The Story of an Hour" written.
1895	"Athénaïse" written; published in 1896.

1897   *A Night in Acadie* (21 stories) published.

1898   Kate Chopin cited as one of the four leading literary figures in St. Louis by the *Star-Times*. "The Storm" written.

1899   *The Awakening* (novel) published. Offensive reviews and local displeasure with the novel and herself affect Kate personally. She travels to Wisconsin.

1900   "The Gentleman from New Orleans" written.

1903   Though ill, Kate moves the family residence to 4232 McPherson Avenue.

1904   Kate visits St. Louis World's Fair regularly; dies on August 22, two days after being taken ill at the fair.

THE
KATE CHOPIN
COMPANION

Dictionary of Characters, Places, Titles, Terms, and People from the Life and Works of Kate Chopin

A

AARON'S STORE   Louisiana (probably Natchitoches Parish). "The Wood-Choppers": It is within walking distance of Léontine's cabin by the (Cane?) river.

ABER   Pseudonym for Fred Evelyn, "A Shameful Affair." *See* Evelyn, Fred.

ABNER, UNCLE   "A No-Account Creole": The elderly black man who gossips with 'Tit-Edouard and Judge Blount in Orville, Louisiana.

L'ABRI   Natchitoches Parish, Louisiana. "Désirée's Baby": The dark and forbidding plantation home of the Aubigny family. *Abri* means shelter or shadow in French. It has a cowllike roof and big stone pillars complemented by the shadows of the nearby trees. The house in its setting suggests the hidden truth, the secret of the Aubigny family, that Armand had a black mother.

ACADIANS   The French people expelled by the British from Nova Scotia in 1755. Many settled in the coastal parishes of Louisiana where they made their living from fishing, hunting, and farming.

ACADIAN YOUTH   *The Awakening*: He offers water from a well on Chênière Caminada to cool Edna Pontellier and Robert Lebrun after the hot Sunday church service.

ACHILLE   Uncle of Athénaïse Miché and Adélaïde Martel. "Athénaïse": He tries to reason with Athénaïse to encourage her to return to her husband Cazeau. "Madame Martel's Christmas Eve": Adélaïde visits him at his home in Iberville Parish. His function in both stories is that of a wise counselor; his distance from the action gives him an oracular quality.

ADAMS AVENUE   St. Louis, Missouri. Two miles northeast of Woodland Park. "A Vocation and a Voice": The story begins with the young protagonist asking, "Is this Adams avenue?" The word Adam suggests the *Bildungsroman* mood of the story.

ADÉLAÏDE   Godmother and guardian of Polydore. "Polydore": The middle-aged woman with brown eyes and a face "fresh with its mignon features" who cares for Polydore after his mother's death. The occasion of a feigned illness by Polydore becomes the moment of their realizing their mutual affection: "She drew him close to her and kissed him as mothers kiss."

"AFTER THE WINTER" (1891)   After 25 years, Monsieur Michel's solitude in his forest retreat is broken by children picking flowers for Easter services. Enraged, he goes to the village to reprimand the offenders. Arriving at church on Easter morning, he is overcome with the spirit of the community. When he visits his old home, Joe Duplan surprises him and convinces him to return to work his old lands.

AFRICA   "A Little Country Girl": Ninette thinks of this very far away continent as she fantasizes about the circus visiting her Louisiana parish.

AGATHE, SISTER   "Lilacs": Adrienne Farival's friend from her school days and now her roommate on her annual spring visit to the convent. She was probably inspired by Chopin's friendship with Kitty Garesché, a schoolmate who entered the convent. Adrienne and Agathe's relationship has romantic overtones.

AGNES, AUNT   *At Fault*: The old black woman who first observed the crumbling riverbank. She had wanted to cross the Red River to be home with her family for supper.

"AH! MAGIC BIRD" (poem, early 1899)   Poem reveals power of a bird's song and closes with "songs of birds that never take their flight / Yonder in fields where flaming poppies grow." See *KCM* for variant lines.

AIKEN, BUD   Husband of 'Tite Reine Choupic. "In Sabine": The crude Texan who married a young Acadian woman. A ne'er-do-well, he treats her harshly in his frustration as he moves his family from place to place. He appears to be defensive in the presence of French people from Louisiana. "Ti Frère" (*KCM*): A big man, Aiken taunts Ti Frère into a fight, loses it, and heads for

Sabine Parish. Chopin uses Aiken not only as a means of exploring male-female relationships but also the contrasting manners of French Louisiana and Texas.

ALBERTA "Two Portraits": The nun who is the embodiment of goodness in this allegorical tale.

ALBERTA "Two Portraits": The wanton's "body was too beautiful to be beaten—it was made for love." A person given over to the beauty, pleasure, and power of her body, she is the opposite of the values and ideals suggested by the nun in the first section.

ALBUQUERQUE, NEW MEXICO *At Fault*: The border town mentioned by Jack Dawson in one of his bragging sessions.

ALEX ("ALECK") "Charlie": The black worker who has some responsibility for supervising others.

ALEXANDRE "Alexandre's Wonderful Experience" (*KCM*): The 14 year old who is thin with round eyes and too-long black hair. His imagination and feeling for others move him to act. A polisher/finisher in Catalan's antique shop, he assists the lady in black, and in turn she rescues him after he is fired for his honesty.

"ALEXANDRE'S WONDERFUL EXPERIENCE" (1900, *KCM*) As Alexandre is polishing furniture at Catalan's, a tall slender lady in black enters to see if anyone had indicated any interest in a small chest she has to sell. The owner denies any interest, but Alexandre remembers the doctor who sought one. He contacts the lady on his own. Noticing her sick child, he goes to see the doctor. Catalan discovers the boy's deed and replaces him. Meanwhile, the doctor and the lady marry and rescue him from a life of selling clothespoles.

ALEXANDRIA, LOUISIANA A town on the Red River southeast of Natchitoches. "Mamouche," "Madame Célestin's Divorce," "Athénaïse," "Vagabonds," "A Night in Acadie," and "Aunt Lympy's Interference."

ALICE "A Turkey Hunt": The housemaid who searches for the turkeys downriver.

ALLEGHENIES "The Maid of Saint Phillippe": The mountain range crossed by the English on their way to Illinois in 1765.

ALMIRY Wife of Si Smith. "The Going Away of Liza": Her husband indicates that she views the Rydon marriage pessimistically.

"ALONE" (poem, 1900)   A love complaint with light and dark imagery as well as conventional romantic sentiments. *See* Per Seyersted's comments in *Kate Chopin: A Critical Biography*, p. 226, note 50.

AMARANTHE   "A Night in Acadie": The woman with fine skin and a slender figure who moves gracefully and swiftly about her affairs. Telèsphore Baquette was on the verge of marrying her when he was distracted by the Valtour girls.

AMBROISE   "Azélie": The black worker on the Mathurin plantation, who receives a buckboard from the owner—a transaction resented by Azélie because he is black.

AMBROISE, M'SIEUR   "La Belle Zoraïde": The mulatto house servant of Dr. Langlé's who is considered an acceptable match for the fair Zoraïde.

AMERICAN CHILD   Daughter of Henri Carambeau and his American wife. "A Matter of Prejudice": Her illness during a birthday party at the residence of Madame Carambeau is the catalyst for the reunion of her own family and that of her father.

AMERICAN QUARTER   New Orleans, Louisiana. The area across Canal Street and upriver from the French Quarter. "A Matter of Prejudice": Used by implication to suggest the conflicts between the Creole French and the Americans. "Athénaïse."

ANDREWS, REV. DR.   "An Embarrassing Position" (one-act play): The minister who is called to the Parkham home after midnight.

ANGÈLE, MADAME   Mother of Marie Louise. "The Lilies": The widow whose calf damages another's property but whose daughter attracts a possible suitor for her. "Mamouche": Reference to the taking down of her fence.

ANGELIQUE, SISTER MARIE   "Athénaïse": The nun who taught Athénaïse at the convent school and encouraged her toward a religious vocation.

ANGELUS   The prayer to the Virgin Mary said by Roman Catholics in the early morning, at noon, and in the evening, usually at the sounding of a bell.

ANIMAL   "Emancipation: A Life Fable": The unspecified creature well cared for all of its life in a cage that discovers an open door and flees to liberty, "seeking, finding, joying, and suffering." Written about 1869, this fable focuses on the subject of liberty to be found in Chopin's later fiction.

ANNIBELLE PLACE   Louisiana (possibly Natchitoches Parish). "Aunt Lympy's Interference": The Annibelle plantation home appears as "the imposing white house through the trees"; it is near the schoolhouse where Melitte taught.

ANNIBELLE, VICTOR   "Aunt Lympy's Interference": The 22-year-old young man of landed gentry who has recently arrived home from a long period away—probably school. This shy fellow loves Melitte.

ANTOINE, MA'AME   *See* Bocaze, Madame.

ANTOINE, PÈRE   "Love on the Bon-Dieu": The Centerville, Louisiana, priest who vouches for Lalie's honesty to a local merchant. "For Marse Chouchoute": He visits Madame Verchette. *At Fault*: The priest who tries to restrain Grégoire from violence. After all the mishaps, he marries Thérèse Lafirme and David Hosmer. His experiences with the extremes of life give him both a sense of humor and an attitude of detachment. He serves several parishes.

ANTOINE'S COTTAGE, PÉRE   In a village (possibly Cloutierville) near Natchitoches, Louisiana. "Love on the Bon-Dieu": Where Lalie and Azenor wait for the priest on the porch; it adjoins the church.

ARAMINTY   *At Fault*: The black servant who avoids working for Melicent Hosmer when she visits Place-du-Bois.

ARCHIBALD   "A Morning Walk," The 40-year-old man whose encounter with Lucy changes his point of view to that of a romantic, a Wordsworthian rustic. "The Unexpected": He dies quickly, probably of tuberculosis.

ARCHITECT   "An Egyptian Cigarette": The urbane traveler who has been to the Far East and who gives an exotic cigarette to a liberal young woman. He seems to be toying with her newfound sophistication.

ARKANSAS   "Doctor Chevalier's Lie": Where the physician meets a country girl at a cabin.

AROBIN, ALCÉE   *The Awakening*: The rake whom Edna Pontellier allows to seduce her. His "reputation" extended from his attention to a consul's wife in Biloxi, Mississippi, to similar activities in New Orleans. Often in the company of ladies, he is seen at gatherings in the homes and at the racetrack. Professionally, he is a lawyer, a partner in the firm of Laitner and Arobin. The name Alcée is derived from Albert, a Cloutierville resident. *See* Laballière, Alcée.

ARSENAL STREET   St. Louis, Missouri; in the south section. "Miss McEnders."

ARTEMISE   "A Turkey Hunt": The distracted 10- to 15-year old black girl who was supposed to help the visitor in the house. It is she who finds the turkeys.

ARTIST "Caline": He sketches Caline during an unexpected stop of the train in the country and this draws her to New Orleans.

L'ARTISTE, MONSIEUR "A Point at Issue": The gentleman in whose company Charles Faraday sees his bride on the boulevard in Paris. However, they later surprise Charles with a portrait of her.

ARTLESS, EVA "An Embarrassing Position" (one-act play): The unconventional, somewhat surprising person who is reared by her father, an eccentric, retired army major.

"AS CARELESS AS THE SUMMER BREEZE" (poem, early 1899) Lyric with images of red wine, red blood, and red rose. *See KCM* for context.

ASSUMPTION, THE The Roman Catholic feast day honoring the belief that the Virgin was assumed into heaven in an uncorrupted state (August 15). Religious life and civil custom were quite integrated in nineteenth-century Louisiana.

ASSUMPTION (PARISH), LOUISIANA Located near the coastal parishes of south Louisiana. "At the 'Cadian Ball": Calixta had gone there for a while. "Madame Martel's Christmas Eve": Gustave Martel was visiting there with a college friend. "The Storm": Alcée Laballière and Calixta recall their rendezvous here.

"AT CHÊNIÉRE CAMINADA" (1893) Tonie Bocaze observes a young lady visiting the island. He falls in love with her and contrives to be in her presence— he takes her sailing once, but she regards him more as a servant. At summer's end she returns to New Orleans. He discovers that Claire Duvigné, the object of his affection, has died during the winter. He keeps the memories of her in his heart and returns to the labors of the living.

AT FAULT (1889–1890) Thérèse Lafirme, having inherited Place-du-Bois from her husband, is managing the plantation. She has just moved and reconstructed the house as the result of the new railroad. Now a lumber mill has begun operation nearby to disturb further the pastoral setting. She and its manager David Hosmer from St. Louis fall in love, but his being divorced affects their relationship. She convinces him to remarry his wife. Meanwhile, Melicent Hosmer, his sister, visits the plantation, and Grégoire Santien, Thérèse's nephew, falls in love with her. This relationship dissolves when Grégoire is involved in a killing at the mill. The Hosmers' reunion does not go well, especially after the return to Place-du-Bois to live. Fanny Hosmer, resentful of Thérèse, fails to achieve any comfort in the South. A visit by the Dawsons and Worthingtons from St. Louis helps a little. One day Fanny drowns crossing the Red River on an errand borne of her frustration. After considerable time has elapsed, Hosmer meets Thérèse on the train from New Orleans, as she had gone abroad to reconcile herself to these troubling events. The impediment to their marriage having now been removed, they are soon married by Père Antoine in nearby Centerville.

"AT THE 'CADIAN BALL" (1892)   Bobinôt goes to the ball to see Calixta and to save her from Alcée Laballière. The lively Calixta is the belle of the ball. However, Alcée, rejected by Clarisse, arrives and courts her on the porch. Meanwhile, he is summoned by Clarisse who accepts him for her husband. Calixta, who previously rejected Bobinôt, accepts him. And ritual shots end the ball.

ATHÉNAÏSE   *See* Miché, Athénaïse.

"ATHÉNAÏSE" (1895)   Married to Cazeau (a widower), the young and immature Athénaïse Miché rejects the daily realities of marriage and returns to her family. Her husband brings her back. With her brother's help, she leaves again, this time for New Orleans. There Gouvernail, attracted to her, helps her know herself through his romantic attentions. And when she discovers her pregnancy, she awakens to a passionate longing to see her husband and returns to him. A reasonable and generous man, he accepts his prodigal wife.

AUBIGNY, ARMAND   Husband of Désirée and father of an infant son. "Désirée's Baby": The issue of a white father and a black mother, he knows only that his is a fine old Louisiana family. Darkly handsome, Armand marries Désirée, who changes his character from one of cruelty and somberness to cheerfulness and generosity. His sullen nature returns on the discovery of his son's Negroid features, and his love for his wife fails. He dismisses them from the plantation and burns their belongings, during which he discovers the truth about himself—that he is black. As the story explores themes of love and miscegenation, Armand reflects the goodness of love and the evil of racism at various stages.

AUBIGNY INFANT   Son of Désirée and Armand. "Désirée's Baby": His Negroid features are discovered when he is three months old. Rejected by the father, both mother and son enter the waters of the swamp never to be seen again. The child is a "Holy Innocent," a catalyst in revealing the evils of racism.

AUBIGNY, MADAME   Mother of Armand. "Désirée's Baby": She lived and died in Paris apart from her family. Armand left her at the age of eight, not knowing that she was black. He discovers the truth at the cost of his own family. She speaks only through the fragment of a letter: "But above all . . . night and day, I thank the good God for having so arranged our lives that our dear Armand will never know that his mother, who adores him, belongs to the race that is cursed with the brand of slavery.'' Her letter provides the denouement; her color the ultimate cause of the conflict.

AUBIGNY, MONSIEUR   Father of Armand. ''Désirée's Baby'': He lived apart from his wife for many years and reared their son alone. Although he was easygoing, his solitude was reflected in the somber atmosphere of L'Abri, the Aubigny plantation, and in the sullen often cruel nature of Armand prior to his marriage. From the beginning, the Aubigny home and son project images of impending doom.

AUGUSTINE   Wife of Lacodie. ''A Sentimental Soul'': Young and pretty, she marries again shortly after Lacodie's death.

''AUNT LYMPY'S INTERFERENCE'' (1896)   Melitte De Broussard from a once-wealthy family is being forced to take a teaching job. Lympy, the old family servant, influences her uncle from New Orleans to rescue her from this degradation and take her to his home. However, Victor Annibelle, of landed gentry, loves her, and when he discovers she is about to leave, asks her to stay, and she does.

AURÉLIA   Daughter of the Jean-Ba's. ''A Little Free Mulatto'': Her parents' concern for her safety and well-being cause them to move from white society into the mulatto community. There is a naïve tone in the description of her happiness that borders on the ironic.

AURÉLIE, MAMZELLE   ''Regret'': The once-satisfied spinster who discovers loneliness after temporarily caring for a neighbor's children.

AVENDETTES   ''At Chênière Caminada'': One of the families living at Chênière Caminada, Louisiana.

AVOYELLES PARISH, LOUISIANA   Located where the Red River joins the Mississippi River. ''A Visit to Avoyelles,'' ''Mamouche,'' and ''A Night in Acadie.'' The area has a large French population.

THE AWAKENING (1897–1898)   Edna, an American, married the Creole French Léonce Pontellier. Now 28 and with two children, she is vacationing on Grand Isle when romantic experiences with Robert Lebrun touch off a realization of her own wishes and feelings. The tropical climate and the waters of the Gulf contribute to her new sense of herself. While Léonce is the first to feel the negative effects of this change, Adèle Ratignolle fears what might be coming. Mademoiselle Reisz offers her an artist's solace. When the Pontelliers return to New Orleans, she is not at home for Tuesday callers. Léonce is angry at her failure to conform to his business needs, as these are ladies related to his clients. After mutual emotional outbreaks, she seeks consolation from Mrs. Ratignolle. She continues to withdraw from her social responsibilities; however, she spends more time on her art while seeking the company of Mademoiselle Reisz. Léonce consults Dr. Mandelet and her father when he visits to determine what the problem might be. With the children in Iberville and Léonce leaving for New York on business, she begins to go to the Jockey Club for the races. There she encounters Alcée Arobin, with whom she has an affair. She quits her family home for a smaller one. When she sees Robret Lebrun after his return from Mexico, she is even more frustrated to realize the difficulties brought about by their love for each other. After witnessing the birth of Mrs. Ratignolle's child and hearing her warnings about the children, she travels to Grand Isle. There she enters the Gulf and allows herself to drown in its waters.

AZÉLIE   *See* Pauché, Azélie.

"AZÉLIE" (1893)   The daughter of a poor Acadian sharecropper, Azélie makes frequent trips to the plantation store where its manager 'Polyte becomes attracted to her and ultimately falls in love with her. When she cannot get supplies for her father on credit, she attempts to steal and 'Polyte apprehends her. With his passion increasing, he suddenly embraces and kisses her. After this scene, she accepts gifts from him, allows his caresses, but refuses to marry him. When she leaves the plantation with her father, 'Polyte follows her.

AZÉMIA   "Ti Frère" (*KCM*): The witness to Ti Frère's accident who gives him aid, resists his attentions, but finally succumbs to her own romantic feelings for him.

AZENOR   "Love on the Bon-Dieu": On the eve of Easter, he meets Lalie on the gallery of the parish rectory. Attracted to her, he makes his path cross hers regularly. He is a persistent and sensitive young man whose affection is made more intense when he fails to see her. He finds and marries her.

AZENOR, MADAME   Mother of Azenor. "Love on the Bon-Dieu": Tranquiline compares Azenor to his mother when it comes to keeping track of the larder.

B

BABETTE "Ripe Figs": The child who yearns to visit her cousins on Bayou Lafourche. She learns patience in having to wait until spring when the figs are ripe.

BABY Child of Raymond and Kitty. "Tante Cat'rinette": The grandchild of the old master who rewarded Cat'rinette.

BAKER "Lilacs": The admirer of Florine, the Farival cook. He sends her flowers, the scent of which inspires Adrienne Farival to make the last journey to the convent.

BAKER "A Sentimental Soul": A suitor of Lacodie's widow Augustine.

BAMBOULA The African-style dance performed by blacks in Congo Square on the edge of the French Quarter in New Orleans. Dramatic beating of a drum was a major part of the music. The occasions drew blacks from a wide variety of national and ethnic backgrounds, Caribbean and African.

BANQUETTE The term used by French Louisianians for sidewalks.

BAPTISTE "Odalie Misses Mass": The black boy who hides in the field.

BAPTISTE "Suzette": The slovenly cattle driver who distracts the other driver and prevents Suzette's catching his eye.

BAPTISTE, JAKE   "A Gentleman of Bayou Têche": He has a cabin near Lake Carencro; Evariste takes the wet Archie Sublet here to get dried off.

BAQUETTE, TELÈSPHORE   "A Night in Acadie": The 28-year-old bachelor weary of the social pressures to marry, who leaves his community for a solitary holiday. However, he inadvertently finds a wife on his visit to Avoyelles Parish. Telèsphore is a man about town, uncomfortable with the older social traditions.

BARATARIA BAY   Located along the southeast Louisiana coast. "At Chênière Caminada."

BARATARIAN ISLANDS   In Barataria Bay east of Caminada Bay and Grand Isle, Louisiana. *The Awakening*.

BARATARIANS   *The Awakening*: Residents of the islands in Barataria Bay, Louisiana, that are rich in the legend of the pirate Jean Lafitte.

BARODA, GASTON   "A Respectable Woman": He encourages his wife, isolated on the plantation, to be hospitable to his friend from the city, Gouvernail, who will be visiting them. Baroda is a distant person concerned only with the courtesies afforded his houseguest; he is not outwardly affectionate with his wife.

BARODA, MRS.   Wife of Gaston. "A Respectable Woman": At first hesitant about Gouvernail, a friend of her husband's who has come to visit, she grows attracted to him. Her romantic impulses are awakened by his charm and courtesy. She tries to convince her husband that she has conquered her reluctance in this ambiguous statement, "I have overcome everything! You will see. This time I shall be very nice to him." The awakening of sexual passion in Mrs. Baroda is a subject treated with more intensity in Chopin's second collection of stories, *A Night in Acadie*. As protocharacters, she and Athénaïse look toward the heroine of *The Awakening*, Edna Pontellier.

BARTNER, FRED   "The Return of Alcibiade": The commission merchant from New Orleans, who feigns the identity of Jean Baptist Plochel's son and falls in love with his granddaughter Esmée. He is one of the several characters that Chopin uses in her fiction to suggest that happiness comes from acts of charity and goodness.

BAT, JULES   "Suzette": The ferryman at Grand Ecore who witnesses Michel Jardeau's drowning in the Red River.

BATON ROUGE, LOUISIANA   Located on the Mississippi River in the south central part of the state. "Azélie": Reference to a nearby prison. "The Gentleman from New Orleans."

BAYOU   Originally from a Choctaw Indian word. A creek or small river that is usually slow, sluggish, and marshy, at least on its edges. It was used for fishing, trapping, and hunting as well as for traveling in certain areas by nineteenth-century Louisianians.

BAYOU BOISPOURRI   Natchitoches Parish, Louisiana. "In and Out of Old Natchitoches": A railroad trestle crossed it next to Alphonse Laballière's new plantation.

BAYOU BONFILS   Natchitoches Parish, Louisiana. Located near the Laborde plantation. "Charlie."

BAYOU BRULOW   Located near Grand Terre Island, Louisiana. *The Awakening*.

BAYOU CHOCTAW   Located near Natchitoches, Louisiana. "Loka": Reference to an Indian settlement here.

BAYOU DE GLAIZE   Located off the Atchafalaya River and Alabama Bayou, in south central Louisiana. "A Night in Acadie."

BAYOU DERBONNE (also Derbanne, now D'Arbonne)   Located south of Natchitoches, Louisiana. The bayou's name comes from St. Denis's companion, Gaspard Derbonne. "Vagabonds": Dr. Jureau lives close by. "A Night in Acadie" and "A Horse Story" (*KCM*).

BAYOU LAFOURCHE   Located in the river parishes of coastal southeastern Louisiana. "Ripe Figs."

BAYOU NATCHEZ COUNTRY   Between Cloutierville and Natchitoches, Louisiana. "A December Day in Dixie": Cotton was the main crop in this area.

BAYOU PIERRE   Located nearly midway between Natchitoches and Shreveport, Louisiana. "In Sabine."

BAYOU ROAD   Located in the vicinity of Bayou Derbonne (Derbanne). "A Horse Story" (*KCM*).

BAYOU ST. JOHN   Located beyond the western edge of the French Quarter, New Orleans, Louisiana. "A Lady of Bayou St. John": The isolated setting for Madame Delisle's struggle with her affections. "La Belle Zoraïde" and "Nég Créol."

BAYOU TÊCHE   Located in the St. Martinville-New Iberia, Louisiana, area made famous by Longfellow's poem "Evangeline." "A Gentleman of Bayou Têche."

BEATON, KITTY   Younger sister of Margaret. "A Point at Issue": The coy and playful girl who is "in love with her own youth, beauty, and happiness." She satisfies Charles Faraday's need for being in the presence of feminine charms.

BEATON, MARGARET   The older Beaton daughter. "A Point at Issue": She has a liberal inclination. Associated with "Women's Suffrage," she serves as the intellectual complement to Charles Faraday during his wife's absence. Chopin uses both Beaton sisters as means of showing masculine emotional and psychological needs.

BEATON, MRS.   Wife of Père and mother of Margaret and Kitty. "A Point at Issue": A traditional mother and wife who is concerned primarily with the well-being of the family.

BEATON, PÈRE   Father of Margaret and Kitty. "A Point at Issue": Charles Faraday's elder and cheerful fellow professor whose family provides comfort for Charles during the absence of his wife. This traditional family operates as a model to contrast with Charles and Eleanor's experimental one.

BEAUDELET, BAPTISTE   "At Chênière Caminada": The ferryman who takes people from Grand Isle to Chênière Caminada for Mass. *The Awakening*: Performing similar services, he appears jealous of old Monsieur Farival's sailing skills.

BEAULIEU, FATHER   The priest at the Catholic church in Cloutierville, Louisiana, during Chopin's residence. He inspired her creation of the fictional Père Antoine.

BEAUREGARD, GENERAL P.G.T.   "A Lady of Bayou St. John": Gustave Delisle died while serving under his command in Virginia during the Civil War.

"BECAUSE" (poem, ca. 1895–1899)   Makes the point that of all nature and her creatures only "man" "chooses because he will."

BEDAUT, AGAPIE   Daughter of Seraphine. "A Dresden Lady in Dixie": The young girl who steals a china figure from the Valtour home. Her public honor is saved when Pa-Jeff admits to the theft.

BEDAUT, SERAPHINE   Mother of Agapie. "A Dresden Lady in Dixie": Madame Valtour interviews her about Agapie's taking the china figure. She is properly defensive and protective in speaking of her child.

BEFURBELOWED   This suggests an exciting or active quality of feminine clothing—petticoats, flounces, ruffles.

BELAIRE, MADAME   "A Point at Issue": Eleanor Gail Faraday studies French with her in Paris as part of a nuptial agreement with her bridegroom.

BELINDY, AUNT   *At Fault*: The wrathful black servant who works for Thérèse Lafirme at Place-du-Bois.

BELLERINE, ST. ANGE DE   "The Maid of Saint Phillippe": The French commander of Fort Chartres who is expected to relinquish it to the British.

"LA BELLE ZORAÏDE" (1893)   Manna Loulou settles Madame Delisle into bed and tells her a true story: La Belle Zoraïde's refusal to marry her mistress's selection and her desire to marry Mézor cause his being sold, but not before she conceives his child. On its birth it is removed to another plantation. Zoraïde is told that the child died. She goes mad and attempts to aid her are futile.

BELLHANGER   "A Sentimental Soul": The customer in Fleurette's store who disapprovingly tells her about Augustine and Gascon's wedding.

BELLISSIME PLANTATION   Located on the Cane River in Natchitoches Parish. "Beyond the Bayou": A geographical and psychological barrier for La Folle.

BELTHROP, MRS.   *The Awakening*: A Tuesday visitor at the Pontellier home on Esplanade Street.

BELTRANS   "Ozème's Holiday": The family who lived along the Cane River. Because Ozème knew that there were many young people there, he was sure of a good time when he visited.

BEN, MR.   "The Godmother": The sheriff or marshall who holds 20 blacks in custody while investigating Everson's death. "A Little Country Girl": He advances Susan a dollar so that she can go to the circus.

BEN, UNCLE   "For Marse Chouchoute": He plays the fiddle at the dance that deters Chouchoute from his duty with the mail.

BEN, UNCLE   "Polly": The benefactor who sends Polly $100 and the promise of another such gift "when Fergusen opens up in St. Jo."

BÊNITOUS, MADAME   "The Bênitous' Slave": The fashionable milliner in Natchitoches, Louisiana, who ultimately has the personal service of Uncle Oswald, who had formerly served her family.

"THE BÊNITOUS' SLAVE" (1892)   Old Uncle Oswald believes long after he is no longer a slave that he still belongs to the Bênitous family. He keeps running away and returning to his servitude. One day he encounters little Suzanne Bênitous and follows her home. Her mother is persuaded to accept his service.

BÊNITOUS, SUZANNE   "The Bênitous' Slave": The little girl Uncle Oswald follows home after being attracted to her family name as one that he had served. "After the Winter": A few years later, she is picking roses for Easter.

BENOIST, MARIE   A relative of Chopin's and a friend of Madame Charleville's who lived on the family estate, Oakland, and had a reputation as a devotée of French authors and the classical tradition.

BÉNÔITE, MILLIE PARKINS   Wife of Thomas "Buddie." "The Gentleman from New Orleans": Faded for her years, she displays a lack of self-assertion. A family conflict has separated her from her parents for a long time. This mother of two sons and a daughter is reunited with her father and mother through a case of mistaken identity.

BÉNÔITE, THOMAS "BUDDIE"   Brother of Sophronie and husband of Millie. "The Gentleman from New Orleans": He is "good looking, energetic, a little too stout, and blustering." He and Millie have conflicts over their families and minor differences over their children—two sons and a daughter—and pets. "Buddie" in the face of Millie's concern for her ill mother becomes reconciled to reuniting the families.

BERTA   "Wiser than a God": The maid who acts in the capacity of a nurse for the ill Mrs. Von Stolz.

BESS   Sister of Nora and Stetson. "A Lady of Shifting Intentions" (*KCM*): At 30, she is as robust and tall as Beverly. She also has round cheeks, light hair, and questioning eyes.

BETSY   *At Fault*: The inoffensive black servant at Place-du-Bois. "The Godmother": She is old and ill and yet working as a maid.

BEVERLY   "A Lady of Shifting Intentions" (*KCM*): The 18-year-old boy who seems impatient waiting for his friend Will. He has impressions that don't measure up to reality.

"BEYOND THE BAYOU" (1891)   When La Folle was a child, the young master was wounded in a military skirmish and arrived at her home to seek aid. The incident "stunned her childhood reason" and ever since she had remained isolated from the plantation on the other side of the bayou. Some years later, when the young master has become the old master, his little boy is injured on a hunt and seeks her aid. She breaks her self-imposed isolation and bears him across the bayou to his home. On this occasion a new world begins to dawn for La Folle.

BÉZEAU, GRANDPA AND GRANDMA "A Little Country Girl": Ninette's stern guardians who are not in favor of her going to the circus with the rest of the community.

BIBI Son of Bobinôt and Calixta. "The Storm": The four year old who waits out the weather with his father at Friedheimer's store and washes at the cistern before returning home.

BIBINE Padue infant. "Loka": The child without a home or a people whom Loka cares for, thus finding love and security.

BICHOU, AURENDELE Sister of Odélia, Nannouche, and Xenophore. "Charlie": The Acadian field hand who is one of Charlie's playmates. She sells poultry door to door and is the recipient of a Sunday dress from Charlie.

BICHOU, FATHER AND MADAME Parents of Aurendele, Odélia, Nannouche, and Xenophore. "Charlie": He dines robustly on pork and greens while his wife stands and serves with her long bare arms. This scene showing the Acadian family dining is indicative of the family structure of this time.

BICHOU, NANNOUCHE Sister of Aurendele, Odélia, and Xenophore. "Charlie": The Acadian child who is interested in the gossip of the day.

BICHOU, ODÉLIA Sister of Aurendele, Nannouche, and Xenophore. "Charlie": The girl buying sundry items at the store.

BICHOU, XENOPHORE Brother of Aurendele, Odélia, and Nannouche. "Charlie": The youngster who finds Charlie Laborde a piece of hickory after dinner and follows her into the woods to protect her. He is a witness to the shooting of Firman Walton by Charlie.

BIDDLE STREET St. Louis, Missouri. *At Fault*: The site of new housing.

BIENVILLE STREET New Orleans, Louisiana. *The Awakening*: Mademoiselle Reisz once lived on this thoroughfare in the Vieux Carré.

BILLY, MR. "The Lillies": the gruff bachelor planter whose sensitivities are exposed by a little girl. "Mamouche": Mamouche recalls his earlier misdeeds to him.

BILOXI, MISSISSIPPI   An early colony established by Pierre LeMoyne, Sieur d'Iberville, in Chopin's time it was a resort and fishing town on the Gulf of Mexico. "The Storm": Clarisse is visiting there when her husband Alcée Laballière has an affair with Calixta. *The Awakening*.

BISHOP, THE   "The Impossible Miss Meadows": He sends the unfortunate Miss Meadows to vacation with the Hyleigh family.

BISHOP OF NATCHITOCHES, THE   *At Fault*: He asks to say a Mass for the dead Grégoire Santien. "Madame Célestin's Divorce": She cites him in a humorous litany of the hierarchy.

BLACK BOY   "Athénaïse": While Athénaïse is at the Miché home, she observes him feeding Cazeau's "brace of snarling, hungry dogs."

BLACK GABE   "Athénaïse": Cazeau recalls the capture of this runaway slave as he accompanies his "runaway" wife homeward. This moment of memory underscores the theme examining the relation of bondage and freedom in marriage.

BLACK-GAL   Daughter of Susan and Pap. "A Little Country Girl": Ninette's yard-friend; Ninette attends the circus with the black girl's family.

BLACK GIRL, LITTLE   *The Awakening*: She operates the treadle of Madame Lebrun's sewing machine and performs various errands for her.

BLACK WOMAN   "A Wizard from Gettysburg": She objects to the young Bertrand Delmandé bringing someone who looks like a tramp onto the veranda to sit in his father's chair. She has a keen sense of social order.

BLACK WOMAN SERVANT   *The Awakening*: Working at the Chartres Street home of the Lebruns, she argues about being able to do her duties, one of which is answering the door bell. Social roles and status are persistent interests in Chopin's fiction.

BLANCO BILL   "A Horse Story" (*KCM*): The master of Ti Démon (the pony) on the Indian "Nation."

BLIND MAN   "The Blind Man": He makes his way without a guide stick to sell pencils from a red box and manages to get safely from place to place, unlike the wealthy, sighted man whose hurried life is stopped by an accident with an electric car. He is nearly an allegorical figure here.

"THE BLIND MAN" (1896)   A blind man makes his way without a stick selling pencils from a red box. On a side street children molest him, but after some confusion a policeman sends him on. A wealthy business man is nearly killed by a street car, but the blind man ambles on.

BLISS, LAURA   "Polly": Recently married, she receives a modern lamp like the one being admired by Mr. Fulton at the party.

BLOOMDALE, MISS   *At Fault*: One of Melicent Hosmer's St. Louis friends and bridge partners, this "fat" woman goes to social events to show off her jewelry.

BLOSSOM   Daughter of Aunt Maryllis and sister of Demins. "Charlie": The black worker at the Laborde house who runs errands and makes much noise doing them.

LE BLÔT   "Love on the Bon-Dieu": He has a home on Bayou Bon-Dieu near Madame Zidore's.

LE BLÔT'S PLACE   Natchitoches Parish, Louisiana. "Love on the Bon-Dieu": The plantation on the Bon-Dieu where Butrand works.

BLOUNT, JUDGE   "A No-Account Creole": The "staid" gentleman, who still manages to exchange country wisdom and gossip with the townspeople of Orville, Louisiana.

BLUDGITT CREEK   Located near Bludgitt Station, Missouri. "The Going Away of Liza": It is unbridged in this area.

BLUDGITT STATION, MISSOURI   "The Going Away of Liza."

BOBINÔT   Husband of Calixta and father of Bibi. "At the 'Cadian Ball": The earnest young fellow, once rejected by Calixta, who finally has his proposal to her accepted. "The Storm": He is absent from his home during a storm and is cuckolded by Alcée Laballière. Bobinôt is good-natured, but he lacks the zeal and passion of Alcée.

BOCAZE, ANTOINE (TONIE)   "At Chêniére Caminada": The Acadian fisherman who is attracted to Claire Duvigné, a Creole young lady visiting the Chêniére. A romantic, he is crushed by the winter death of Claire. *The Awakening*: He is described as shy and unwilling to face any woman except his mother. His situation is used to explore the differences between Acadians and Creoles and the implications of these differences.

BOCAZE, MADAME ANTOINE   Mother of Antoine. "At Chênière Caminada": She comforts Tonie after he returns from his luckless pursuit of Claire Duvigné. *The Awakening*: She offers Edna Pontellier a room in which to sleep and later regales her and Robert Lebrun with stories.

BODEL, MR.   "A Night in Acadie": His home is the setting for a card game with Wat Gibson and a fight between André Pascal and Telèsphore Baquette over Zaïda Trodon.

BOISDURÉ, AGLAÉ (LA CHOUETTE)   Stage name: Mademoiselle de Montallaine. "Nég Créol": A Creole woman in financial, social, and physical decline. Chicot devotes himself to her, but fails to acknowledge her death.

BOISDURÉ JEAN   "Nég Créol": The old master of the Boisduré family who was revered by Chicot (*see* Xavier).

BOLTONS, MRS. ELEANOR   *The Awakening*: A Tuesday visitor at the Pontellier home on Esplanade Street.

BON-ACCUEIL PLANTATION   Located in west central Louisiana. "A Wizard from Gettysburg." The Delmandé family home and the setting for the post-Civil War restoration of the family.

BONAMOUR, EVARISTE ANATOLE   Father of Martinette. "A Gentleman of Bayou Têche": Visitors see him as part of the local Acadian color, but he and his daughter are concerned that he not be offended as an individual.

BONAMOUR, MARTINETTE   Daughter of Evariste. "A Gentleman of Bayou Têche": Concerned about a possible indignity to her Acadian father, she expresses herself on the matter.

BON-DIEU, THE   A bayou in Natchitoches Parish, Louisiana. "Love on the Bon-Dieu": Lalie lives near this bayou. "Athènaïse": Reference is made to the rigolet of the Bon-Dieu.

BONFILS, DR.   "The Bênitous' Slave": He decides that it is time to put the old man, Uncle Oswald, in an institution. "Beyond the Bayou": He attends Chéri.

BONHAM ROAD   Natchitoches Parish, Louisiana. "A Horse Story" (*KCM*): Perhaps this is the Texas Road.

BONNEAU, ARISTIDES   "Ti Démon": He is nearly beaten to death by the friend whom he tricked.

BORDON, JACQUES   Son of Sylveste and brother of Lolotte, Nonomme, and Sylveste. "A Rude Awakening": The middle child.

BORDON, LOLOTTE   Daughter of Sylveste and sister of Nonomme, Sylveste, and Jacques. "A Rude Awakening": The eldest child who cares for the younger children and accepts responsibility beyond her capacity.

BORDON, NONOMME   Son of Sylveste and brother of Lolotte, Jacques, and Sylveste. "A Rude Awakening": The youngest son who is sickly. He is finally cared for by Madame Duplan.

BORDON, SYLVESTE   The father of Lolotte, Nonomme, Sylveste, and Jacques. "A Rude Awakening": Disorderly in the care of his children, he is shocked into becoming a responsible father by the planter Joe Duplan.

BORDON, SYLVESTE (VEVESTE)   Eldest son of Sylveste and brother of Lolotte, Nonomme and Jacques. "A Rude Awakening": The small child who is in sympathy with his father's good humor at breakfast.

BOREDOMVILLE   An imaginary town near St. Louis, Missouri. "Miss Witherwell's Mistake."

BOTTON, MR. BILLY   "The Gentleman from New Orleans": It is on his place in Natchitoches Parish that good wine is made, although it is said to be not as good as that in New Orleans.

BOULÔT AND BOULOTTE   "Boulôt and Boulotte": Twelve-year-old twins who go to town to buy shoes.

"BOULÔT AND BOULOTTE" (1891)   These twins save their picayunes to go to town to buy new shoes. The children await their return. When the two are spied through the branches, the children grow excited. However, they are amazed to see the new shoes—not on the twins' feet but in their hands. In answer to the surprised looks, Boulotte states that they are not going to ruin their shoes in the dust.

BOY (QUADROON)   *See* La Blanche.

BOY, THE   Later Brother Ludovic. "A Vocation and a Voice": The orphan in search of love and security who is seduced by Suzima. He leaves her and the gypsies for a monastery, but one day returns to her.

BOWER, NAT   "Ti Frère": The "half-breed" who runs regular card and dice games at his cabin on the lake, the scene of drinking and fighting as well as playing.

BOWER'S CABIN   Located in Natchitoches, Louisiana, area on the rim of a lake fed by the bayou that runs along the road through the fields. "Ti Frère": A type of boathouse where regular card and dice games take place.

BRADLEY, GUS   "Charlie": The son of a planter near Les Palmiers and friend of the Labordes who is shy and patient in his romantic attentions to Charlie. A big and awkward fellow, he has fine hair and a smooth face. He is responsible not only in his treatment of the sisters but also in his concern for their father.

BRAINARD, GEORGE   "Wiser than a God": The cheerful and energetic ivy-leaguer who while on vacation from school falls in love with Paula Von Stoltz when he hears her play the piano. Despite her attraction to him, she rejects his proposal of marriage.

BRAINARD, MISS   Sister of George. "Wiser than a God": She is concerned that Paula Von Stoltz be able to play dance music on the piano, for she has a good reputation as a popular singer who performs regularly at family affairs. Miss Brainard is a light contrast to the serious Paula.

BRAINARD, MRS.   Mother of George and Miss Brainard. "Wiser than a God": Wealthy and "radiantly attired," she hosts a party for which Paula von Stoltz has been hired to play the piano. Her characterization is sketchy and bordering on caricature.

BRAINARD, MRS.   Wife of George. "Wiser than a God": The "little black-eyed wife" who is unhappy about her husband's loss of his musical talents.

BRANTAIN, MR.   "The Kiss": The successful suitor for Nathalie's hand in marriage who is described as "insignificant," "unattractive," and "enormously rich."

BRANTONNIERE, ADÈLE   Sister of Bosé and Fifine. "A Family Affair."

BRANTONNIERE, BOSEY (BOSÉ)   Daughter of Madame Solisante's sister and sister of Adèle and Fifine. "A Family Affair": She comes to her aunt's home to help her in her distress and to help her own mother by recovering misappropriated items from her grandmother's estate. This spunky young woman forces her aunt to take charge of her life once again.

BRANTONNIERE, FIFINE   Sister of Bosé and Adèle. "A Family Affair.

BRANTONNIERE, MRS.   Mother of Bosé, Fifine, and Adèle; sister of Félicie Solisante. "A Family Affair": She interests her daughter Bosé in going to the country to help her older sister who is nearly crippled.

BREAZEALE, MARIE   Sister of Oscar Chopin and wife of Phanor (m. 1884). In a letter Chopin comments on the intensity of her wifely affection for Phanor (*KCM*).

BREAZEALE, PHANOR   Brother-in-law of Chopin and husband of Marie Chopin. As the district attorney of Natchitoches, Louisiana, he told Chopin much about the political and social conditions of the region. He also was a member of the U.S. Congress.

BRIGHTMAN, NATHAN   "Elizabeth Stock's One Story": The wealthy man of the town who receives mail at his home on the hill during winter weather from Elizabeth Stock, whose assistance enables him to meet an appointment. The son of one of his business friends takes her job in the post office.

BRIGHTMAN, MARGARET   Wife of Nathan. "Elizabeth Stock's One Story": She helps Elizabeth recover from the winter trek to deliver the mail to the Brightman home.

BRIGITTE   "Nég Créole": The Irishwoman who lives with Janie and others on the floor below Aglaé Boisduré's room and who offers help to the ailing Creole woman.

BRINKE, MRS.   *At Fault*: The friend and card partner of Melicent Hosmer's who has read a paper on Hegel and published one on Dante. She lives in St. Louis, Missouri.

BRITTON, SALLIE   The schoolmate of Chopin's who was not a Catholic; as a result, Chopin was not allowed to stay overnight at her home.

BROTHER OF FEDORA AND CAMILLA   "Fedora": He is disappointed that he can't drive the horse to pick up Miss Malthers at the station.

BROTHER LUDOVIC   *See* Boy, the.

BROZÉ, MADAME   Related to Gamiche. "Dead Men's Shoes": She rears her poverty-stricken family in Caddo Parish. She and her two daughters as well as Septime are Snopes-like characters.

BROZÉ, SEPTIME   "Dead Men's Shoes": The crippled man who is one of Gamiche's surviving kin.

BRUCE   "At the 'Cadian Ball": The black worker who tells Clarisse of Alcée Laballière's destination.

BRUNO   ''A Harbinger'': The artist who falls in love with his model.

BUTRAND   ''Love on the Bon-Dieu'': ''He works on Le Blôt's Bon-Dieu place.'' Père Antoine has recently spoken with him of Madame Zidore.

''BY THE MEADOW GATE'' (poem, 1898)   A 24-line romantic lyric in the manner of an ode with maiden, dream, grass, birds, and evening star. See *KCM* for line variants.

BYARS, WILLIAM VINCENT   A St. Louis poet (b. 1857) who published a number of books of poetry and prose. Chopin admired the music of his verse.

C

CADDO PARISH, LOUISIANA Located in the northwestern corner of the state. "In Sabine" and "Dead Men's Shoes": An economic and cultural wasteland.

CADIAN BAYOU Not far from the village (Cloutierville, Louisiana). "Ti Démon: The body of water that is close to the protagonist's home.

CAIRO, EGYPT "An Egyptian Cigarette": Visited by the architect.

CAJUN The corruption of the word Acadian that is frequently used by Acadians to describe themselves.

CALIFORNIA *At Fault*: Melicent intended to visit this state for its flora.

CALINE "Caline": Drawn by the romance of the artistic life, she finds disillusionment. She never finds the boy who made her picture when the train stopped near her home. She has long brown legs and black hair—a pretty Acadian girl.

"CALINE" (1892) Asleep outside in the country, Caline awakens to a train stopped nearby. One of the passengers milling about has a sketchbook in which he begins a picture of her, but the train departs before he is finished. She yearns for romance and goes to the city where she is disillusioned to find that her attraction is for the young man and not for the city.

CALIXTA   "At the 'Cadian Ball'": The young lady of Spanish descent (her mother was from Cuba) and coquettish charm who is attracted to Alcée Laballière. After an escapade in Assumption Parish and the evening at the ball, she marries Bobinôt. "The Storm": After five years of marriage to Bobinôt, she responds amorously to Alcée when he comes by for shelter during a storm and during the absence of her husband and four-year-old son Bibi. Chopin uses her to portray the Spanish presence in French Louisiana.

CALVARY CEMETERY   St. Louis, Missouri. Burial Place of Chopin; grave marker has incorrect birthdate.

CAMI   "After the Winter": The cobbler's son who warns Trézinie about Michel's place and picks flowers with her there anyway. "Mamouche": The heavy and stupid child who sleeps with his mouth open.

CAMILLA   Sister of Fedora. "Fedora": She went to school with the Malther's girl, to whose brother Fedora is attracted.

CAMINADA BAY   Located on the leeward side of Grand Isle, Louisiana. *The Awakening*: Edna sails across this bay with Robert; it is the prelude to an awakening.

CAMPBELL DOCTOR   "For Marse Chouchoute": The physician Mr. Hudson calls to treat the injured Wash.

CAMP STREET   New Orleans, Louisiana. The upriver side of Canal Street in the American Quarter. "A Matter of Prejudice."

CAMPTE, LOUISIANA   A community across the Red River near Natchitoches (current spelling: Campti). "Tante Cat'rinette": It is large enough to support a store.

CANAILLE   A French expression of disapprobation. It suggests that someone is a blackguard, scum, or scoundrel.

CANAL STREET   New Orleans, Louisiana. The main thoroughfare dividing the French Quarter from the newer American section. "A No-Account Creole" and *The Awakening*.

CANE RIVER   This and the Red River are the two main bodies of water in the Natchitoches area of Louisiana. It connects Natchitoches and Cloutierville. "A No-Account Creole," "The Return of Alcibiade," "In and Out of Old Natchitoches," "Ozème's Holiday," "Polydore," "Athénaïse," "Vagabonds," and *At Fault*.

CARAMBEAU, HENRI "A Matter of Prejudice": After marrying an American young lady, he becomes alienated from his mother, whose French Creole disposition does not allow for such mixing of nationalities. Henri is described as "big, goodlooking, honest faced, [with] tender brown eyes, [and] firm mouth." *See* American child.

CARAMBEAU, MADAME Mother of Henri. "A Matter of Prejudice": An old Creole woman who rejects the change brought about by the newly arrived Americans, but who after an encounter with a little American girl (her granddaughter) and great personal turmoil accepts it by attending Christmas Mass in an American church and calling on her son's family. *See* Carantelle, Madame.

CARAMBEAU, MRS. Wife of Henri. "A Matter of Prejudice": This young American lady has a "sweet, fresh face" and speaks "school French." She is the mother of "the American child."

CARANTELLE, MADAME Mother of Mrs. Duplan. "A No-Account Creole": Euphraisie Manton stays at her home on a visit to New Orleans. She is "a delightfully conservative old lady" who had not been to the American side of Canal Street in many years. *See* Carambeau, Madame, and La Folle for similar behavior patterns.

CARENCRO LAKE Located in southwestern Louisiana near Bayou Têche. "A Gentleman of Bayou Têche": Close to the Hallet plantation, it is the setting for much of this story.

CAROLINAS North and South Carolina. "La Belle Zoraïde."

CARONDELET STREET New Orleans, Louisiana; in the American Quarter. *The Awakening*.

CARROLTON, LOUISIANA (CARROLLTON) Then a distant town or suburb in the upriver vicinity of New Orleans. *The Awakening*.

CASSIMELLE, PÈRE "Polydore": The priest who hears Polydore's confession when he visits Adélaïde, gives him a long penance, and tells him that he deserves a beating; Adélaïde is outraged at his comments.

CATALAN, MR. G. "Alexandre's Wonderful Experience" (*KCM*): The shady proprietor of an antique furniture store in New Orleans who deceives the lady in black. After discharging Alexandre for his revelation of the fraud, he hires a stout German boy to replace him. There seems to be a social interest in Chopin's having Catalan (Spanish) choose a German youth to replace a Creole one.

CAT ISLAND   Located east of Last Island near Timbalier Bay. *The Awakening*.

CATALAN'S ANTIQUE SHOP   New Orleans, Louisiana. "Alexandre's Wonderful Experience" (*KCM*): The place where Alexandre meets the lady in black.

CATEAUS   "At the 'Cadian Ball": Calixta walks to the ball with this family, but she leaves without them.

CATICHE   *The Awakening*: In the suburbs of New Orleans. The mulattress who operates a garden cafe within walking distance of Esplanade Street.

CATO   "An Embarrassing Position" (one-act play): The old black servant.

CAT'RINETTE, TANTE   "Tante Cat'rinette": The old black recluse who gives up her home and some of her independence to help the descendants of her old master. Essentially, she executes a contract with them.

CAVALRY OFFICER   *The Awakening*: The sad-eyed gentleman the young Edna (later Pontellier) had once been attracted to when he visited her father. His image recurs as she slips beneath the Gulf waters to her death.

CAVANELLE   Brother of Mathilde. "Cavanelle": The storekeeper, who lives his life through his ambition for his sister, then through his concern for his aunt. His seemingly selfless nature has a dark psychological aspect.

CAVANELLE, FELICIE   "Cavanelle": She comes from Terrebonne Parish after Cavanelle's sister Mathilde dies, so that he can care for her.

CAVENELLE, MATHILDE   Sister of Cavenelle. "Cavenelle": A sickly person and a singer of little talent whose brother seems to have pretensions for her singing in the opera. Cavanelle cares for her until her death.

"CAVANELLE" (1894)   A lady is in love with Cavanelle, who for years has looked after his sister with hopes of establishing her as a professional singer. When she dies, the lady, seeking companionship, visits him again, only to find that he is now caring for his aunt. At first angry, she becomes resolved to his self-sacrificing ways.

CAWEIN, MADISON (1865–1914)   A poet and friend of Chopin's who wrote works that reflected his affection for his native state of Kentucky, and his appreciation of Keats and Swinburne.

CAZEAU   Husband of Athénaïse. "Athénaïse": A patient and generous man, he is a widower of ten years when he marries the young Athénaïse. Not only does he draw on his own marital experience, but he also considers the nature of marriage in the light of other relationships of bondage. He allows his wife the opportunity of a second chance and a second decision after her frightened flight from him soon after their marriage.

CEDAR BRANCH   An imaginary location. "A Mental Suggestion." *See* Cedars, The.

CEDARS, THE   Located near St. Louis, Missouri. The city's society often spent summers on this former plantation. Chopin cites the Banhardt family in one instance (*KCM*). She herself composed "The Night Came Slowly" and "Juanita" there in July 1894.

CÉLESTIN   "Madame Célestin's Divorce.": After working and lying about for six months in Alexandria, he returns to his wife, who changes her mind about divorcing him.

CÉLESTIN, MADAME   "Madame Célestin's Divorce": The good woman with a sense of humor who is married with two children. She responds to Lawyer Paxton's flirtations during her husband's absence but then rejects his suggestion that she get a divorce.

CELESTINE   *The Awakening*. The black servant who accompanies Edna Pontellier when she moves to the little "pigeon house." Old and discreet, she cooks and looks after Edna's domestic affairs.

CÉLINA'S HUSBAND   *The Awakening*. Mariequita sullenly speculates on running away with him.

CENTERVILLE, LOUISIANA   Located on the railroad five miles from Place-du-Bois. *At Fault*: The town where Grégoire Santien raises "Cain."

CHALON, DR.   "Tante Cat'rinette": Interested in receiving pay for his work, he refuses to come to Kitty's aid.

CHARLEVILLE, FREDERICK ALEXANDER   A relative who had moved to California and for whom Eliza Faris O'Flaherty was concerned.

CHARLEVILLE, VICTOIRE VERDON (1780–1863) Maternal great-grandmother of Chopin. As the family storyteller, she taught Chopin about her family and region (St. Louis).

CHARLIE   *See* Laborde, Charlotte "Charlie."

"CHARLIE" (1900)   Of the seven Laborde daughters, Charlie causes the most difficulty with her tomboy ways. The governess has unusual trouble with her studying. When she manages to shoot a plantation visitor, she is sent to a convent school in New Orleans, where she excels. When her father is seriously wounded in an accident, Charlie returns to take over his responsibilities while Aunt Clementine makes arrangements for her sisters.

CHARTRAND   "Suzette": The landowner with hired hands.

CHARTRAND, LOUIS, MR.   *At Fault*: The owner of a store. "Love on the Bon-Dieu": One of his interests is promissory notes for credit agreements. He is based on Charles Bertrand, whose store was burned by Union troops in 1864.

CHARTRAND'S STORE   Centerville, Louisiana. *At Fault*: Twenty yards from Grammont's store, it is the place where Grégoire tries to get the blacks to drink with Louis Chartrand.

CHARTRES STREET   New Orleans, Louisiana. Runs through the French Quarter, parallel to the Mississippi River. "A Sentimental Soul": A place of small shops and living quarters. *The Awakening*: Where the Lebruns live when away from Grand Isle.

LA CHATTE   "A No-Account Creole": The older white-haired black woman who has been instrumental in rearing the Santien boys. She functions to provide accounts of family history and behavior. Her lively characterization is in the tradition of a black mammy.

CHENE   Child of Mademoiselle Salambre. "Miss McEnders": Through this child Georgie McEnders first comes to some new understandings.

CHÊNIÈRE   A small rise of land in a marshy coastal area that has live and water oak trees growing on it. In the vast Louisiana lowlands along the coast, chênières became sites of small settlements.

CHÊNIÈRE CAMINADA   An oak-filled island across Caminada Bay from Grand Isle, Louisiana. "At Chênière Caminada": Where Tonie Bocaze meets Claire Duvigné. *The Awakening*: Where Edna Pontellier experiences an awakening of the senses and her emotions.

LES CHÊNIERS   Natchitoches, Louisiana, area. *At Fault*: The Joseph Duplan plantation on the Cane River some distance from Place-du-Bois. "A Rude Awakening" and "After the Winter."

CHÉRI   ''Beyond the Bayou'': The master's son who is wounded by accident and triggers La Folle's recovery from her fear of crossing the bayou.

CHÉRIE   Daughter of the lady in black. ''Alexandre's Wonderful Experience'' (*KCM*): Small and delicate, she is an invalid. Both Alexandre and the doctor are moved by her condition to become involved with her mother.

CHEVALIER, DR.   ''Dr. Chevalier's Lie'': He acts nobly in the situation of a young woman's suicide, as he covers up the deed.

CHICAGO, ILLINOIS   ''The Impossible Miss Meadows.''

CHICOT   *See* Xavier, César François.

CHILD   ''Beyond the Bayou'': The youngster calls public attention to La Folle's crossing the bayou. Chopin uses children frequently in this way as narrative devices.

CHOCTAW JOE   ''Loka'': Loka remembers him as an Indian given to revelry and violence.

CHOPIN, FELIX (1878–1955)   Son of Kate and Oscar Chopin. His description of his mother appears in *KCM*.

CHOPIN, FREDERICK (1876–1953)   Son of Kate and Oscar Chopin.

CHOPIN, GEORGE (1874–1952)   Son of Kate and Oscar Chopin. His wife commented on the importance of writing in his mother's life. He was a physician.

CHOPIN, JEAN-BAPTISTE (1871–1911)   Son of Kate and Oscar Chopin.

CHOPIN, JULIA BENOIST (1820–1870)   Wife of Victor Jean-Baptiste Chopin and mother of Oscar Chopin. She was born in Cloutierville; shortly after her marriage, she moved to the McAlpin plantation.

CHOPIN, LAMY   Brother of Oscar Chopin. He managed the Chopin plantation, which had been divided by the railroad.

CHOPIN, LELIA (HATTERSLEY) (1879–1962)   Daughter of Oscar and Kate Chopin. In 1880 the Cane River packet was named for her. A letter quoted in Seyersted's biography shows her to be understanding of the joy and sadness that her mother found in her life.

CHOPIN, OSCAR (1845–1882)   Son of Julia Benoist and Victor J.B. Chopin; husband of Kate O'Flaherty; brother of Lamy and Eugenie; father of Jean, Oscar, George, Frederick, Felix, and Lelia. As a boy he suffered under his father's demanding nature and left home after the family's return from France at the close of the Civil War. He moved to St. Louis, where he met Kate at Oakland. After their marriage and European tour, they settled in New Orleans where he worked as a cotton factor, and then Cloutierville, where he contracted swamp fever and died. His politics were conservative, and he participated in the Battle of Liberty Place (New Orleans) as a member of the White League.

CHOPIN, OSCAR, JR. (1873–1933)   Son of Oscar and Kate Chopin. He provided a sketch or description of his mother's parlor in St. Louis where she worked and gathered her literary friends (St. Louis *Post Dispatch*, November 26, 1899).

CHOPIN, DR. VICTOR JEAN-BAPTISTE   Husband of Julia Benoist and father of Oscar, Lamy, and Eugenie. He had a reputation for being cruel and dictatorial to his wife, family, and slaves. His wife separated from him for a few years and the slaves made consistent attempts to escape. During the Civil War, while he was in France, his profits grew as the wealth of his neighbors in Natchitoches dwindled and he met considerable resentment on his return. His son Oscar, who was forced to work as an overseer, left for St. Louis. At first he objected to Oscar's marriage because Kate was Irish, but she won him over with her personality, French, and music. The doctor died in 1870 during the first year of the marriage.

CHOPPIN, DR.   "A Sentimental Soul": The expensive physician who treated Lacodie the week before the locksmith died.

CHOTARD, MADAME   Mother of Odalie. "Odalie Misses Mass": She leaves Odalie with Aunt Pinky on the Assumption and goes to Mass. "Ti Frère" (*KCM*): Azémia goes to Mass with her and her family on Sunday.

CHOTARD, ODALIE   "Odalie Misses Mass": The 13-year-old who gives up the pleasure of showing off her dress at the Mass celebrating the Assumption and assumes the role of Miss Paulette as she cares for and entertains the old black woman.

CHOUCHOUTE   *See* Verchette, Armand.

CHOUPIC   Son of Baptiste. "Mamouche": One of the undesirable candidates for younger companion of Dr. John-Luis.

CHOUPIC, BAPTISTE   Father of 'Tite Reine. "In Sabine" and "Mamouche." *See* Reine, 'Tite.

CHOUTEAU, LIL   Daughter of Marion A. Baker. Probably related by marriage to Laclede's lover Marie Thérèse Bourgeois Chouteau. Chopin received a letter from her during her European wedding trip.

CINCINNATI, OHIO   *At Fault.*

CINDY   "A Wizard from Gettysburg": The black servant on the Bon-Accueil plantation who is wary of strangers and concerned about the silver when the youngest Delmandé brings this old man into the house.

CISTERN   An artificial reservoir of water often located near the house so that the rain could run into it from the roof. Usually of wooden construction, it required periodic cleaning and the removal of foreign objects, which sometimes included lizards and snakes in Louisiana.

CITÉ   *The Awakening*: The young black woman who understood French and helped Mrs. Ratignolle with sorting the laundry.

CITY OF MEXICO   *See* Mexico City.

CLAIRE   "The Godmother": She and her cousin Lucie are not getting along well, and as a result she is not invited to her cousin's card party.

CLAIRGOBEAU   "A Point at Issue": The old couple who let a room on the Rue Rivoli in Paris to Edna Gail Faraday while she studies French.

CLARISSE   Goddaughter of Madame Laballière. "At the 'Cadian Ball": She is "dainty as a lily; hardy as a sunflower; slim, tall, graceful, like one of the reeds that grow in the marsh . . . cold and kind and cruel." After difficulties she marries Alcée Laballière who had startled her with his passion. "The Storm": Now Alcée's wife, she is in Biloxi, Mississippi, without him for a holiday. "In and Out of Old Natchitoches": Alphonse Laballière is her cousin.

CLÉMENTINE   "Ma'ame Pélagie": The old black nurse who looks after Pauline Valmêt.

CLÉMENTINE   Aunt of the Laborde daughters and Esmée (Plochel). "Charlie": The formal somewhat pompous lady who lives in New Orleans. Her plans include educating the Laborde daughters in Europe. She looks after them as a mother would. Julia Laborde is compared to her angellike character. "The Return of Alcibiade'': Esmée is to go to her when her grandfather dies if there is no one to care for her. Chopin makes frequent use of parent substitutes in her fiction.

CLÉOPHAS   "A Very Fine Fiddle": The old man who loves to play his fiddle, which was a gift from a late Italian friend.

CLERK   "A Pair of Silk Stockings": "He could not reconcile [Mrs. Sommers's] shoes with her stockings."

CLOUTIERVILLE, LOUISIANA   Located on the Cane River in Natchitoches Parish, Kate Chopin lived here in the early 1880s. "For Marse Chouchoute": The town three miles from the railway station. "Mamouche," "The Return of Alcibiade," "In Sabine," "Ozème's Holiday," and "Madame Martel's Christmas Eve." When Chopin refers to "the village" in other stories, she often means Cloutierville, "two long rows of very old frame houses."

COCHON DE LAIT   A suckling pig was a major culinary delight among the Acadians; it was split and roasted as it hung turning before the hot coals of a bonfire. The term was sometimes used as an expression of endearment for a child.

COLFAX, LOUISIANA   *At Fault*: Rufe Jimson intended to stop here on his way from Place-du-Bois to Grant Parish, Louisiana.

COLFAX WOMAN   "A Night in Acadie": She killed her old husband, cut him up, and salted him in a barrel.

COLIMARTS   Located near Natchitoches, Louisiana. "Charlie": The plantation not far from Les Palmiers that had a dance teacher.

COLLINS   "Elizabeth Stock's One Story": Nathan Brightman's business correspondent whose son becomes postmaster of Stonelift.

COLLINS   "Elizabeth Stock's One Story": The son of an influential St. Louis businessman and the new postmaster of Stonelift who is sensitive and poetically inclined.

COLONEL, THE   *The Awakening*: The widower and Confederate veteran who is Edna Pontellier's father. He has a plantation in Mississippi and is a devoted Presbyterian. Tyrannical and self-centered, he has little feeling for others and preaches on authority and the Bible. His manner caused his wife's death.

COOK   *The Awakening*: She often needs Mrs. Pontellier's supervision in the preparation of meals.

"COME TO ME" (poem, early 1899)   An erotic sentiment with images of eyes, lips, and cheeks. *See KCM* for line variants.

CONGO SQUARE   New Orleans, Louisiana. Located across from the western rampart (Rampart Street now). "La Belle Zoraïde": Where the blacks gathered to dance and to enjoy music and singing.

CONSHOTTA, LOUISIANA (probably Coushatta)   Located between Natchitoches and Shreveport. "The Godmother": Everson came from this town; he had a brother here.

CORBEAU   "The Return of Alcibiade": This "grif" boy waits tables at Jean Baptiste Plochel's.

CORNSTALK, TEXAS   *At Fault*: The raw and rough town where Grégoire Santien is killed.

CÔTE JOYEUSE   Natchitoches Parish, Louisiana, on the Cane River. "Ma'ame Pélagie": Where the ruins of the Valmêt plantation stand. "Vagabonds."

COTON MAÏS   "Désirée's Baby": He operates a ferry boat just below the Valmondé plantation on the Red River. Chopin used the name of a real person here, a *gens de couleur*.

COTURES   "At Chênière Caminada": A family residing on the Chênière.

COULON   *At Fault*. A piney-wood sage who has the reputation of a mystic healer.

COURT BOUILLON (courtboullion)   A stew with a heavy tomato gravy that is made with the fillets of a large fish (a redfish for example), onions, green pepper, and various seasonings. It is frequently served with rice.

CORBEILLE   The French term for the wedding presents the bridegroom presents to the bride.

COUSINE   Cousin of Azémia. "Ti Frère" (*KCM*): Azémia plans to go to her cousin's for a veillée on Saturday night.

CREOLE   A descendant of the original French and Spanish settlers who came to New Orleans in the seventeenth and eighteenth centuries. There was considerable intermingling of races and nationalities to the point that some Germans,

Irish, and blacks became a part of this group. However, despite the variety of mixture, the dominant cultural tone was and is French.

CRISSY, AUNT   "The Gentleman from New Orleans": The black elder on the Bénôite plantation who has a comic style. A careless pipe smoker, she prefers to talk and remain in the midst of people rather than do such tasks as shelling peas where she is out of the way.

"CROQUE-MITAINE" (1892)   The nursery governess from Paris warns P'tit Paul about a hideous ogre, the Croque-Mitaine, that lives in the woods. One night, the children go out and discover that the ogre is just Alcée Laballière going to a costume ball.

CROQUIGNOLES   Flat cakes that are deep-fried and often served with café au lait (coffee with milk).

CURÉ   "A Lady of Bayou St. John": The priest who comes to Madame Delisle's home to offer consolation on her husband's death.

CURÉ   "At the 'Cadian Ball": He makes peace between Clarisse and Calixta as they fight on the church steps. This priest could possibly be Père Antoine. "Aunt Lympy's Interference": He is happy that the family estrangement is ended.

CURÉ, MONSIEUR LE   "The Maid of Saint Phillippe": He waits to perform the marriage that Marianne ultimately refuses to allow.

CUSTOMERS IN FLEURETTE'S SHOP   "A Sentimental Soul": They include a child, a gentleman, a mulattress, and a young girl.

CYNTHY, AUNT   Aunt of Betsy. *At Fault*: The black woman who is a domestic servant at Place-du-Bois. "Mamouche": The formidable housekeeper for Dr. John-Luis.

CYPRESS JUNCTION   Located south of Natchitoches, Louisiana. "A December Day in Dixie": The railroad stop near Emile Sautier's saloon.

D

DAINEAU "The Godmother": Gabriel Lucaze's old schoolmaster.

DANIEL Husband of Mandy. "A Family Affair": The black field worker who drives the wagon on Madame Solisainte's plantation.

DANNY Son of Martha and nephew of Elizabeth. "Elizabeth Stock's One Story": Elizabeth uses her pay as postmistress to send him to school. When her job ends, he is apprenticed to Mr. Filmore Green, a grocer in Stonelift.

DAUPHINE STREET New Orleans, Louisiana. "Athénaïse": Sylvia's boarding house, where Athénaïse, Gouvernail, and Montéclin stay, is on this French Quarter street. *The Awakening*.

DAVIDSON, GRACE An editor and friend of Chopin's in St. Louis.

DAWSON, MR. JACK *At Fault*: The traveling salesman with an outgoing personality and a tendency toward anecdotes who is past thirty, "short, round, young, blond, good-looking and bald." When he is at home, he creates parties and activities like a dinner at a restaurant near Forest Park.

DAWSON, MRS. JACK ("LOU") *At Fault*: The friend of Fannie Larimore's and Belle Worthington's who is strangely handsome and a professional timewaster. Tall and thin, she, like her husband, is amiable and outgoing, but at times she is a flirt.

"DEAD MEN'S SHOES" (1895)   When old Gamiche dies, Gilma, who had "adopted" him a few years before, finds himself put out of house and horse by the relatives. In seeking recovery of his horse, he discovers from lawyer Paxton that he has inherited everything. People begin to treat him better immediately, but he is concerned about the poor, though unkind, relatives. He resolves the crisis by claiming his horse and leaving the house and property to the relatives from Caddo. Gilma leaves a free man.

DE BROUSSARD, MELITTE   "Aunt Lympy's Interference": The 18-year-old attractive and extroverted member of a once-wealthy family who seems always on the edge of the good life but must consider becoming a schoolteacher to make her own way, a clear step down in status. Her love for Victor Annibelle prevents her being "rescued" from her situation by her uncle in New Orleans.

"A DECEMBER DAY IN DIXIE" (1900)   The narrator arrives early in the morning at the station, hears a story in the saloon about a baby falling into a cistern, rides the train into Natchitoches, observes the snow-covered fields and the confusion of the town, and experiences the welcome thaw on the next day.

DELARIVIÈRE, MADAME   "La Belle Zoraïde": The owner of Zoraïde who prevents her marriage to Mézor and gives away their child, hoping to make a better match for Zoraïde.

DELASIDAS, THE MISSES   *The Awakening*: Tuesday visitors at the Pontellier home.

DELISLE, GUSTAVE   "A Lady of Bayou St. John": After dying in battle in Virginia with Beauregard's Confederate forces, he is mourned "forever" by his widow, who was less than faithful while he was away fighting.

DELISLE, MADAME   Wife of Gustave. "La Belle Zoraïde": Every evening she listens to Manna Loulou's stories. She appears to have a childish disposition and an inability to occupy herself in a mature fashion. "A Lady of Bayou St. John": She toys with a lover, rejects him when her husband is killed, and devotes her life to her deceased mate.

DELMANDÉ, BERTRAND   The elder. Father of St. Ange. "A Wizard from Gettysburg": An old man long thought dead at Gettysburg, he returns with a shattered memory to his home and saves it from peril when he remembers the location of the family treasures, hidden during the Civil War. Chopin often uses the interaction of the old and the young as a narrative device.

DELMANDÉ, BERTRAND   Son of St. Ange. "A Wizard from Gettysburg": The student, about 15 years old, who is about to leave school because of his family's weakening finances when he discovers and aids an old man on the plantation. It happens that the stranger is his grandfather, Bertrand Delmandé.

DELMANDÉ, MADAME   Wife of the elder Bertrand. "A Wizard from Gettysburg": She recognizes her husband, long thought dead, and drags herself toward him as she demands his own recognition of her.

DELMANDÉ PLANTATION   *See* Bon-Accueil plantation.

DELMANDÉ, ST. ANGE   Father of Bertrand; son of the elder Bertrand. "A Wizard from Gettysburg": In a financial crisis during the aftermath of the Civil War, he is trying to save the plantation when his father returns and reveals the necessary resources.

DELONCE   Brother of Fifine. "The Godmother": He is attracted to the blonde schoolteacher from Louisiana Normal School.

DELONCE, FIFINE   "The Godmother": She gossips and carries tales.

DEMENIL, ALEXANDER (1849–1928)   The editor of the St. Louis publication *The Hesperin* who knew Chopin from her childhood. He refused at first to review *The Awakening*, but later did so with a mild rebuke. He wrote about Chopin in the *Missouri Historical Review* (*KCM*).

DEMINS   Son of Aunt Maryllis and brother of Blossom. "Charlie": The black fellow who does odd jobs about the Laborde plantation—sharpening tools and carrying the family mail.

DENNISON STREET   St. Louis, Missouri. "A Vocation and A Voice."

DÉSIRÉE   "Désirée's Baby": Found as a toddler on the road to Texas, she is adopted and reared by the Valmondés. She later marries the impulsive Armand Aubigny. However, his love for her disappears with the discovery of the Negro characteristics of his son, for he blames her. She has brought the loving aspects of the Valmondé home to L'Abri and has marvelous effects on all those about her. Recovering from the birth of the child, she appears to be an idealized figure reclining with the baby on a throne. Except for her brown hair—golden in the sun—and gray eyes, white is the only color associated with her. She stands in contrast to the darkness about her—the shadows of the house, the pigment of the blacks, and the swarthiness of Armand. When Désirée, the very symbol of love, is denied love, "She disappeared among the reeds and willows that grew thick along the banks of the deep, sluggish bayou; and she did not come back again.''

"DÉSIRÉE'S BABY" (1892)   An orphan, Désirée is adopted by the Valmondés. Maturing into a beautiful young woman, she marries Armand Aubigny. Soon after their child is born, his Negroid characteristics become apparent. The father rejects mother and son; and Desirée takes the baby and enters the swamp never to be seen again. Armand, in disposing of their effects, discovers that his mother was black.

DEYO, CHARLES L.   An editorial writer for the St. Louis *Post-Dispatch* who was an admired member of Chopin's literary circle in St. Louis. Chopin sought critical advice from him, an exception to her general inclination to make her own decisions in these matters.

DIANTHA   "A Harbinger": The model who after her initiation into love marries another man.

DICEY, AUNT   Mother of Wilkins. "A Gentleman of Bayou Têche": The black servant on the Hallet plantation who is socially conscious.

DILLON, JOHN   The cofounder and editor of the St. Louis *Post-Dispatch*. His attitudes were liberal and intellectual. He was a friend of Chopin's and a member of her salon. His career took him to the New York *World*.

DIMPLE   "A Family Affair": The young black girl who is Madame Solisainte's personal maid.

"A DIVORCE CASE"   Translation from the French of "Un Cas de Divorce" by Guy de Maupassant, 1894. See translation in this volume. A lawyer argues for a divorce on behalf of his client, whose husband has a "strange sensual perversion." The framed story centers on fragments of letters. The narrative includes erotic images of dreams, eyes, and flowers.

DOCTOR   "Alexandre's Wonderful Experience" (*KCM*): In search of a chest of drawers, he meets the lady in black through Alexandre's aid. Struck by the infirm Chérie, he marries the lady and is grateful to the boy for making it possible. The generous doctor lives in the country near New Orleans.

DOCTOR, THE   "The Godmother": He is a frequent nocturnal visitor to Widow Nicholas's quarters and the man she marries. "Polydore": He comes to assist Adélaïde.

DOCTOR'S WIFE   Possibly the wife of Dr. Bonfils. "Loka": At the Band of United Endeavor meeting, she fastidiously suggests that Loka be bathed even before the group discusses her future.

DODSWELL, MR.   "An Embarrassing Position" (one-act play): The person who leaks information on Willis Parkham to the *Paul Pry*.

DONNELLY, MRS.   "A Vocation and a Voice": The orphan boy goes on an errand for her.

DORALISE   "The Return of Alcibiade": The young mulatto girl who waits on Jean Baptiste Plochel's table.

DORAN, FATHER   "A Vocation and a Voice": The parish priest who says Mass with the orphan boy as the server.

DOROTHEA   "The Unexpected": Her love for Randall disappears when she observes the disfigurement his illness has caused.

DORTRAND GIRLS   "Athénaïse": According to Athénaïse, these young women would have liked to marry Cazeau.

DOUDOUCE   "A Visit to Avoyelles": The bachelor who fails in his romantic quest to rescue his lost love, Mentine, from the continued drudgery of married life.

DOUTÉ   "A Night in Acadie": The old black woman who makes a gumbo for Foché's ball and puts up with his animated behavior.

"DR. CHEVALIER'S LIE" (1891)   The doctor hears the report of a pistol shot. When he investigates, he finds a young woman dead by her own hand. He recognizes her as someone whom he'd met in Arkansas and who had yearned for the romance of the city. He buries her decently and writes to her home that she had become ill and died.

DRAKE, MISS   *At Fault*: The St. Louis resident who is a friend of Melicent Hosmer's and who has been to Europe for an extended stay.

"A DRESDEN LADY IN DIXIE" (1894)   Madame Valtour misses a china Dresden lady from its accustomed place; it had belonged to her deceased daughter. Agapie Bedaut's mother finds it among her daughter's things, and the child is banned from the Valtour house. However, black Pa-Jeff saves her from disgrace by taking the blame. The youngster is accepted by the Valtours as a result.

DRIVER, THE "Suzette": Young and straight-backed, he wears a white shirt, coarse trousers, leggings, and a gray felt hat as he rides his horse in the cattle drive. He fails to see Suzette as he passes by her.

DRUGGIST "A Sentimental Soul": His place of business is on Chartres Street, where Fleurette and Lacodie have their shops.

DRUGGIST "Ti Demon": He stocks gifts appealing to the feminine taste.

DRUG STORE BOY *At Fault*: The adolescent with glasses and mustache who had once been intent on caramels and chewing gum and now works at a St. Louis corner store.

DUCHERON, PÈRE "Madame Celéstin's Divorce": Madame Celéstin's confessor who cautions her about scandal and bad example in the matter of divorce.

DUMAY, HENRY A Frenchman who taught his country's literature at Washington University in St. Louis. A liberal member of Chopin's circle, he translated her "Story of an Hour" into French.

DUMONT'S FIELD Natchitoches Parish, Louisiana. *At Fault*: Marie Louise lives here, across the Red River from Place-du-Bois.

DUPLAN, JOE "A Rude Awakening": The plantation owner who rescues Lolotte and the children then shocks their father into being more responsible. He is known by all in the Natchitoches area to be a good and generous man. "After the Winter": He provides encouragement to his neighbor, old friend, and former comrade-in-arms—Monsieur Michel. *At Fault*: He and his family are guests at Place-du-Bois for a party honoring the visitors from St. Louis. "A No-Account Creole" and "Ozème's Holiday." *See* Duplan, Mrs. and Les Chêniers.

DUPLAN, MRS. JOE *At Fault*: The old-fashioned but strong woman who accompanies her husband to a party at Place-du-Bois. "A No-Account Creole": She helps rear Euphrasie Manton after her mother's death. "A Rude Awakening": Lolotte and her brothers are in her care. Mrs. Duplan, even more than her husband, has a reputation throughout the community for helping those in need.

DUPLAN, NINETTE Daughter of Mr. and Mrs. Joe Duplan. *At Fault*: She is personable and outgoing, in many ways a reflection of her parents. "A No-Account Creole."

DUPLAN'S LANDING Natchitoches Parish, Louisiana. A riverboat landing area. "A Rude Awakening": Adjacent to Les Chêniers.

DUVIGNÉ, MADAMOISELLE CLAIRE   ''At Chênière Caminada'': Her family lives on Rampart Street in New Orleans, where her father is a well-known attorney. A young Creole coquette, she inadvertently becomes the object of Tonie Bocaze's affections while visiting the Chênière during the summer. In the subsequent winter, she dies and Tonie is disconsolate. *The Awakening*: For two summers Robert Lebrun devotes himself to her; her death leaves him emotionally wrought. Like Désirée, she has an idealized and mystical quality, for she has drawn music from an old organ and love from the hearts of two men.

E

EAST ILLINOIS "The Maid of Saint Phillippe": The region that was ceded to England by France.

"AN ECSTASY OF MADNESS" (poem, 1898)   Night imagery and passion dominate this four-line lyric. *See CW* for variant of title and version.

EDMONDS, PAULINE (POLLY) "A Mental Suggestion": The young lady whose interest in art is unimaginative. Her emotional attachment shifts during Don Graham's experiment, and she marries Faverham.

"AN EGYPTIAN CIGARETTE" (1897)   An architect who has traveled gives a lady friend a box of exotic cigarettes. With some teasing, she smokes one in his office and dreams of yearning for Bardja and struggling through hot sands for a cool river. Afterward, she destroys the cigarettes and observes that it is "worse for a dream."

ELIOT, CHARLOTTE Mother of T. S. Eliot. She founded the Wednesday Club of St. Louis, a literary and service group for whom Chopin read a paper on German music. Mrs. Eliot was driven to improve social conditions and to demonstrate the effectiveness of women in society.

"ELIZABETH STOCK'S ONE STORY" (1898)   The 38-year-old woman who dies of consumption and among whose papers a summer visitor discovers a story. She had been the postmistress for six years when she lost her job, despite the delivery of a letter in difficult weather to Nathan Brightman. Ironically, she loses her job to his business friend's son, Collins. Vance Wallace, her admirer, protests in vain. No longer can she support her sister's son in school, and she leaves to go to St. Louis for medical care.

ELLEN   *The Awakening*: The black maid in the Pontellier household who wears a white fluted cap. She witnesses the aftermath of Edna's throwing her wedding ring on the floor.

ELODIE   "Regret": A baby in arms.

ELODIE, TANTE   "The Godmother": Her love as a godmother makes her an accomplice to a crime. She is grief-stricken with the effects of guilt and concern for her godson, Gabriel Lucaze. Chopin uses Elodie to explore the power, limit, and damaging effects of love.

ELVINA   "A Night in Acadie": She has beautiful eyes, but is swarthy with slow and heavy body movements. Telèsphore Baquette is attracted to her, but not enough to marry her. There is a suggestion of racism in his view of her.

"EMANCIPATION: A LIFE FABLE" (1869–1870)   An animal, born into a cage, lives well with food and straw in abundance. One day the door to the cage is left open, and he sees the light of freedom. He departs, never to return, although he must seek and fight for his subsistence.

"AN EMBARRASSING POSITION" Comedy in One Act (1891)   Eva Artless, whose father is kept from home by a rail accident, goes late at night to stay with her friend Parkham, a political figure concerned about the impropriety of their being together. A reporter arrives and discovers them. Parkham is forced to propose to Eva, and a minister arrives to marry them.

ENGFELDER, HERR   "Wiser than a God": The rigorous professor of music at the conservatory who rejects the Brainard daughter as a voice student. He claims that "his system was not equal to overcoming impossibilities."

ENGLAND   "The Maid of Saint Phillippe."

ENGLISH COACHMAN   "A Matter of Prejudice": The stiff gentleman employed by Henri Carambeau.

ERNST   Brother of Sophie and son of Papa Konrad. "With the Violin": "Ten years old going on eleven," he is active and imaginative as Papa Konrad restrains him for the duration of his story.

ESMÉE   Granddaughter of Jean Baptiste Plochel. "The Return of Alcibiade": Fred Bartner begins to fall in love with her while both try to make the old fellow happy.

ESPLANADE STREET   New Orleans, Louisiana. The downriver border of the French Quarter. "A No-Account Creole": Euphrasie stays in a house on this street. *The Awakening*: The Pontelliers live on this street. "Aunt Lympy's Interference."

"EUPHRAISIE" (1888–   )   Story never finished. Barbara Ewell suggests that "A No-Account Creole" might be a revision of the original (*Kate Chopin*, p. 55). *See* Manton, Euphrasie.

EUROPE   "A Point at Issue": The continent visited by the Faradays on their wedding trip.

EUSÈBE   "Tante Cat'rinette": The "free mulatto" from Red River (Parish).

EVELYN, FRED   "A Shameful Affair": The rugged and aggressive young man from the upper class whose desire for varied experiences leads him to work as a summer laborer. He awakens passion in Mildred Orme when they kiss. Evelyn is a device Chopin uses to examine the desires and passions of a young woman just being awakened to herself.

EVERSON   "The Godmother": The card-game companion whom Gabriel Lucaze kills and whose body Tante Elodie rifles to shift the blame for the killing.

F

FAGET, DR. JEAN CHARLES The old physician who assisted in delivering Chopin's son Jean-Baptiste on May 22, 1871, in New Orleans.

FAIR HAIRED GIRL UP AT THE NORMAL ''The Godmother'': The recipient of Gabriel Lucaze's romantic attentions. Part of her attraction is her northern fairness.

''A FAMILY AFFAIR'' (1897) Bosey Brantonniere goes to the country to help her mother's sister Madame Solisainte, who is crippled and having difficulty running her home effectively. Bosey also intends to correct an imbalance of the inheritance and to force her to walk once again. Bosey departs for home with her aunt walking and raving on her gallery.

''A FANCY'' (poem, ca. 1892) A meditation on a temptation ''born of fate and wishing'' though now ''naught remains of it.''

FARADAY, CHARLES Bridegroom of Eleanor Gail. ''A Point at Issue'': The professor of mathematics who tries a new approach to marriage by ''allowing'' his wife to live apart from him in Paris so that she can learn French. Although lonely, he finds solace in the Beaton family, especially the daughters— Kitty Beaton becomes a point of jealousy with Eleanor. Fortunately, their good intentions prevail over the foibles of their very human natures.

FAR NIENTE   Located in Wisconsin. "The Impossible Miss Meadows": The Hyleigh summer cottage on the lake.

FARIS, ATHÉNAÏSE CHARLEVILLE (d. 1897)   Mother of Eliza and grandmother of Chopin from whom she learned the Creole language.

FARIS, CHARLY   Related to Eliza Faris O'Flaherty. A clerk on the Mississippi River.

FARIS, WILSON   Husband of Athénaïse Charleville and father of Eliza. He was from Kentucky.

FARIVAL, ADRIENNE   "Lilacs": The opera star in Paris who returns annually to visit her convent school in the countryside near the city. She lives a full life of worldliness as she is surrounded by people and their attentions. However, she brings the world with her to this peaceful convent. Sister Agathe is especially intense in her affection for her, and the Mother Superior responds by not allowing the annual visits and purging the institution of reminders of her former presence.

FARIVAL, MONSIEUR   *The Awakening*: The elderly grandfather of the twins who is the constant seeker of the lady in black at Grand Isle. He had been quite a sailor; Beaudelet, who ferries the island guests to the Chênière, is jealous of his skills even now.

FARIVAL TWINS   *The Awakening*: The musically inclined girls of 14 who are always dressed in blue and white, "the Virgin's colors." Their precocity irks Mademoiselle Reisz.

"FATHER AMABLE"   Translation from the French of "Le Père Amable" by Guy de Maupassant, 1898. See translation in this volume. Over the objections of his old, deaf father, Césaire marries Céleste, who has a child out of wedlock. They live in the same house as father Amable, who is cold and distant. Césaire works himself literally to death. Then to keep the farm going, Céleste has the baby's father move in. Shortly after, the old father commits suicide.

FATUM, STEVEN   A Confederate soldier who secretly crossed Union lines to marry a relative (Puss) of Eliza Faris O'Flaherty.

FAVERHAM   "A Mental Suggestion": Don Graham's wealthy, charming, and popular friend who receives a suggestion and marries Graham's fiancée. Chopin shows persistent interest in themes touching on the psychological and scientific.

FAVETTE, MADEMOISELLE "At Chênière Caminada": The young lady who visited Grand Isle and the Chênière during the summer. She marries during the subsequent winter in New Orleans.

FÉDEAU "Ozème's Holiday": Ozème planned to visit him on his trip up the Cane River. "A Night in Acadie": There is a reference to the Fédeau family.

FEDORA "Fedora": Vainly in love with a younger man, she transfers her affection to his sister. She has a masculine aspect with emphasis on her strength and forcefulness. Chopin uses this passionate young woman to explore the nature of love and to touch on its androgynous and homosexual aspects.

"FEDORA" (1895) Fedora falls in love with a younger man. When his sister visits Camilla, she insists on picking her up at the station. And she aggressively kisses the unsuspecting Miss Malther, who seems the substitute for her brother.

FÉLICIE, MISS "For Marse Chouchoute": The Acadian maiden whom Chouchoute leaves on the dance floor.

FÉLICITÉ "Athénaïse": The old black woman who manages the house and cooks for Cazeau during Athénaïse's absences and periods of inattention. Her sympathy lies with Cazeau.

FELIX "Ma'ame Pélagie": In her dream Pélagie recalls her suitor who went to war and did not return.

FERGUSON'S STORE St. Louis, Missouri. *At Fault* and "Polly": A branch is expected to open in St. Joseph.

FERRINGER, MISS A singer in New Orleans who went on the stage to support her indigent parents. She married a wealthy merchant, Mr. Boder. In a diary entry (*KCM*), Chopin admires her for her "talents and womanly attractions."

FERRIS, MRS. "A frank, wholesome woman, amiable and natural," whom Chopin met at the Deyos' and for whom she wrote a poem ("For Mrs. Ferris," Christmas 1895).

FERRY, 24-MILE Across the Red River some distance from Cloutierville, Louisiana. "Mamouche" and "Ozème's Holiday."

FERRYMAN "Vagabonds": He takes Valcour across the Red River so he can go on to Alexandria.

FIACRE   A small horse-drawn coach.

FIFINE   Daughter of Cléophas. "A Very Fine Fiddle": Her dislike of her father's playing the fiddle drives her to sell it.

FILÉ   The seasoning made from sassafras leaves used in the preparation of gumbos.

FILIPS, JUDGE   "The Godmother": He had once been the target of lawyer Morrison's pistol shot.

FILMORE, MISSOURI   A very small town that looked to St. Louis for commerce and excitement. "Polly."

FITCH   "A No-Account Creole": A business associate of Wallace Offdean's who meets him at their New Orleans club prior to Offdean's venture into north Louisiana.

FLAGMAN   "Caline": He helps Caline by recommending that she seek his sister when she gets to New Orleans.

FLEURETTE, MAMZELLE   "A Sentimental Soul": The shopkeeper who loves Lacodie, a married man, without guilt only after his death. Like Madame Delisle, she makes an altar memorial to him. Chopin emphasizes the eccentric nature of her affection for Lacodie.

FLORENCE, ITALY   "Charlie."

FLORENTINE   Daughter of Bertrand and Madame Delmandé, and sister of St. Ange. "A Wizard from Gettysburg": Married, she lives in town; her daughter goes with her mother and brother to Bon-Accueil.

FLORINDY, AUNT   "A Turkey Hunt": The black cook who doubts the honesty and veracity of Artemise.

FLORINE   "Lilacs": The cook at the Farival house in Paris who is the object of the baker's affection and Sophie's supervision.

FOCHÉ   "A Night in Acadie": Fat, red, and emotional, he gives a ball at which Telèsphore Baquette and Zaïda Trodon dance. His emotions and frustrations are vented on the people who assist him.

FOCHELLE, FATHER   At Fault: The priest at the New Orleans Cathedral and an old friend of Thérèse Lafirme's. "A Sentimental Soul": He is Mamzelle Fleurette's old confessor at the Cathedral. The Awakening: Father Fochel (variant spelling) unsuccessfully explains the meaning and limits of an indulgence to the lady in black. He is quite traditional but capable of applying his sense of humor on the appropriate occasion.

FOREMAN   *At Fault*: He supervises the crew at the lumber mill near Place-du-Bois. David Hosmer is his immediate superior.

FOREST PARK   St. Louis, Missouri. *At Fault*: Located outside of the city in Chopin's time, it was a favorite recreation area.

"FOR MARSE CHOUCHOUTE" (1891)   Chouchoute is awarded a paying job to carry the mail from Cloutierville to the train. One night he stops for entertainment, and his young black friend seeing the horse with the mail bag takes it and rides for the train. However, as he rides along the moving train, the horse stumbles and Wash falls and dies.

"FOR MRS. FERRIS" (poem, 1895)   A meditation on being and seeming; with bird images.

"FOR SALE"   Translation from the French of "A Vendre" by Guy de Maupassant, 1896. See translation in this volume. A man walks through the fields along the sea, comes upon a house for sale, enters it, sees the portrait of the now-fled owner's mistress, and experiences a feeling of déjà vu as well as joy for her freedom. Intense images. *See The Awakening*.

FORT CHARTRES   Missouri-Illinois area of the old Louisiana territory. "The Maid of Saint Phillippe": A French outpost.

FORT LEAVENWORTH   Kansas. *At Fault*: An army post.

FOURTH DISTRICT   New Orleans, Louisiana. The uptown section of the city, upriver of Canal Street; a contrast to the downriver suburb of the French Quarter known as Faubourg Marigny, a main street of which was Goodchildren Street (now St. Claude Avenue). "Cavanelle."

FRANCE   *At Fault*: Often a place of refuge for Louisianians, Grégoire Santien's mother goes here. "The Maid of Saint Phillippe," "Miss McEnders," and "Alexandre's Wonderful Experience" (*KCM*). Oscar Chopin's father brought his family here for refuge during the Civil War.

FRANCISCO   *The Awakening*: According to Mariequita, he ran away with Sylvano's wife.

FRANÇOIS "A Matter of Prejudice": Madame Carambeau's coachman who is surprised at her change of plans for Christmas Mass.

FRANÇOIS "The Wood-Choppers": The black worker, younger than Peter, who refuses to follow his elder's request to work at Léontine and her mother's. *At Fault*: He works at Chartrand's store.

FRANÇOISE, PIERRE "At Chênière Caminada": The common topic among the islanders is whether this old man lives or does not live.

FRANKLIN, DR. *At Fault*: Fanny Larimore's physician in St. Louis, Missouri.

FRENCH MARKET Located on the river side of the French Quarter, New Orleans, Louisiana. It provides a populous and varied setting for the social and commercial life of the old city. "At Chênière Caminada," "A Sentimental Soul," "Athénaïse," "Nég Créol," "Alexandre's Wonderful Experience" (*KCM*).

FRENCH QUARTER New Orleans, Louisiana. The oldest section of the city, it is bounded by Canal Street, Rampart Street, Esplanade Street, and the Mississippi River. "Athénaïse": The heroine stays in a boarding house on one of its narrow streets. *The Awakening*: Edna walks its streets looking for Mademoiselle Reisz's home.

FRICASSÉE A stew made of cut-up pieces of chicken or veal in a light stock or roux gravy.

FRIEDHEIMER'S STORE Natchitoches Parish, Louisiana. "At the 'Cadian Ball": Where Bobinôt overhears that Alcée Laballière is going to the ball. "The Storm": Where Bobinôt waits for the weather to clear while Alcée has an affair with his wife, Calixta.

FRIEND OF EDNA PONTELLIER *The Awakening*: At school she was Edna's most intimate acquaintance, and like her she was self-contained. Her "exceptional intellectual gifts" showed up in "fine-sounding" essays. She was moved to discussion by literature as well as religious and political controversies. She was probably modeled on Kitty Garesché, Kate Chopin's childhood friend.

LA FRINGANTE "After the Winter": The black child who is among those picking flowers for Easter.

FROBISSAINT   ''Loka'': The owner of an oyster house who hires Loka as a ''tumbler-washer.'' He is considered a ''practical philanthropist''; however, when she begins breaking glasses over his customers' heads, he takes her from his place of business to the Band of United Endeavor.

FROBISSAINT'S "OYSTER SALOON"   Natchitoches, Louisiana. ''Loka'': Where Loka finds food and employment.

FRONIE   ''At the 'Cadian Ball'': Having fought Calixta over a mutual lover on the steps of the church, this Acadian girl continues to rival her at the ball.

FROSINE, TANTE   ''Ripe Figs'': She lives on Bayou Lafourche; Babette and Maman-Nainaine are anxious to visit her.

FRUIT VENDOR   *The Awakening*: He sells his produce on the street in New Orleans.

FULTON, MR.   ''Polly'': When the deliveries from the St. Louis shopping spree are made, he keeps order at the McQuade home in Filmore as the crowd gathers.

G

GAIL, ELEANOR   The bride of Charles Faraday. "A Point at Issue": As part of a new approach to marriage, when Eleanor marries Charles, both decide that she should not be encumbered by the married state and that she should grow intellectually in a way that her single life had prevented. Human nature prevails in the experiment, but Eleanor makes some of the strongest statements on the institution of marriage to be found in Chopin's fiction.

GAIL, MR.   "Charlie": According to Xenophore, he had killed a bear some time ago.

GALLERY   A porch, covered or uncovered, that encircles a house.

GALOPIN, STÉPHANIE   Wife of Théodule Peloté and grandmother of Mamouche. "Mamouche": She is the lost love of Dr. John-Luis.

GALWAY, MOTHER   A member (madam) of the Sacred Heart order at the St. Louis Academy of the Sacred Heart. Chopin notes a gathering of students on her feast day in 1867.

GAMARCHÉ'S STORE   Natchitoches Parish, Louisiana. Possibly Cloutierville. "Ti Démon": When Ti Démon came into the town, he tied his horse in the lot next to this store.

GAMICHE, LE VIEUX   "Dead Men's Shoes": The elderly planter, who "adopted" Gilma Germain as a youngster. He dies when Gilma is 19 and leaves the plantation to him. He shows little regard for his relatives. Gamiche is one of several characters who contribute to an adoption motif in Chopin's fiction.

GANACHE'S WIDOW   "A Night in Acadie": Seductive but not handsome, she has property and Telèsphore Baquette finds her attractive.

GARESCHÉ, KATHERINE (KITTY)   A childhood friend of Chopin's. Their relationship was "interrupted by her entering the Sacred Heart Convent as a religious in 1870" (*KCM*). She was a perceptive observer of Chopin, seeing more of a likeness to her Irish father. Chopin visited her after the death of Oscar and later dedicated a poem "To the Friend of My Youth: To Kitty." Garesché entered the novitiate at Maryville, St. Louis, served there, then later went to the convent in Grosse Pointe Farms, Michigan.

GASCON   "A Sentimental Soul." The butcher who marries Lacodie's widow.

GAUCHE, MRS.   *At Fault*: The friend of Melicent Hosmer's who spilled something on a gown of Melicent's last season.

"THE GENTLEMAN FROM NEW ORLEANS" (1900)   A visitor from the city is expected. When a strange man arrives, Aunt Crissy assumes that he is the person. However, it turns out to be Mr. Parkins, the father of Mrs. Bénôite, who is to bring her home to visit her ill mother. Meanwhile, Mr. Sneckbauer does arrive much to the delight of Mr. Bénôite's sister Sophronie. A reconciliation between the estranged Bénôites and Parkins occurs as a result of the mistaken identity.

"A GENTLEMAN OF BAYOU TÊCHE" (1893)   Mr. Sublet, a visitor to the Hallet plantation, desires to sketch Evariste Bonamour; at first he agrees to pose, but then he refuses when informed that it might not be dignified to do so. He does not arrive for the sitting, but instead goes fishing and rescues the visitor's son from drowning. Afterward, a bargain is struck guaranteeing him dignity in exchange for posing.

GENTLEMAN, OLD   "At the 'Cadian Ball": Cultivating a world view and pose, he reads the papers from Paris and thinks that Alcée Laballière's conduct is chic, with more panache than Boulanger's.

GENTLEMEN, THREE   "A Very Fine Fiddle": Musicians from the city (New Orleans) who are performing at the plantation. When they come upon Fifine selling the fiddle, they buy it from her with money and another instrument.

GENTLEMAN VISITOR   *The Awakening*: Edna (Pontellier), just entering "her teens," became infatuated with him. He was engaged to a young lady at a neighboring plantation. As she was so young, Edna meant nothing to him, and this fact is "a bitter affliction" to her then and later.

GEORGE   "Polly": The blond young man who eventually marries Polly and "opened [a store] in St. Jo."

GEORGE, HENRY   "Miss McEnders": Georgie McEnders plans to hear him lecture on "Single Tax."

GEORGIA   "La Belle Zoraïde": Possibly where Mézor is sold; it is referred to as one of those "distant countries."

GERMAIN, GILMA   "Dead Men's Shoes": The "adopted" son of Gamiche who inherits property from the old planter. When he realizes that the elderly man's relatives have received nothing, Gilma overlooks their boorishness to him and gives them nearly all that he has received. He is moved by their poverty and his own happiness with little.

GERMAN BOY   "Alexandre's Wonderful Experience" (*KCM*): This stout fellow was hired by Catalan to replace Alexandre in the antique shop.

GERTRUDE, MISS   *At Fault*: According to Johannah, Melicent Hosmer's maid, Miss Gertrude had beautiful golden hair.

GETTYSBURG   Pennsylvania. "The Wizard from Gettysburg": The battle in which Bertrand Delmandé was wounded and suffered a loss of memory.

GIBSON, ROBERT EDWARD LEE (1864)   A poet ostensibly admired by Chopin. He worked as the head clerk at the St. Louis Insane Asylum. Madison Cawein and he were friends.

GIBSON, WAT   "A Night in Acadie": A kind of justice of the peace who is supposed to officiate at the marriage of Zaïda Trodon and André Pascal, but is playing cards at Mr. Bodel's.

GIESTIN, ANDRÉ   Son of Giestin. "In and Out of Old Natchitoches": The boy Alphonse Laballière attempts to use to integrate the local school (on his land) which is directed by Suzanne St. Denys Godolph.

GIESTEN, MADAME   "In and Out of Old Natchitoches": The mulattress who lives with her extended family on Alphonse Laballière's newly bought plantation.

GIESTIN, MONSIEUR   "In and Out of Old Natchitoches": The free mulatto who works on Alphonse Laballière's land.

GILBERTA, LA PETITE   "Lilacs": Adrienne Farival's rival in the Paris opera.

GILDER, RICHARD WATSON   An editor at *Century* who had contact with Chopin and her work over much of her career. On women's issues he was unusually conservative, and it was not exceptional that "The Story of an Hour" was rejected.

GIRL FROM ARKANSAS   "Doctor Chevalier's Lie": The young woman from the country who commits suicide. Having despaired of finding her fortune in New Orleans. she had turned to prostitution. Dr. Chevalier saves her honor.

GIRL HIRED BY THE DAWSONS   *At Fault*: Mrs. Dawson keeps her uncommonly busy—day and night. She suggests the exploitive nature of her employer.

GIRLS, TWO   "Lilacs": Sophie apparently let them in the Farival house to play with the bird in its cage.

GLENCOE   Located near St. Louis, Missouri. A pastoral landscape of hills, sloping meadows, and cattle along the Meramec River. Chopin visited the Carr family here on May 28, 1894, when a storm interrupted the afternoon. *See* "The Storm: A Sequel to 'At the 'Cadian Ball'."

GODFREY, DOCTOR   "A Family Affair": The young physician who loves Bosey and plans to marry her. He is "youngish," "good-looking," with "a loud and cheery voice."

"THE GODMOTHER" (1899)   Gabriel Lucaze kills Everson, a companion from a card game. When he tells Tante Elodie, her love for him compels her to cover up this crime. Life continues about them as usual except for Gabriel (whose guilt drives him from his girl, his apprenticeship, and his community) and Elodie (whose health and emotional life deteriorate). Gabriel dies in a fall from a horse.

GODOLPH, MADAME ST. DENYS   Mother of Suzanne. "In and Out of Old Natchitoches": Alphonse Laballière persuades her to sell him a piece of land along the bayou and to assist him in his romantic quest for her daughter.

GODOLPH, SUZANNE ST. DENYS   "In and Out of Old Natchitoches": Of a once privileged and wealthy family, she is now a schoolteacher, a position of little status. She is insulted when Alphonse Laballière tries to enter a mulatto pupil in her school, and she leaves her position to go to New Orleans. There, even more of her illusions are shattered, as Alphonse and Hector Santien seek her affection.

"THE GOING AWAY OF LIZA" (1891)   When the stern and hard Abner Rydon married Liza-Jane, there was some question about their suitability for each other. According to the fellows at Bludgitt Station, there were many quarrels and she left him after one. Her name was usually not mentioned in Abner's presence. However, on a cold Christmas Eve, she returns to her home, and Abner, with some coaxing from his mother, goes to her.

GOLF GIRL, THE   "A Mental Suggestion": A visitor at a resort who is a satirical device.

GOODCHILDREN STREET   New Orleans, Louisiana. A street in Faubourg Marigny near the French Quarter; it is now called St. Claude Avenue. "Cavanelle": Cavenelle's yellow cottage is located here.

"GOOD NIGHT" (poem, undated; published 1894)   A love poem with dark and light imagery and images of the eyes.

GOTRAIN PLACE   Natchitoches Parish, Louisiana. "Athénaïse": Near the Bon-Dieu, where Miché lives.

GOTRAIN SWAMP   Natchitoches Parish, Louisiana. Next to or part of the Gotrain tract. "Athénaïse": Where Black Gabe, the runaway slave, had been caught.

GOUVERNAIL   "Athénaïse": The charming gentleman, editor of a New Orleans newspaper, who is infatuated with the heroine. Ordinarily detached and urbane, he is moved by Athénaïse's vulnerability, and his passion is stirred. "A Respectable Woman": He attracts the wife of a friend, Gaston Baroda. He uncovers a romantic need in her that she had not recognized before meeting him. *The Awakening*: He attends Edna Pontellier's dinner with Miss Mayblunt as his dinner partner. Under his breath he utters the lines from Swinburne. Like Arobin, he is a device or catalyst used to bring about change or at least emphasize it in another character; unlike Arobin, who is a stereotypical rake, Gouvernail is an individual who is not only one of the more interesting of Chopin's characters, but also one of the more memorable.

GRAHAM, DON   "A Mental Suggestion": The college professor who experiments with hypnosis and people, even his fiancée.

GRAMMONT   *At Fault*: The owner of a store in Centerville, Louisiana.

GRAMMONT'S STORE   Centerville, Louisiana. Located near the Cane River and Place-du-Bois. *At Fault*: Grégoire Santien disturbs the peace here.

GRAND AVENUE   St. Louis, Missouri. *At Fault*.

GRAND COTEAU, LOUISIANA   A college town in the southwestern part of the state during the nineteenth century. "A No-Account Creole" and "A Wizard from Gettysburg."

GRANDDAUGHTER OF MADAME DELMANDÉ   Daughter of Florentine. "The Wizard of Gettysburg": She comes to visit and play at Bon-Accueil.

GRAND ECORE, LOUISIANA   Located near Natchitoches. "Tante Cat'rinette": Kitty and Raymond are married here, and Cat'rinette has an epiphany on the Grand Ecore Road. "Suzette": Michel Jardeau falls from the Grand Ecore flat and drowns in the Red River. A ford and a cut-off are nearby.

GRAND ISLE, LOUISIANA   An island on the Gulf Coast, across from Caminada Bay. "At Chênière Caminada": Claire Duvigné is one of the summer visitors from here. "Cavanelle": Cavanelle intends to send his sister here for the summer. *The Awakening*: Edna Pontellier's awakening begins during the summer here, and her life ends later in the year off its beach.

GRANDMÈRE OF AZÉMIE   "Ti Frère": (*KCM*): Fat and often fanning herself, she is eager to accept Ti Frère's romantic attentions—at first more than Azémie is.

GRAND TERRE, LOUISIANA   An island east of Grand Isle along the Gulf Coast. "At Chênière Caminada": The farthest Tonie's mother had traveled. *The Awakening*: Robert Lebrun mentions to Edna Pontellier that he wishes to spend the day with her at the old fort here.

GRANDMOTHER OF AZÉLIE AND SAUTERELLE   "Azélie": Like a witch, she wears a black shawl over her head.

GRANT PARISH, LOUISIANA   East of Natchitoches Parish. *At Fault*: Rufe Jimson, the Texan, was on his way here when he stopped at Place-du-Bois. "In Sabine": The Aikens lived here for a while.

GREEN, FILMORE   "Elizabeth Stock's One Story": The grocer Danny is apprenticed to when Elizabeth can no longer financially assist him with his education.

GRETNA, LOUISIANA   Located across the Mississippi River from old New Orleans. "In and Out of Old New Orleans": Where Hector Santien meets Suzanne St. Denys Godolph at the train as she flees to New Orleans.

GRIESMANN, MRS.   *At Fault*: Melicent Hosmer writes that this pretentiously intellectual woman is leading her on a scientific trip to the West. There is something of the confidence man in the character.

GRIFFE ("GRIF")   The offspring—boy or girl—of a mulatto and a black or a black and an American Indian.

"GRIFFE" GIRL   "La Belle Zoraïde": The infant daughter of Zoraïde who is taken from her mother just after birth.

GRISGRIS (GRIGRI)   The talismans and charms used by those who practice voodooism in Louisiana and the Caribbean. People use them as means of security, wish fulfillment, and aggression.

GRISSEL   Grandchild of Papa Konrad. "With the Violin": The youngest of the three grandchildren.

GROCER   *The Awakening*: Having disliked Mademoiselle Reisz, he is happy to see her gone from his neighborhood.

GROSBEC   A game bird with a large bill. Hunting it was a ritual of Louisiana culture.

GROSBOEUF   "At the 'Cadian Ball": The host of the ball.

GROS-LÉON   "For Marse Chouchoute": The host of the dance which caused Chouchoute to wander from his duties. "Love on the Bon-Dieu": Azenor mentions doing work for him.

GROSSE TANTE (MARIE LOUISE)   *At Fault*: The old and wise black Creole woman who lives on the bank of the Red River and from whom Thérèse Lafirme seeks counsel. She dies when the high bluff with her cabin crumbles into the river.

LA GUERRE   The French term for war. In late nineteenth-century American literature it meant the American Civil War.

GULF OF MEXICO   The body of water along the coast of Louisiana and Mississippi. "At Chênière Caminada," it affects the romantic inclinations of Tonie Bocaze. *The Awakening*: It has a mystical presence for Edna, especially when she learns to swim in its waters.

GUMBO   From the African word for okra. This combination of soup and stew is made from a roux base and includes seafood and/or meat, seasoning, vegetables, filé or okra (the latter two for thickening). Both the cooking and the eating of it were often social occasions among the Acadians and Creoles. Chopin offers an unusually good description in "A Night in Acadie."

GUSTAVE   "For Marse Chouchoute": The mulatto who with others forms a chorus indicting Chouchoute for his irresponsibility in leaving the mail unattended.

GUTRO   "A Vocation and a Voice": The ever-scowling gypsy, who is often referred to as a beast and is frequently rough with Suzima and the orphan boy.

H

HALIFAX, AUNT "Dead Men's Shoes": The old black woman whose aid Gilma seeks.

HALLET, MR. "A Gentleman of Bayou Têche": The master of a plantation in the Acadian country who is host to a visitor interested in the local color.

HALLET PLANTATION Louisiana. Along Bayou Têche near Carencro Lake. "A Gentleman of Bayou Têche": When Mr. Sublet visits here, he is anxious to sketch an Acadian.

HANK, MARSE (PARKHAM) "An Embarrassing Position" (one-act play): Cato is loyal to him when the Yankee troops come during the Civil War.

HANNAH "Miss McEnders": A housemaid.

"A HARBINGER" (1891) The artist Bruno falls in love with his model, Diantha. After he introduces her to the nature of love, she marries another gentleman.

HARDING & OFFDEAN "A No-Account Creole": Business partners in a New Orleans firm. Fitch is probably Harding's first name; Wallace Offdean is the junior partner. However, there is some ambiguity at times regarding their relation to the firm. It could be argued that Wallace might be the son of the partner Offdean and that Fitch has no relation to the firm. "Athénaïse": Mr.

Harding advances Athénaïse money from her husband's accounts; he appears perceptive in observing human nature.

HARRY, OLD   "For Marse Chouchoute": Mr. Campbell refers to him when describing Wash's speed on the horse ride.

HARVARD UNIVERSITY   Cambridge, Massachusetts. "Wiser than a God": Where George Brainard might have studied before his return home.

HARVEY, MR.   "The Kiss": Nathalie's romantic interest before her marriage.

HATTAN, OLD   *At Fault*: The carpenter who wanted work at Place-du-Bois.

"THE HAUNTED CHAMBER" (poem, 1899) *See CW* for context. It is one of Chopin's longer poems—22 lines—and has a Poe-like setting, mood, and subject: the death of a woman. Chopin makes distinctions between male and female responses. *See The Awakening*.

HAVANA, CUBA   *At Fault*: The weather and flowers of Place-du-Bois are compared to the climate and flora of this Caribbean city.

HAYWARD, FLORENCE   A journalist and friend of Chopin's in St. Louis.

HE   "Two Summers and Two Souls": At first he is rejected, but later, on receipt of a letter, he returns to his love.

HEBREW NOTION VENDER   "Nég Créol": He gives Nég a metal pail in exchange for shrimp down at the French Market.

HECTOR   *At Fault*: One of the black workers on Place-du-Bois.

HEINRICH   "Mrs. Mobry's Reason": The gardener Mrs. Mobry reminds of the importance of work.

HENRI, MONSIEUR   "Lilacs": One of Adrienne Farival's faithful but scorned lovers.

HENRY   *At Fault*: A clerk for Hosmer at the mill near Place-du-Bois.

HENRY, EUGENIE CHOPIN   Sister of Lamy and Oscar Chopin; daughter of Julia Benoist and Victor Jean-Baptiste Chopin. She lived on the Baxter estate not far from Grand Ecore, Louisiana. Her husband's family owned Melrose plantation.

"HER LETTERS" (1894)   A wife has kept her and her lover's letters bound in her desk with a note to her husband that should he find them, they should be destroyed unseen. After she dies, he finds them, and with much concern, he follows her instructions. But his curiosity is aroused and he slowly drives himself to the point of madness as he seeks to know the degree of her fidelity (or infidelity). Finally, he is pushed by these circumstances to commit suicide from the same bridge from which he disposed of her letters.

HERMINIA   "A Horse Story" (*KCM*) The 18-year-old Acadian girl with calico dress, sunbonnet, and black eyes who comes from the Bayou Derbanne settlement. When her horse goes lame, she walks with her goods to sell to the Labatier house. Solistan comes upon her pony wandering near his farm, finds her at Labatier's, and later marries her.

D'HIBOUT, NID   "Love on the Bon-Dieu": His home is near Lalie's on Bayou Bon-Dieu.

HIGHCAMP, MISS   *The Awakening*: After dinner she plays Grieg on the piano, mechanically rather than poetically. Her playing seems a common entertainment after the Highcamps' dinner.

HIGHCAMP, MR. JAMES   *The Awakening*: The plain, bald-headed, and unresponsive man whose manners lack graciousness. He makes a "lame offer" to escort Edna Pontellier home after the dinner and recital at his home.

HIGHCAMP, MRS. JAMES   *The Awakening*: The high-living woman of questionable reputation and delicate courtesies who befriends Edna Pontellier. Although she gives considerable attention to her own husband, she is often in the company of Alcée Arobin.

THE HILLS   Several miles west of Natchitoches and Cloutierville, Louisiana. "After the Winter": Where Monsieur Michel is said to have killed several people.

HIRAM   *At Fault*: A black worker at Place-du-Bois. "Odalie Misses Mass": Aunt Pinky once wanted to marry him while he was a servant of Mr. Bênitous's. He is a good storyteller and the source of local news. "Polly": He is described as old, and is probably the same character from the previous stories. Here he looks for hammer and nails to fix the planks that gave way to the weight of the coal.

HOLT, MEREDITH   "Miss McEnders": Georgie McEnders's not-so-respectable fiancé.

HOMEYER   *At Fault*: The friend of David Hosmer's and his alter ego who is a reasonable and often wise person. One knows him only through whatever Hosmer says about him or his ideas because he does not physically take part in the action of the novel. There is a slight suggestion that Homeyer may not exist except as a psychological vehicle or device.

"A HORSE STORY" (unfinished, 1898: *KCM*)   Herminia, riding Ti Démon, goes to sell eggs. The pony develops a limp, and she leaves it by the road to walk to Monsieur Labatier's. The pony frees itself, and Solistan finds it in disheveled condition. He searches for Herminia and while doing so realizes his affection for her. But Solistan finds her and later marries her—much to the dismay of the pony who runs off and dies.

HOSMER, DAVID   *At Fault*: Forty and tall, he is a northern lumberman who is in charge of the mill near Place-du-Bois. His earlier marriage and divorce from Fanny Larimore cause him problems when he becomes romantically attracted to the Catholic Thérèse Lafirme, the mistress of the nearby plantation. However, despite setbacks at the mill and with his intentions for Thérèse, he finally marries her and settles on the plantation.

HOSMER, MELICENT   Sister of David. *At Fault*: The Unitarian who becomes romantically involved with Grégoire Santien, Thérèse Lafirme's nephew, but a shooting ends her enthusiasm for him and she moves back to St. Louis, Missouri, where she plans a trip to the West. She is a fickle sort who seems to have settled somewhat, although her naïveté is intact.

HOSMER INFANT   Son of David and Fanny Larimore. *At Fault*: He died at the age of three; his photograph is on his father's desk at the mill.

HOTEL ROYAL   New Orleans, Louisiana, in the French Quarter. "In and Out of Old Natchitoches": The hotel where Alphonse Laballière stays when he comes to see Miss Suzanne Godolph.

"AN HOUR" (poem, before 1899)   A love lyric with a time motif: past, present, and future. *See KCM* for contextual plot.

HOUSTON, TEXAS   *At Fault*: Visited by Jack Dawson.

HUDSON, MR.   "For Marse Chouchoute": The master of the railroad station who provides aid for the injured Wash and calls for the doctor.

HULL, MRS.   A St. Louis neighbor of Chopin's who was interested in being a writer. One of her stories is about how a black girl gets her name (*KCM*).

HUSBAND   ''Her Letters'': Perplexed by the bound letters from his wife, and mindful of his promise to dispose of them, he commits suicide.

HYLEIGH, EVADNE   ''The Impossible Miss Meadows'': Mrs. Hyleigh's daughter who nearly equals her mother in pretentiousness.

HYLEIGH, MAX   Brother of Evadne and Mildred. ''The Impossible Miss Meadows'': Mrs. Hyleigh's son who is a stereotype of his high social class and at 19 is fashionably bored.

HYLEIGH, MILDRED   Sister of Evadne and Max. ''The Impossible Miss Meadows'': Mrs. Hyleigh's daughter who uses slang and mumbles.

HYLEIGH, MRS.   Mother of Evadne, Max, and Mildred. ''The Impossible Miss Meadows'': A lady of social rank and pretense. Because Miss Meadows was a person of little consequence, she sent the second best trap to the station for her.

HYPPOLITE   ''Mamouche'': Dr. John-Luis considers him an ugly child, an unfit choice for his young companion.

I

I "The Bênitous' Slave": The female narrator. "Cavanelle: The female narrator who has an Emersonian inclination with a preference for nature, contemplation, and simplicity, and an antipathy for Christianity and organized religion. "An Idle Fellow": The narrator who is exhausted from formal studies. "Juanita": The female narrator in the guise of a summer visitor. "Vagabonds": The female narrator who is a cousin of Valcour's, and owns a plantation on the Cane River. "An Egyptian Cigarette": The sophisticated female narrator who experiments with smoking an exotic cigarette. "Elizabeth Stock's One Story": The narrator, a summer visitor who discovers the story. "The Night Came Slowly: The narrator who has a philosophical perspective and relies on nature rather than religious orthodoxy. "A Reflection": The narrator who functions as a detached observer. "A Turkey Hunt": The amused female narrator, a visitor to the plantation. "A December Day in Dixie": The narrator who is a winter traveler and visitor.

"I WANTED GOD" (poem, 1898) A witty couplet in which the speaker discovers God "in my inmost thought." *See CW* for context.

IBERVILLE PARISH, LOUISIANA Upriver from New Orleans between St. Martin and West Baton Rouge parishes. "Madame Martel's Christmas Eve": Uncle Achille lives here. *The Awakening*: The location of the Pontellier family home and plantation.

"AN IDLE FELLOW" (1893)   The narrator, a student and reader, sits beside her friend Paul and learns from him about experience with nature. Then they walk down the slope as they speak of human nature.

"IF IT MIGHT BE" (poem, ca. 1888)   Touches on love, death, and suicide.

"IF SOME DAY" (poem, 1895)   Has another version with different title; *see CW.* A romantic poem using images of eyes, fingertips, and "swarthy cheek."

"IF THE WOODS COULD TALK" (poem, 1893)   A memory poem with a walking motif and images of the summer woods. *See KCM* for variants.

ILLINOIS   "Juanita."

"THE IMPOSSIBLE MISS MEADOWS" (1903)   The bishop asks Mrs. Hyleigh to allow a poor young lady, Miss Meadows, to share some of their summer vacation at Far Niente. She and her children object to this person of no social consequence being thrust upon them. Homely and pale, she suffers from a recent illness and her father's death. Mrs. Hyleigh is sympathetic but uncomfortable as the visit begins.

"IN AND OUT OF OLD NATCHITOCHES" (1893)   After Alphonse Laballière attempts to enroll a mulatto in a Natchitoches school for whites, Suzanne St. Denys Godolph, the schoolmistress, closes it and departs for New Orleans, where she is met by Hector Santien, whom she grows to love. Alphonse also begins to love her and visits her to give a message from her mother. He advises her not to be seen with Hector in public, a matter of respectability. She discovers Hector to be Deroustan, the gambler.

"IN DREAMS THROUGHOUT THE NIGHT" (poem, 1893)   A love lyric using the image of eyes in a conventional romantic manner.

"IN SABINE" (1893)   Grégoire Santien, traveling westward, stops at the Aiken place to rest. Struck at the decline of Aiken's wife, once a pretty Acadian girl, he realizes her husband's harsh treatment of her. He steals her away from him and continues on his journey.

IOWA   "The Godmother."

IRISH MAID   "A Matter of Prejudice": The red-cheeked employee of the Henri Carambeaus who comes to pick up the little Carambeau daughter from the old madame's French Quarter home. She is one of the very few nonblack servants in Chopin's fiction, and she is probably one of two in the Louisiana fiction. *See* White Maid.

IRON MOUNTAIN, MISSOURI   Located southwest of St. Louis in the Ozark plateau. "A Shameful Affair": Location of the Kraummer farm.

L'ISLE DES MULÂTRES   Natchitoches Parish, Louisiana. "A Little Free Mulatto": A Mulatto colony, the destination of the move by Jean-Ba's family.

"IT?"   Translation from the French of the short story "Lui?" by Guy de Maupassant, 1895. See translation in this volume. The narrator in this epistolary story explains a mystical presence he experiences when he is alone. He hopes to dispel the presence by marrying a young woman. Elements of visions and images of light.

"IT MATTERS ALL" (poem, ca. 1893)   Light verse on love.

J

JACOBS, MR. ''Tante Cat'rinette'': The owner of a store in Campte, Louisiana. Raymond clerks for him.

JAKE, UNCLE ''For Marse Chouchoute'': Gros-Léon's neighbor.

JAMBALAYA Oysters, shrimp, ham, and sausage are among the seafoods and meats combined with a tomato gravy and various seasonings to produce this dish, which is usually served with rice. Food and its preparation are intrinsic to the way of life in south Louisiana, the French country.

JAMES ''Miss McEnders'': The coachman.

JAMES ''Wiser than a God'': The butler for the Brainards who answers the door for Paula Von Stoltz and shows her into the music room.

JANE ''The Recovery'': After 15 years her sight is restored and she must face the reality masqued by her illusions.

JANET Younger sister of Edna Pontellier. *The Awakening*: Edna had once quarreled with her, but it was not for this reason that Edna was refusing to attend her wedding. Léonce and Edna were sending gifts, but she offered no explanation for their absence.

JARDEAU, MICHEL   "Suzette": The young suitor who drowns in the Red River.

JASPER, UNCLE   *The Awakening*: The Pontellier children enjoy his company when they visit Iberville. He takes them fishing on the lake.

JEAN-BA' (BAPTISTE?), MONSIEUR AND MADAME   "A Little Free Mulatto": The free mulatto couple who move to an island in the Cane River area to make their small daughter secure and happy. Race is the cause of the move. This family could be related to the one on the Santien place.

JEANNE, SISTER   "Lilacs": The baker at the convent in the Paris countryside. Her baking gives rise to memories of first communion.

JEAN-PIERRE, PAPA   "In and Out of Old Natchitoches": Hector Santien reads that this old man has died in Natchitoches.

JELLEBY, MRS.   "Miss Witherwell's Mistake": The female writer who, according to the narrator, brings discredit on her sex.

JIMSON, RUFE   *At Fault*: The rawboned Texan who brings the message of Grégoire Santien's death to Thérèse Lafirme. He has "long knotty hands," "scraggy yellow hair and beard." He is "rawboned . . . lank and long of leg." His manners and dress are crude. Colfax, Louisiana, is his next stop. When Thérèse thinks of him as an animal, she is not far from Chopin's sense of the wilderness and its inhabitants beyond the borders of French Louisiana.

JOÇINT   Son of Morico. *At Fault*: The rebellious youngster who sets fire to the mill. Grégoire kills him for it.

JOCKEY CLUB   Located near New Orleans, Louisiana. *The Awakening*: The fashionable race track where Arobin meets Edna Pontellier. The horses serve as a memory of youth and as agents of passion. This race track is now known as the Fair Grounds and the city limit encompasses it.

JOE   Son of Pap and Susan; brother of Black Gal. "A Little Country Girl": He earns money for the circus by picking cotton. His clothing is a cakewalk dress.

JOE   *The Awakening*: The young mulatto who is a waiter in the Pontellier household.

JOHANNAH   *At Fault*: Melicent Hosmer's maid in St. Louis. She is given instructions that Melicent is not at home to Mrs. Van Wycke.

JOHN-LUIS, DOCTOR   "Mamouche": After an unhappy love affair in his youth, he has stayed single for many years. Loneliness has taken him, and he is anxious to have a substitute child. In seeking someone, he interviews several boys to no avail. Then Mamouche, who had earlier awakened him to his loneliness (which brought about the search) is brought to him for damaging his property. The doctor adopts this boy whom he discovers is the grandson of his former love.

JOHNS, GEORGE S. (b. 1857)   From 1883 he served in several editorial capacities on the St. Louis *Post-Disptach*. Liberal and unprejudiced, he was a member of the literary circle that inspired Chopin. He introduced her to William Byars's poetry.

JOHNS, ORRICK   Son of George S. Johns. He praised Chopin's treatment of the complexities of marriage in the *Mirror* (July 20, 1911 reprinted, *KCM*). A poet, he also published *Time of Our Lives* (1937) about the St. Louis his family had experienced.

JONAH, UNC'   "The Lilies": The black man on Mr. Billy's place who according to Pompey turned over the cream on the windowsill.

JONES, HUDSON   "Miss Witherwell's Mistake": The former assistant editor at the Boredomville Battery whom Frances Witherwell finds objectionable.

JOSÉ, MONSIEUR   "Polydore": The old man who is concerned about the "ill" youngster.

JOSEPH, OLD   "The Going Away of Liza": One of the gang at Bludgitt Station, Missouri.

JOSEPHINE   Sister of Louise Mallard. "The Story of an Hour": She tells Louise of her husband's "death," based on the reports that had come.

JOSÉPHINE   *The Awakening*: The griffe girl who is Mrs. Ratignolle's nurse.

JOSIE   A blouselike garment for women and girls; it was frequently made of coarse cotton.

JUANITA   "Juanita": The fat girl who "married" the one-legged man. In reading this story, one will find it appropriate to compare the characters with those in Flannery O'Connor's "Good Country People."

"JUANITA" (1894)   A summer visitor inquires about a fat girl named Juanita, who somehow attracted men. She discovers that Juanita married a one-legged man and bore his baby.

JUBA, UNC' "Croque-Mitaine": The old black man on the plantation who allays the children's fears of the Croque-Mitaine.

JUDE "Polydore": The black boy who rides to get the doctor.

JUDGE MORSE'S WIFE "Aunt Lympy's Interference": The woman Lympy was nursing in Alexandria before returning to the Cane River area.

JUDGE'S WIFE "Loka": She is not concerned about Loka's age. *See* Blount, Judge and Parkerson, Judge.

JUDY, AUNT "Loka": The Padues are about to go down the road to her cabin when Françoise spots Loka.

JULIE "Lilacs": The crippled woman who sits knitting by a sunny window— a memory of Adrienne Farival's childhood.

JULIETTE "Athénaïse": The young black woman whose baby is crying when Athénaïse returns home to stay. She and her child appear ominous in this context, almost an ironic reflection.

JUREAU, DR. "Vagabonds": Valcour falls asleep drunk on his gallery.

K

KANSAS "The Godmother."

KASKASKIA The western Illinois part of the French territory of Louisiana. "The Maid of Saint Phillippe."

KENRICK, ARCHBISHOP PETER RICHARD A close friend of Thomas O'Flaherty's, Chopin's father. He arranged for him to be buried from the cathedral in St. Louis and he delivered the address. He confirmed both Chopin and Katherine Garesché on May 1, 1861.

KENTUCKY "A Rude Awakening": Aunt Minty's home state. *The Awakening*: Imagery of Edna Pontellier's native state recurs throughout as the tall grass and the cavalry officer bind her early experiences to those on Grand Isle.

KITTY Wife of Raymond; daughter of Vieumaite. "Tante Cat'rinette": Ill and in need, she is aided by Cat'rinette, who had served her father for many years.

"THE KISS" (1894) Nathalie, a beautiful and conniving young lady, seeks the romantic attention of Mr. Harvey and marriage with the wealthy Mr. Brantain. Her open and affectionate manner with Harvey bothers Brantain at first, but he accepts the friend-of-her-brother explanation. When Brantain marries her, she expects a continuing relationship with Harvey, but he politely withdraws.

KLAYTON, COLONEL BILL   *At Fault*: The Texan with somewhat of a wild and eccentric reputation who calls Grégoire "Frenchy" in his store. A fight ensues and the colonel shoots and kills him.

KLEIN'S HOTEL   Grand Isle, Louisiana. *The Awakening*: The resort hotel that is the site of regular card games, dances, and concerts. Mademoiselle Reisz in a rare public appearance plays the piano here one evening; one of the pieces is "Solitude."

KNAPP, VERNON (BUNNY) (1847–1930)   Son of Colonel George Knapp, owner of the St. Louis *Republic*. The newly married Chopins encountered him in Europe during their wedding trip. This attorney probably wrote the article on Chopin that appeared in the *Republic* on September 11, 1910 (*KCM*).

KOLBENHEYER, DR. FREDERICK (1843?–1921)   Born in Austrian Poland, he came to St. Louis in 1840 and practiced medicine—obstetrics and family practice—for 47 years. Because he was a neighbor of her mother's, Chopin and he came to know and enjoy each other. He assisted in the delivery of three of her children. As an agnostic and liberal, he had a strong influence on tempering Chopin's practice of Catholicism. With his interest in philosophy and literature, he became her literary confidant.

KONRAD, PAPA   "With the Violin": He appears first as an elderly, grateful man and then as a young man rescued from despair at Christmas. This seasonal story reveals Konrad as a symbolic character, a version of Santa Claus.

KRAUMMER, FARMER   "A Shameful Affair": He is observed speaking with the young fellow who turns out to be Fred Evelyn.

KRAUMMER FARMHOUSE   Near Iron Mountain, Missouri. "A Shameful Affair."

KRAUMMER, MRS.   "A Shameful Affair": The mistress of the house and farm and hostess to Mildred Orme, a summer visitor.

KUNSTLER, MAX   "Wiser than a God": The middle-aged teacher of harmony who is in love with his student, Paula Von Stoltz. He pursues her with "the dogged patience that so often wins in the end."

L

LABALLIÈRE, ALCÉE   Brother of Didier and Alphonse. "At the 'Cadian Ball'': The rice planter who seeks Clarisse's hand in marriage, but is also attracted by Calixta, with whom he has a mysterious rendezvous. Clarisse marries this dashing and experienced gentleman in the end. "Croque-Mitaine'': He is temporarily mistaken for an ogre. "The Storm'': As Calixta's former beau, he has a brief affair with her, despite their being married to others. "In and Out of Old Natchitoches'': Cited as a sugar and rice planter. The Laballière family is one of several influential Creole families in the Cane River region. *See* Arobin, Alcée.

LABALLIÈRE, ALPHONSE   Brother of Alcée and Didier. "In and Out of Old Natchitoches'': The "liberal'' plantation owner who loves Suzanne St. Denys Godolph and who alienates her with his attempt to "integrate'' her school. "At the 'Cadian Ball'': Cited as a cotton planter. "Ozème's Holiday'': Alluded to. Alphonse generally shows Creole bravado and style, reason, and determination.

LABALLIÈRE, DIDIER   Brother of Alcée and Alphonse. "At the 'Cadian Ball'': Madame Laballière's son who lives in New Orleans.

LABALLIÈRE, MADAME   Mother of Alcée, Alphonse, and Didier. "At the 'Cadian Ball'': She oversees with Clarisse's help the social aspects of plantation life for Alcée. "Loka'': Her recommendation to place Loka with the Padues, an Acadian family, is accepted by the Band of United Endeavor.

LABATIER, MONSIEUR AND MADAME   Parents of Prospère. "A Horse Story" (*KCM*): The planter family whose summer house is in the pine hills west of the low, mosquito-infested bayous.

LABATIER, PROSPÈRE   "A Horse Story" (*KCM*): Herminia hopes for his attentions when she visits the Labatier home. The plan does not work, but she is rescued from Prospère's inattention by Solistan.

LA BLANCHE   "Désirée's Baby": The mulatto who lives in a cabin near L'Abri and whose son, described as a quadroon boy, fans the Aubigny child with an instrument made of peacock feathers. Both serve as objects of comparison in the scenes involving the discovery and discussion of Negroid characteristics in the Aubigny child.

LABLATTE, ZÉPHIRE   "A Family Affair": He runs a store, and previously he bought Madame Solisainte's carriage.

LABLATTE'S STORE   Natchitoches Parish, Louisiana. "A Family Affair": Near the Solisainte plantation. Bosey sends Fannie's boy here for lemons and ice.

LABORDE, AMANDA   One of seven sisters. "Charlie": The 16 year old who has long, narrow, dark eyes and a habit of locking things up. Self-conscious and particular, she goes with her Aunt Clementine to Paris.

LABORDE, CHARLIE (CHARLOTTE)   One of seven sisters. "Charlie": At 17 she is a lively, attractive, tomboyishly active girl. She shows a keen sense of the tall tale, and she wounds a visitor with a pistol shot. Charlie then becomes more conventional in dress (she had worn trouserlets) and manner. When her father loses his arm and his health, she takes over many of his responsibilities. Her affection for Gus Bradley develops throughout. However, she is celebrated for having written an ode on her grandmother's birthday and for having saved the levee in her father's absence. Clearly, she is a remarkable character and a believable one. Chopin shows Charlie as strong and able, but she is very much a woman in her feeling and intuition.

LABORDE, FIDELIA   One of seven sisters. "Charlie": The 10-year-old who is thick-waisted. She breathes hard and has some ailments of the throat. Charlie thinks that she is lazy.

LABORDE, GRANDMOTHER   "Charlie": On her seventieth birthday, Charlie writes an ode in her honor.

LABORDE, IRENE One of seven sisters. "Charlie": At 14 she is excitable and interested in romantic intrigues.

LABORDE, JULIA One of seven sisters. "Charlie": At 19 she is the eldest Laborde daughter. Beautiful with blue eyes and a flair for fashion, she is also generous. When the aftermath of her father's being wounded begins to be resolved, she leaves for New Orleans with Aunt Clementine. Later, she marries Firman Walton, who had been shot by her sister.

LABORDE, MR. A widower and the father of seven daughters. "Charlie": He favors Charlie throughout, and she, after exasperating him by accidentally shooting a visitor, begins to conform to his hopes for her. When he loses an arm in an accident at the sugar mill, Charlie takes charge of Les Palmiers and his health. His brother had died in Mexico earlier.

LABORDE, PAULA AND PAULINE Two of seven sisters. "Charlie": The six-year-old twins who are the youngest of the sisters. The former is mischievious and the latter timid. Charlie ultimately looks after them as daughters.

LABRIE, JACQUES "The Maid of Saint Phillippe": A suitor of Marianne's.

LAC DU BOIS Natchitoches Parish, Louisiana. *At Fault*: "These hills extended in a long line of gradual descent far back to the wooded borders of Lac du Bois; and within the circuit which they formed on the one side, and the irregular half circle of a sluggish bayou on the other, lay [Place-du-Bois]." *See* Lafirme Lake.

LACLEDE "The Maid of Saint Phillippe": Reference is made to Pierre Laclede Liguest who founded the village that became St. Louis, Missouri.

LACLEDE'S VILLAGE The site of the city of St. Louis, Missouri. "The Maid of Saint Phillippe."

LACODIE Husband of Augustine; and father of a five-year-old son. "A Sentimental Soul": The locksmith that Fleurette, a shopkeeper, loves even though he is married. When he becomes ill and dies, she loves him anew, especially after his widow remarries. A mild sort of man, his name suggests a tension between being bound and being free.

LACROIX "A No-Account Creole": His mules break the fence often at the old Santien place.

LADIES OF THE SACRED HEART   ''A No-Account Creole'': The nuns of the Sacred Heart order who taught at the boarding school in Grand Coteau. They also taught Chopin in St. Louis, Missouri, and maintained a convent in New Orleans.

"A LADY OF BAYOU ST. JOHN" (1893)   Madame Delisle is alone with her slaves during the Civil War. Young and beautiful, she attracts the affection of a neighbor, Sepincourt. At first she only jests about going away with him, then suddenly she awakens to his charms and agrees. When she hears of her husband's death in battle, however, her mood changes. When Sepincourt later seeks her hand in marriage, she refuses and dedicates her life to her dead husband. She grows old in this service.

"A LADY OF SHIFTING INTENTIONS" (1895; fragment *KCM*)   Young people gather in the parlor while waiting for mother to return from a club meeting and father to arrive from his office. Beverly's illusions of Bess tumble when he meets her in the foyer.

LADY, OLD   ''Wiser than a God'': The person who lives upstairs from Paula Von Stoltz and who tells George Brainard that Paula has gone to Leipsic—the message that is, in effect, the rejection of his proposal.

LADY IN BLACK   *The Awakening*: The silent woman who is observed alone, reading from a velvet prayer book, but who more often is seen following the lovers about Grand Isle. She also seems to have an unusual interest in an indulgence associated with her prayer beads.

LAFIRME, JÉRÔME   Son of the elder Jérôme: husband of Thérèse. ''Ma' ame Pélagie'': He plays checkers with Léandre Valmêt. *At Fault*: Thérèse takes over his responsibilities at Place-du-Bois following his death.

LAFIRME, JÉRÔME   Father of Jérôme and Jules. ''Ma' ame Pélagie'': He converses with Lucien Santien.

LAFIRME, JULES   Son of the elder Jérôme; brother of the younger. ''Ma'ame Pélagie'': He listens to his father's conversations with Lucien Santien, and is interested in marrying Pélagie.

LAFIRME, THÉRÈSE   Widow of Jérôme. *At Fault*: At 30 she is mistress of Place-du-Bois. Although she is childless, she looks after her nephew Grégoire Santien with keen and loving interest. There is every reason to believe that she was a Santien before her marriage. Thérèse has an extraordinary concern for the well-being of others. Her care for those who work on the plantation is nearly maternal. Her love for Hosmer is tempered more by the justice that his divorced spouse requires than by the demands of Roman Catholic orthodoxy in the matter of divorce. After failing in her attempt to reunite the Hosmers, and after the unfortunate death of his wife, she marries Hosmer after a suitable pause. When she asks for his help in running the plantation, he defers to her natural gift of managing it, but the likelihood of his taking a part is evident.

LAFIRME LAKE   Possibly Lac du Bois. Natchitoches Parish, Louisiana. "A Rude Awakening." A lake near the Bordon home where Sylveste fished.

LAFIRME STORE   On Place-du-Bois plantation, Natchitoches Parish, Louisiana. *At Fault*: The Lafirmes owned the plantation.

LA FOLLE (JACQUELINE)   "Beyond the Bayou": As a result of a violent incident in her youth, this black woman lives in self-imposed isolation on the side of the bayou across from the main house of the plantation. Considered mad to some extent, she crosses the bayou when a similar act of violence recurs, as she acts to save a little boy's life. In La Folle Chopin merges her exploration of alienation and the psychological effects of fear.

LAFORCE, MADAME   *The Awakening*: A Tuesday visitor at the Pontellier home.

LAGNIAPPE   Now virtually accepted as an expression meaning something extra, it was once confined to French Louisiana. Grocers and merchants kept their customers loyal by small gifts, often simply extra items. This practice added vitality to the ordinary activities of the day and frequently was a subject of conversation.

LAIDPORE   *The Awakening*: The artist-teacher and dealer who teaches Edna Pontellier and sells some of her sketches.

LAITNER   *The Awakening*: An attorney and partner in a law firm with Arobin.

LAKE   Lake Pontchartrain, Louisiana. Over 20 miles across, it borders New Orleans on the north. It was and still is a resort area with picnicking, dining, and boating places along its shore. "Charlie," "Athénaïse," and *The Awakening*. *See* Lake End.

LAKE END   Probably Lake Port, near New Orleans, Louisiana (now, within the city limits). A railroad ran from the French Quarter down what is now Elysian Fields Avenue to Lake Pontchartrain. "Athénaïse": Gouvernail takes Athénaïse on an outing here.

LALIE   "Love on the Bon-Dieu": The poor girl who lives with her grandmother at the edge of the swamp. She meets Azenor on the gallery of the local priest's home at Easter. Azenor woos and wins her in the freshness of the spring and returns her to the life of the community.

LALONDE, CÉCILE   Daughter of Madame Carambeau. "A Matter of Prejudice": The widow who is described as being "pretty, blonde, plump, [and] little."

LALONDE, GUSTAVE   Son of Madame Cécile Lalonde. "A Matter of Prejudice."

LAMBEAU, MIMI   "Nég Créol": She worked in the French market and gave Nég coffee.

LAMÉRIE   "Ozème's Holiday": The storekeeper who with Bodé welcomes Ozème back from his travels.

LAMÉRIE'S CROSSROADS STORE   Natchitoches Parish, Louisiana. "Ozème's Holiday": Ozème stops at this store by the Cane River to buy a cigar.

LANGLÉ, DOCTOR   "La Belle Zoraïde": The neighbor who is anxious to marry Madame Delarivière. His two black servants are emotionally involved with Zoraïde, Madame's servant. Zoraïde and Ambroise are light-skinned and their match would be a reflection of the Langlé-Delarivière bond.

LA RICANEUSE   "Ma'ame Pélagie": The black servant who is abusive at the beginning of the Civil War.

LARIMORE, FANNY   David Hosmer's first wife. *At Fault*: Of weak intellect and character, she lost her son when he was three years old and turned to alcohol. A divorce soon followed, and her rather empty friends now fill up her life. Her health is unsteady. David returns to marry her again at Thérèse's insistence; the remarried couple move to Place-du-Bois, where Fanny is plagued with jealousy and where in the nearby Red River she drowns.

LA ROCHELLE, FRANCE   "The Maid of Saint Phillippe": Where Picoté had lived and where Captain Vaudry wishes to take Marianne.

LARONCE, PICOTÉ   Father of Marianne. "The Maid of Saint Phillippe": He dies before the village and outpost are evacuated by the French.

LATELY, COOL   "An Embarrassing Position" (one-act play): The reporter for the *Paul Pry*.

LAWYER "A Sentimental Soul": The rich lawyer with an office around the corner from Lacodie's and Fleurette's shops in the French Quarter of New Orleans.

LEBRUN, MADAME ALINE Mother of Victor and Robert. "At Chênière Caminada": The widow from Grand Isle who, accompanied by her mother, informs Tonie Bocaze of Claire Duvigné's death. *The Awakening*: She rents cottages at Grand Isle during the summer to help maintain her comfortable level of living. Her husband died early in their marriage, and the luxury of the summer house on the Gulf soon came to mean opportunity for income. She still maintains a home in New Orleans.

LEBRUN, ROBERT Son of Aline; brother of Victor. *The Awakening*: Attracted to Edna Pontellier during the summer at Grand Isle, this 26 year old comes to love her, but in the end custom and morality require him to reject her. Employed at a mercantile house in New Orleans, he leaves it for a sojourn in Mexico, ostensibly for business, but in reality to come to a firm decision about Edna. For two summers he had been involved with Claire Dubigné, who died during the winter; now he faces another unfulfilling love. He speaks English, French, and Spanish and displays considerable charm, making him a favorite among the ladies visiting the island.

LEBRUN, VICTOR Son of Aline; brother of Robert. *The Awakening*: The 19 year old who has the reputation of being rugged and romantic, an extrovert. Mariequita is attracted to him, but he teases her with descriptions of the splendor of Edna Pontellier and the marvelous dinner she had given him.

LECOMPTE STABLES New Orleans, Louisiana. *The Awakening*: Dr. Mandelet recalls "the good old times" when these stables flourished.

LEGREE, SIMON The cruel master in Harriet Beecher Stowe's *Uncle Tom's Cabin*. *See* McAlpin and McFarlane.

LEIPSIC, AUSTRIA "Wiser than a God": The native city of the Von Stoltz family.

LENT The Roman Catholic liturgical season that extends from Ash Wednesday to Easter Sunday. Catholicism was a part of the culture of French Louisiana, and fasting, abstinence, and penance were a part of the inhabitants' daily lives. They looked forward to Easter, when they could resume the robust social activities of dining, dancing, and gambling that had been suspended or reduced during Lent.

LÉON   Husband of Odile. "Regret": He is away in Texas.

LÉONCE   "Ti Frère" (*KCM*): He grows fine peaches and makes a gift of them to Azémia.

LÉONCE, MR.   "A Gentleman of Bayou Têche": Martinette tells her father, Evariste, to have Léonce cut his hair.

LÉONTINE, MISS   "For Marse Chouchoute": The Acadian maiden who dances with Chouchoute. "The Wood-Choppers": the young schoolteacher whom George Willet rescues from her futile attempts to chop wood. Although she criticizes his social class (planter), she ultimately succumbs to his kindness and marries him.

"LET THE NIGHT GO" (poem, 1897)   *See CW* for other titles and versions. The poem suggests a life within the self. *See* "A Pair of Silk Stockings."

LEPLAIN, GERVAIS   "Aunt Lympy's Interference": The rich uncle from New Orleans on her mother's side who offers Melittte aid.

LIBERTY PLACE, BATTLE OF   New Orleans, Louisiana. September 14, 1874. The White League, an organization of Democrats of which Oscar Chopin was a member, fought against the Republican Radicals, who were defeated. Forty men died in this fray. The site of the conflict is at the foot of Canal Street across from the ferry landing.

LIDIE   *The Awakening*: The black servant whose children play with the Pontellier children at Iberville.

"LIFE" (poem, 1899)   A lyric on the mysteries of living that closes with "To love a little and then to die! / To live a little and never know why!"

"LILACS" (1894)   Each year Adrienne Farival visits the convent where she went to school in her youth. The nuns look forward to the arrival of this famous opera singer and the gifts she brings. Her affect on Sister Agathe is notable, for she is young and impressionable. Suddenly, the Mother Superior refuses to allow her visits and returns her gifts. While she turns sadly from the door, Sister Agathe cries in the room above the chapel.

LILIA   A polka for piano composed by Kate Chopin and published for her by Rollman and Sons. St. Louis, in 1888 (*KCM*).

"THE LILIES" (1892)   Mamouche releases Widow Angèle's calf and allows it to eat up part of Mr. Billy's planted field. Furious, he warns the widow. Her daughter Marie Louise brings him Easter lilies for reparation. Asked to dine with him, she criticizes the quality of his dinner. Touched by her generosity and precocity, Mr. Billy determines to make the acquaintance of the widow.

LINDELL AVENUE   St. Louis, Missouri. *At Fault*: On Sunday people often thought it fashionable to walk this avenue to Forest Park.

"LINES SUGGESTED BY OMAR" (poem, 1898)   Five quatrains with imagery from *The Rubaiyat*. *See KCM* for variants of titles and lines as well as comments on context.

"LINES TO HIM" (poem, 1898)   A witty look at male play and its effects.

"A LITTLE COUNTRY GIRL" (1899)   Nearly everyone is going to the circus, but Ninette's grandparents are reluctant to let her go. The little one in frustration says that she hopes that it will rain; she is corrected by her grandmother Bezeau. Jules Perrault convinces her guardians to let her go, but a storm hits the circus and she blames herself for the destruction. She is inconsolable. Jules convinces the Bezeaus that she would improve in the company of young people. The next day she is to go to a birthday party.

"A LITTLE DAY" (poem, ca. 1899)   A witty, Dickinson-like reflection on a summer moment. See *KCM* for variants.

"A LITTLE FREE MULATTO" (1892)   Jean-Ba', a mulatto who could nearly pass for white, has a daughter who cannot play with the white children. Concerned about her situation, he moves his family to L'Isle des Mulâtres, where she can be happy.

LITTLE RIVER   Divides Grant and La Salle parishes to the east of Natchitoches Parish, Louisiana. "Azélie": The Pauchés live along this river most of the year: Chopin suggests that there is something less desirable about living here than in Natchitoches Parish.

LITTLE ROCK, ARKANSAS   *At Fault*.

LIZA JANE   Wife of Abner Rydon. "The Going Away of Liza": She leaves and returns after months of "sin or suffering."

LIZETTE, TANTE   "Beyond the Bayou": A black mammy type who prepares tisane tea for La Folle after she collapses.

"THE LOCKET" (1897)   A locket, found on a dead soldier lying on the battlefield, is returned to the family with the news of Edmond Pillier's death. However, this sorrowful fiancée and his father are happily surprised by Edmond's appearance some time later. He explains that it had been stolen from him the night before the military engagement by his messmate.

LOKA "Loka": The half-Choctaw woman who suffers prejudice and insult, but prevails by means of her love for Bibine Padue, an infant placed in her care. She is more a thematic device than a fully developed character, as Chopin explores alienation and the role of love in achieving community. Through her treatment by the Band of United Endeavor, Chopin criticizes philanthropy.

"LOKA" (1892)   A half-breed Indian girl has fled Indian country and is working at a saloon where she is soon fired. The Band of United Endeavor paroles her to the Padue home to learn responsibility. She grows to love the baby placed in her care there. In a struggle between her desire for freedom and her love of the child, she nearly runs away. As a prodigal, she is accepted once again into family service, but with reluctance.

LOLO "Tante Cat'rinette": The person who attracts Cat'rinette's attention and helps shift her thinking.

LORD AND PELLEM "Polly": An accounting firm in St. Louis, Missouri. Pellem is the junior partner reluctant to release Polly for the afternoon. However, both partners are generous in their gift when she marries.

LOUISE "A Matter of Prejudice": Madame Carambeau's black maidservant who assists in caring for the sick American child. She is old and wears a tignon on her head and golden rings in her ears.

LOUISIANA The state in which *At Fault* and *The Awakening* along with many of the short stories are set.

LOUISIANA TERRITORY "Maid of Saint Phillippe": The eastern province is cited.

LOURDES The town in France where the Virgin Mary is said to have appeared. Water from this shrine was frequently kept in Catholic homes. A miraculous quality was attributed to its devotional use. *See CW* 2:695–99.

"LOVE ON THE BON-DIEU" (1891)   Lalie, who lives with her grandmother in the swamp, meets Azenor at the church rectory the day before Easter. Attracted to her, he literally makes his paths cross hers. After several rendezvous, he realizes his love for her. One day she is absent from church, and he goes to her home to find her ill. He rescues her and then, perceiving her love for him, he marries her.

LOVERS, THE *The Awakening*: The couple who stroll Grand Isle nearly always accompanied by the lady in black. They contribute to a motif of romantic love marred by accompanying guilt and arbitrary limits.

LUCAZE, GABRIEL Son of Justin. "The Godmother": Attractive and healthy, he has curly, short black hair and a drooping mouth. Tante Elodie, his godmother, once had a romantic attachment for his father. With his mother dead and his father away on the plantation, he lives in town in a room of a relative and reads law at Mr. Morrison's law office. He commits murder, and after much torment he is killed.

LUCAZE, JUSTIN Father of Gabriel. "The Godmother": He and Tante Elodie are romantically involved before his marriage to someone else. She responds by shifting her affection to his son. His wife dead and his son in town, he stays and works in the country at his plantation.

LUCIE "The Godmother": The young Lady who does not invite her cousin Claire to her card party because of an argument.

LUCY Sister of Amanda and cousin of Jane. "A Morning Walk": The young woman of 20 who awakens the fancies of a 40-year-old man.

LUDWIG, HERR "With the Violin": The leader of the opera who 12 years ago saved Papa Konrad from suicide and who is to come to Christmas dinner. His picture is in a place of honor over the mantel. He is the "Angel" about whom the children learn in Papa's story.

LUGGER A small fishing boat with at least one sail that was popular in the coastal areas of Louisiana. It was often used to ferry people among the islands and bays.

LULIN "Charlie": The crew member of the paddle steamer who generally answers for the contents under transport, though he occasionally errs.

"THE LULL OF SUMMER TIME" (poem, ca. 1898) A dreamy reflection on a summer moment. *See KCM* for variants.

LYMPY, AUNT (OLYMPE) "Aunt Lympy's Interference": The interfering old family servant who is proud and unbending. This light-colored black with bandana and gold earrings prods Gervais Leplain's conscience to look after Melitte, his niece. However, her act brings different results from her intentions. Melitte responds to Victor Annibelle's need for her to stay; so she does not go to her uncle in New Orleans.

M

"MA'AME PÉLAGIE" (1892)   Madame Pélagie and her sister Pauline live in a cabin beside the ruins of the family plantation, which they hope to rebuild along with the life that once surrounded it. When Léandre sends his daughter to stay with them, Pauline awakens to life. When the child seeks to return to the city, Pauline's response causes her sister to cease living in the past and to build a new but modest home and life.

"MAD?"   Translation from the French of the short story "Fou?" by Guy de Maupassant, 1894. See translation in this volume. A man is driven intensely and erotically toward his new wife. He perceives her loss of interest in him and her fulfillment in the horse she rides daily. He ensnares the horse during one of her rides, kills it, and in a struggle with his wife kills her as well. The narrative has a frenzied tone.

"MADAME CÉLESTIN'S DIVORCE" (1893)   Lawyer Paxton on his way to work in the morning often stops to speak with Madame Célestin. Attracted to her and aware of her complaints about her husband, he urges her to divorce Célestin. Her husband being away, she toys with the idea—all of this encouraging Paxton. Finally, her husband returns and makes promises: she then decides against divorce.

"MADAME MARTEL'S CHRISTMAS EVE" (1896)   At Christmas time Madame Martel always prefers to be alone, so her family visits others during this time. However, one night she sees a figure like her dead husband's in a room. She is stunned. Then she discovers that it is Gustave, her son who has returned to be with her. And she reveals her need for her children's presence.

"THE MAID OF SAINT PHILLIPPE" (1891)   When the British are about to arrive to claim the village of Saint Phillippe, the French soldiers are preparing for their return to France and the colonists are readying for the move across the Mississippi to Laclede's village. In the upset Marianne's father dies. A colonist and a soldier both offer her the security of marriage, but she rejects their proposals and strikes off alone into the wilderness.

MAIGRE-ÉCHINE   The French expression suggesting a generally ineffective person or ne'er-do-well.

MAJE (MAJOR)   Son of Minervy. *At Fault*: He helps the remarried Hosmers at Place-du-Bois.

MALLARD, BRENTLY   Husband of Louise. "The Story of an Hour": He is reported dead in a railroad accident but turns up alive.

MALLARD, MRS. LOUISE   Wife of Brently. "The Story of an Hour": She has a most unconventional response when she hears the news of her husband's death: she feels relief, a freedom, and a kind of happiness. However, when she realizes the error of the news, that her husband is, indeed, alive, she herself dies. Louise Mallard shows Chopin's daring in the creation of characters who do not conform to the conventional.

MALTHERS   "Fedora": The young fellow Fedora falls in love with; he is the brother of her sister Camilla's schoolmate.

MALTHERS, MISS   "Fedora": The sister of Malthers and school friend of Fedora's sister Camilla who is suitably disturbed by the loving ardor Fedora displays toward her.

MAMAN CHAVAN   "In and Out of Old Natchitoches": When Suzanne St. Denys Godolph comes to New Orleans, she boards and lodges at her home in the French Quarter. "A lovable, fresh-looking, white-haired, black-eyed, small, fat little body, dressed all in black," she is Santien's friend who understands no English.

MAMAN-NAÍNAINE   "Ripe Figs": Babette's godmother who promises the youngster a visit to her cousins.

MAMOUCHE   Son of Mathurín Peloté and grandson of Théodule Peloté and Stéphanie Galopin. "The Lilies": The young prankster who releases a calf into a planted field. "Mamouche": He ultimately finds refuge from his mischief-filled life at the home of Dr. John-Luis. Chopin uses him to show the salutary effects of love and security.

"MAMOUCHE" (1893) Mamouche finds refuge from bad weather at the home of Dr. John-Luis. The doctor offers him hospitality for the night, and by morning the boy has slipped away. Having enjoyed the youngster, the physician decides to seek a young companion who will inherit his property. He searches without finding anyone. However, Mamouche is brought to him for injuring his property, and the doctor offers him a new home. The grandchild of his former love accepts.

MAMZELLE "Croque-Mitaine": P'tit Paul's governess from Paris who uses the fear of the Croque-Mitaine to discipline the children.

MAN DISTRIBUTING THE DEATH NOTICES "The Godmother": A fixture of the period and a device that brings about the denouement.

MANAGER "Lilacs": He manages opera singer Adrienne Farival; Sophie is always citing him.

MANDELET, DR. *The Awakening*: A man of experience and sensibilities who attends Madame Ratignolle and suspects the nature of Edna Pontellier's difficulties. He advises Léonce: "Let your wife alone for a while." He is a foil to her father's authoritarian way and advice.

MANDOLIN PLAYERS *The Awakening*: The musicians at Edna Pontellier's farewell dinner.

MANDY *At Fault*: The black servant at Place-du-Bois who is mischievous and lively. "The Wood-Choppers": Possibly a younger version of this character.

MANDY Wife of Daniel. "A Family Affair": The black cook who worked for discriminating families; she replaces Susan in Madame Solisainte's kitchen. Mandy was a common name for black servants of this period; while there is a possibility that she could be the same Mandy in *At Fault*, a question still exists.

MANNA LOULOU "La Belle Zoraïde": The old black companion of Madam Delisle. In the evening she tells her stories to soothe her for sleep. "A Lady of Bayou St. John": She continues as a storyteller for Madame Delisle. Manna Loulou serves as a mother figure for her mistress, whose childlike disposition requires maternal affection and care.

MANNING, MRS. *At Fault*: The St. Louis friend of Melicent Hosmer's who is involved with charitable activities, so much so that she is hardly home and even then with little time for a social life.

MANTON, EUPHRASIE   Daughter of Pierre. "A No-Account Creole": Though engaged to Placide Santien, she falls in love with Wallace Offdean during a visit. Placide ultimately withdraws so that she can follow her inclinations. Euphrasie has definite ideas about the use of the plantation land and spends much of her time with Mrs. Duplan. Attractive, with chestnut hair, she has a pure heart and a simple sense of responsibility. "After the Winter": She is riding in the Duplan carriage. Mrs. Duplan had reared her since her mother's death when she was 10 and had even sent her to the school run by "the ladies of the 'Sacred Heart.'"

MANTON, PIERRE   Father of Euphrasie. "A No-Account Creole": The manager of the old Santien place for Harding & Offdean who is a "small, square man with mild, kindly face, brown roughened from healthy exposure." His hair is gray and long. He shows Wallace Offdean around the property.

MANY, LOUISIANA   "In Sabine": Bud Aiken claims to have bought a pig in this Sabine Parish town. It is the last town of any consequence between Natchitoches and the Texas border.

MARAIS   The French word for swamp or lowland grass describes much of the countryside near New Orleans and Natchitoches. (There are fewer areas like this since a levee system was subsequently installed.) These areas often have cypress trees shrouded in Spanish moss, various floating plants, palmettoes, mud flats, grasses, reptiles, birds, deer, bear, and insects.

MARCELINE, SISTER   "Lilacs": Adrienne Farival uses her bed when she visits the convent. The nun eagerly anticipates her visit.

MARCÉLINE AND MARCÉLETTE   The older daughters of Odile. "Regret": The former laughs regularly and the latter weeps when addressed loudly.

MARDI GRAS   A pre-Lenten celebration in New Orleans, this "Fat Tuesday" festivity held the day before Ash Wednesday includes parades, masking, and balls. The Ball of Proteus, the dance of a private club called a "krewe," is one of the older events. The season itself starts on Twelfth Night (Epiphany) and ends on Mardi Gras Day.

MARGARET   Older sister of Edna Pontellier and Janet, and daughter of the Colonel. *The Awakening*: She is matronly, dignified, and practical.

MARIANNE   Daughter of Picoté Laronce. "The Maid of Saint Phillippe": The strong young pioneer woman whose love for the primitive gives her resolve when her father dies, when she refuses marriage, and when she departs into the wilderness before the arrival of the British.

MARIANNE   ''Athénaïse'': The young lady who, according to Athénaïse, is anxious to marry Cadeau. ''Ti Démon'': The pretty girl with the personality of a coquette who refuses to consider Ti Démon's affection for her seriously because of his ''irrationality.''

MARIE ANNE, SISTER   ''Lilacs'': One of the younger nuns who looks forward to the excitement of Adrienne Farival's annual visit to the convent.

MARIE LOUISE   *See* Grosse Tante.

MARIE LOUISE   Daughter of Madame Angèle. ''The Lilies'': She soothes Mr. Billy's anger.

MARIEQUITA   *The Awakening*: The Spanish coquette of Grand Isle who tends toward jealousy. She is pictured as young, barefooted, and with a red kerchief on her head during the summer. The red covering suggests not only her liveliness but also her short temper. Both Lebrun brothers are attracted to her. She is with Victor while he is repairing the cottages on the island during the winter.

MARKSVILLE, LOUISIANA   ''A Visit to Avoyelles'': Jules and Mentine Trodon live here. ''A Night in Acadie'': Telèsphore Baquette goes here for a Sunday holiday to escape social pressures.

MAROT   ''Loka'': The Choctaw squaw ''who drank whiskey, plaited baskets, and beat'' Loka.

MARSHALL   ''Mamouche'': Dr. John-Luis's black servant who is responsible in the search for a suitable young companion to help alleviate the doctor's loneliness.

MARSHALL, TEXAS   Located near the Louisiana border. ''In and Out of Old Natchitoches'': The farthest west that Suzanne St. Denys Godolph had ever gone.

MARTE, UNCLE   ''The Godmother'': He notices the small footprints—a lady's—near the Nigger-Luke cabin, where Gabriel Lucaze killed Everson.

MARTEL, ADÉLAÏDE   Sister of Gustave and Lulu. ''Madame Martel's Christmas Eve'': She is in Iberville with Uncle Achille's family, where the atmosphere is usually festive, regardless of the season.

MARTEL, GUSTAVE   Brother of Adélaïde and Lulu. ''Madame Martel's Christmas Eve'': For a moment Madame Martel thinks her 19-year-old son is her husband who had been dead for some time. He had been celebrating Christmas in Assumption and had returned to be with his mother. A secure and sensitive type, he tells his mother, "Oh, well, if we can't be gay, there's nothing to keep us from being happy, mom."

MARTEL, LULU   Sister of Adélaïde and Gustave. "Madame Martel's Christmas Eve": The youngest daughter of Madame Martel who is staying with intimate friends on the other side of the village for a few days of celebration.

MARTEL, MADAME   Mother of Adélaïde, Lulu, and Gustave. "Madame Martel's Christmas Eve": Since becoming a widow, she has not celebrated the feast of Christmas. Her children usually go off to other family and friends, as they know her inclination to be alone. A Creole, she is slender and blonde. The memory of her husband's outgoing, boyish, and exuberant spirit stands in stark contrast to the mourning clothes she wears during his favorite season.

MARTIN, DR.   *At Fault*: The Unitarian minister who officiates at the re-marriage of David Hosmer and Fanny Larimore in St. Louis, Missouri. His sexton and housekeeper are witnesses.

MARYLLIS, AUNT   Mother of Demins and Blossom. "Charlie": The black cook for the Laborde family. Vibrant and fat, she controls her kitchen and children with a strong voice.

MASS   The principal ritual and ceremony of Roman Catholicism was and is an important part of daily life in the French parishes of Louisiana. Attendance is required on Sundays and Holy Days, and is encouraged on others. Chopin's stories include references to parts of the celebration of the Mass: the Confiteor, Gloria, Credo, and Sanctus. Also, there are frequent references made to the sacraments of Penance and Holy Eucharist (Communion).

MATHURIN, MR.   "Azélie": The genial, generous, and urbane plantation owner for whom Azélie's family sharecrops.

MATTEO'S WIFE   "Nég Créole": A friend of Chicot's.

"A MATTER OF PREJUDICE" (1893)   Madame Carambeau, a near re-cluse, takes care of an American child who becomes ill during a birthday party at her home. The child stays on for nursing care, and this old French woman becomes fond of her. When she returns her to her family, the madame, lonely now, thinks of her prejudice against Americans. On Christmas she goes to the American church and visits her son, his American wife, and her granddaughter for whom she had unknowingly cared. All return to her home for a reunion dinner.

MAURY, CORNELIA FIELD   A St. Louis artist with whom Chopin corresponded. Children were a favorite subject of her paintings.

MAYBLUNT, MISS   *The Awakening*: Looking at the world through lorgnettes with the keenest interest, she gives the appearance of being an intellectual at Edna Pontellier's dinner party. Gouvernail is her escort for the evening.

McALPIN PLANTATION   Near Cloutierville, Louisiana. It consisted of 4,367 acres and 94 slaves when Dr. Victor Jean-Baptiste Chopin and his wife Julia moved there. Until 1852 Robert McAlpin had owned it. *See* McAlpin, Robert.

McALPIN, ROBERT   According to tradition, he had been the inspiration for the cruel Simon Legree of Harriet Beecher Stowe's *Uncle Tom's Cabin*. *See* McFarlane, Robert, *At Fault,* and McAlpin Plantation.

McBRIDE, MR.   "The Going Away of Liza": One of the gang at Bludgitt Station, Missouri.

McENDERS, GEORGIE   "Miss McEnders": The disillusioned daughter of a prominent St. Louis family who is about to be married. Her concern about correctness and propriety seems ironic when the shadowy sources of her family's wealth are made known to her.

McENDERS, HORACE   Father of Georgie. "Miss McEnders": His reputation in the community is tarnished when it becomes known how he acquired his wealth.

McFARLANE'S GRAVE   Natchitoches Parish, at Chopin, Louisiana, the site of Little Eva plantation. *At Fault*: Grégoire takes Melicent here on a sunny day. McFarlane was modeled after Harriet Beecher Stowe's Simon Legree from *Uncle Tom's Cabin*.

McFARLANE, ROBERT   *At Fault*: Grégoire Santien takes Melicent to his grave on a sunny day; he indicates the dark nature of the deeds associated with his activities on his plantation. "The Return of Alcibiade": Jean Baptiste Plochel remembers this nearby plantation owner who had wanted to buy one of his slaves. He is cast after McAlpin, who inspired Harriet Beecher Stowe's Simon Legree of *Uncle Tom's Cabin*.

McQUADE, ISABEL   Sister of Phoebe and Polly. "Polly": The gregarious sister who is the organizer of a party to celebrate the good fortune of her sister Polly.

McQUADE, MRS. LOUISE   Mother of Isabel, Phoebe, and Polly. "Polly": She lives in Filmore and is the recipient of many of Polly's purchases.

McQUADE, PHOEBE   Sister of Isabel and Polly. "Polly": A schoolgirl.

McQUADE, POLLY   Sister of Isabel and Phoebe. "Polly": A gift from Uncle Ben brings her new fortunes. She buys gifts for her family. An assistant bookkeeper, she prepares for marriage and a move to St. Joseph, Missouri, site of a new store.

MEADOWS, MISS   "The Impossible Miss Meadows": The girl whose misfortunes cost her nearly everything. The bishop asks the Hyleighs to let her visit them at a fashionable summer resort. The contrast between her simplicity and their pretense suggests a moral allegory.

MELROSE PLANTATION   On the Cane River near Natchitoches, Louisiana. Owned by the Henry family during Chopin's residence in Cloutierville. *See* Henry, Eugenie Chopin.

MELVERN, MISS   "Charlie": The governess from Pennsylvania who has a rigid temper. She works with horses also, perhaps an ironic comment on her teaching responsibilities with the Laborde girls at Les Palmiers.

MEMPHIS, TENNESSEE   On the Mississippi River. *At Fault*: Fanny comments to Hosmer that a visit to Memphis convinced her that no one could really live in the South.

MEN'S CLUBS   New Orleans, Louisiana. *The Awakening*.

"A MENTAL SUGGESTION" (1896)   Don Graham makes a mental suggestion to his friend Faverham that he will be attracted to Pauline Edmonds. In the hypnotic experiment, Faverham, indeed, pays her much attention. However, Graham does not count on Pauline, his fiancée, falling in love with Faverham. They are married. When Graham removes the suggestion, Faverham embraces Pauline with fervor.

MERAMEC RIVER   "Mrs Mobry's Reason": It "twines like a silver ribbon through the green slopes of Southern Missouri." "A Shameful Affair": An especially clear body of water near the Kraummer farmhouse.

MERRIMAN, MR. MORTIMER   *The Awakening*: A "jovial fellow, something of a shallow-pate, who laughed a good deal at other people's witticisms." He attends Edna Pontellier's dinner with his wife, who cuts off his lame jokes and anecdotes.

MERRIMAN, MRS. MORTIMER   *The Awakening*: A companion of Edna Pontellier's at the races and a pretty and vivacious guest at her dinner party.

"A MESSAGE" (poem, ca. 1893)   A romantic sentiment with the imagery of birds. See *KCM* for variant texts.

METAIRIE RIDGE   A stretch of high ground running southwest to northeast on the lake side of New Orleans, Louisiana. "A Sentimental Soul."

MEXICO CITY, MEXICO   *The Awakening*: Robert Lebrun writes letters to Mademoiselle Reisz from here, and Edna Pontellier is permitted to read them.

MEXICO, OLD   "Charlie": Mr. Laborde's brother dies in Mexico. *The Awakening*: Robert Lebrun goes to Vera Cruz via steamer ostensibly to pursue a business adventure. *See* Mexico City. The lady in black had once received a pair of Mexican prayer beads.

MÉZOR   "La Belle Zoraïde": One of Dr. Langlé's field workers. The very black lover of Zoraïde and the father of her child, he is sold to prevent their union. He had attracted Zoraïde with his dancing at Congo Square.

MICHÉ, ATHÉNAÏSE   Sister of Montéclin. "In and Out of Old Natchitoches": Her upcoming marriage is cited. "Athénaïse": The rebellious bride who bolts from her husband Cazeau, at first to her family home and then with the aid of her brother to New Orleans. There she receives the romantic attentions of the newspaperman Gouvernail and begins to awaken to a mature emotional life. When she discovers her pregnancy, she is moved passionately toward Cazeau and returns home to him. Athénaïse approaches maturity with difficulty, and this narrative explores the complexities of growing into young womanhood and the very real challenges and fears that marriage represents.

MICHÉ, MONSIEUR AND MADAME   Parents of Athénaïse and Montéclin. "Athénaïse": They live on the old Gotrain place, running it for a merchant in Alexandria. The mother is defensive about what caused her to come back home. They are ill at ease with Cazeau despite the smooth appearance of jovial normality. There appears to be more dancing and dining than working on this plantation. The fields and house are suffering neglect.

MICHÉ, MONTÉCLIN   Brother of Athénaïse. "Athénaïse": The disrespectful fellow who holds Cazeau to ridicule. When his sister returns home, he questions her vigorously about the reasons. And he aids her flight to New Orleans to leave Cazeau once again. He too has a problem coping with the expectations of maturity.

MICHEL, MONSIEUR   "After the Winter": Disillusioned after the Civil War, he lives the life of a hermit, but the contacts of children and his comrade-in-arms Joe Duplan draw him back into the life of the community.

MICHIE   A frequently used corruption of Monsieur.

MICHON   "Love on the Bon-Dieu": The former occupant of the cabin near the swamp where Madame Zidore lives.

MIDDLEBURG, MISSOURI   "Mrs. Mobry's Reason": Edward's uncle put him in charge of the business here.

MILL, LUMBER   Natchitoches Parish, near Place-du-Bois. *At Fault*: Joçint burns the mill that Hosmer had been supervising.

MILLER, MISS   "The Impossible Miss Meadows": The name mistakenly used for Miss Meadows. The accident suggests an attitude toward the common people.

MIMOTTE   "Nég Créol": The woman who sells voodoo charms and powders from a shanty.

MINERVY   Wife of Moses: mother of Maje (Major). *At Fault*: The black servant on Place-du-Bois who like the other blacks is reluctant to help Melicent Hosmer with domestic duties—in her case, cooking.

MINISTER   "A Morning Walk": He intones the words, "I am the Resurrection and the Life." This statement serves as a catalyst for Archibald's spirit.

MINISTER'S WIFE   "Loka": She estimates Loka's age at 16 during the meeting of the Band of United Endeavor.

MINNESOTA   "The Godmother."

MINTY, AUNT   "A Rude Awakening": The "fat black negress" who assists Lolotte in caring for the children.

MISSISSIPPI   *The Awakening*: Edna Pontellier's father, the Colonel, had a plantation here.

MISSISSIPPI RIVER   A location of major importance, directly and indirectly, in Chopin's fiction. "The Maid of Saint Phillippe": The village of Saint Phillippe is near the river. "A Matter of Prejudice": The river is viewed across the green levees. "Her Letters." "Alexandre's Wonderful Experience" (*KCM*). *The Awakening*: A view of the river's crescent.

"MISS McENDERS" (1892)   Georgie McEnders, preparing for her marriage to Meredith Holt, discovers from her seamstress, whom she has criticized, that both her father and her fiancé have tarnished reputations. Interested in social reform and belonging to "society," she must face disillusionment.

"MISS WITHERWELL'S MISTAKE" (1889)   When her engagement to Roland Wilson is broken off, Mildred Witherwell is sent by her father to stay with his sister. She writes a column for the Boredomville *Battery*. One day the niece goes to the *Battery* for her aunt and discovers her former beau. Their reconciliation is carefully nurtured by the aunt.

MOBRY, EDITHA PAYNE   Mother of Naomi and Edward; wife of John. "Mrs. Mobry's Reason": Trying to cover a strain of insanity in the family, she worries that her daughter might inherit it and discourages the possibilities of her marrying.

MOBRY, EDWARD   Brother of Naomi; son of John and Editha. "Mrs. Mobry's Reason": His mother's objections fail to prevent his marriage.

MOBRY, JOHN   Father of Naomi and Edward; wife of Editha. "Mrs. Mobry's Reason": A determined sort of man who goes after what he wants and gets it. He marries Editha after her initial rejection of his suit. And he is concerned about Naomi's health and happiness—in that order.

MOBRY, NAOMI   Sister of Edward; daughter of Editha and John. "Mrs. Mobry's Reason": A seemingly healthy young lady who has beauty and talent. In love with her cousin Sigmund, she is happy. Suddenly, she becomes distant and confused and childlike. The mental illness feared by her mother strikes, and the joy of her youth and spring is shattered.

MONSEIGNEUR   "Madame Célestin's Divorce": "Not a mo' eloquent man in Natchitoches Parish," he urges patience and tolerance in the person of an understanding cleric.

MONSIEUR   "The Bênitous' Slave": The employer of Uncle Oswald who copes with his desire to return to the service of the Bênitous' by allowing the old black man to assist Madame Bênitous and her daughter.

MONSIEUR AND MADAME   "A Turkey Hunt": Madame directs the hunt for the missing turkeys. "Old Aunt Peggy": They are the owners "in bondage" to their former slave.

"MONSIEUR PIERRE"   Translated from the French of a short story by
Adrien Vely, 1890. See translation in this volume. A soldier has a chance
encounter with a young matron to whom he has previously been attracted. Her
husband secretly witnesses their expressions of affection and her declaration that
they must never see each other again. Afterward, François, the husband, confronts and baits the soldier Pierre. Later that same evening, he *thinks* he confronts
the soldier Pierre at his post, but it is another soldier who shoots the intruder
dead.

MONTEL   *The Awakening*: For 20 years he has been the suitor of Madame
Lebrun. He is in Mexico developing business, and he meets Robert Lebrun in
Vera Cruz.

MONTREVILLE, MADEMOISELLE   "Cavanelle": Cavanelle mistakes
her for the narrator of the story while he and his sister are at the opera.

MOORE, SUE V.   Editor of *St. Louis Life* (later *Criterion*). She invited Chopin
to write for the magazine. The two women were cordial to each other as they
participated in the literary community of St. Louis. She probably wrote the
sketch of Chopin in *St. Louis Life,* June 9, 1894 (*KCM*).

MOREAU'S   New Orleans, Louisiana. A tavern or bar. "Cavanelle": The
narrator muses on the possibilities of Cavanelle's enjoying himself for a change.
Food and drink are often served in these neighborhood establishments.

MORGIN, MR.   "Mamouche": Mamouche lets his horse loose.

MORICO   Father of Joçint. *At Fault*: The wise old black man who lives within
a short horse ride of Place-du-Bois. His Indian wife is dead.

"A MORNING WALK" (1897)   Archibald, a practical man of 40, takes a
constitutional walk and meets Lucy, a young lady who enlivens his spirit. He
follows her into church on this Easter morning and experiences a revitalized
vision of life.

MORRISON   "The Godmother": The attorney at whose office Gabriel reads
law before the murder. He once shot at Judge Filips on the street.

MORTIMER   "In Sabine": The black man who does yard work for Aiken.
He is sympathetic with 'tit Reine.

MOSE   Husband of Minervy; father of Maje (Major). *At Fault*: A black
fieldworker on Place-du-Bois.

MOTHER OF CHÉRI AND WIFE OF P'TIT MAÎTRE   "Beyond the Bayou": She receives La Folle's inquiry about Chéri's health the morning after the accident.

MOTHER OF LÉONTINE   "The Wood-Choppers": She is without a fire at home, for there is no cut wood. Léontine tries to help her, but Mr. Willet relieves her. White-haired and feeble looking, she is grateful for any assistance, even if it might be thought patronizing by her daughter.

MOTHER OF MADAME ANTOINE LEBRUN   "At Chêniére Caminada": She crosses on the lugger from Grand Isle to the Chênière for Mass.

MOTHER OF ODILE   "Regret": Because she is ill, she requires her daughter Odile's presence.

MOTHER SUPERIOR   "Lilacs": The strict nun who is leery of Adrienne's reputation as well as her affection for Sister Agathe and refuses the opera singer further admission to the convent. She also orders all signs of her influence returned.

MOUTH, THE   Natchitoches Parish. *At Fault*: Pierre Pardou lives here, not far from Dumont's field.

"MRS. MOBRY'S REASON" (1891)   Editha Payne reluctantly marries John Mobry, a man who usually acquires what he seeks. From their union come two children whom Mrs. Mobry worries over and tries to prevent from marrying when they reach maturity. Edward marries to her dismay. Her daughter Naomi, in love with her cousin Sigmund, suddenly shows symptoms of mental illness. And the cause of Mrs. Mobry's reluctance to marry and her fears become clear: There had been insanity in her family.

MULÂTRESSE   "A Rude Awakening": Lolotte recalls her being at the hospital.

MULATTO   "After the Winter": Indignant over Michel's wearing his hat in church, she says to him, "Take off yo' hat!"

MULATTO BOY   "A Night in Acadie": He helps Foché prepare for the ball, and is the object of his wrath.

MULATTO, MULATTRESS   A person of mixed Caucasian and Negro ancestry; the terms apply to first-generation offspring especially.

MURPHY   ''Polly'': He brings the coal to the McQuade home in Filmore.

"MY LADY ROSE POUTS" (poem, late 1898-early 1899)   Playful personification of flowers. See *KCM* for line variants.

N

NARRAGANSETT, RHODE ISLAND   *At Fault*: Where Mr. Bert Rodney's wife and daughter are vacationing. "A Shameful Affair": The Orme family is on vacation here.

NATCHITOCHES, LOUISIANA   The oldest French settlement in Louisiana and the center of the Cane River region. Established originally as a military and trading post in 1714, it was named Fort St. Jean Baptist; it was later renamed for a Caddo Indian tribe. A French soldier, Louis Juchereau de St. Denis, founded the post. Chopin uses many of the names associated with the early history of this city in her fiction. The parish and the city share the same name and are mentioned in the following: "A No-Account Creole," "A Rude Awakening." "Boulôt and Boulotte," "The Bênitous' Slave," "Loka," "At the 'Cadian Ball," "A Visit to Avoyelles," "The Return of Alcibiade," "In and Out of Old Natchitoches," "Madame Célestin's Divorce," "In Sabine," "Tante Cat'rinette," "Polydore," "A Night in Acadie," "A December Day in Dixie," and *At Fault*. The Natchitoches setting is also suggested in other works.

NATCHITOCHES PARISH, LOUISIANA   Bordered by the Red River and De Soto and Sabine parishes on the west; Bienville on the north; Winn, Grant, and Rapides on the east; and Vernon on the south. The Red River and the Cane River are its major bodies of water. A series of hills slope from the west to the flat bottom lands along the rivers. *See* Natchitoches, Louisiana.

NATHALIE "The Kiss": A beautiful and conniving young woman who nearly succeeds in acquiring both a husband and a lover.

NATHAN *At Fault*: The black servant who plays the violin at Place-du-Bois. Grégoire once hit him with a crow bar, and he helps on the ferry crossing when the bank crumbles into the river.

NED *See* Pillier, Edmond.

NEELY, PETER "Polly": His rheumatism leaves and never returns during the excitement surrounding Polly's homecoming in Filmore.

NÉG *See* Xavier, César François.

"NÉG CRÉOL" (1896) Chicot (Xavier) has illusions of grandeur about his ancestry and the family of his old master. He works in a fish market where he trades and begs for food and materials. These he offers to Aglaé Boisduré as she is in decline physically and financially. One day he finds her dead. He refuses to attend or even recognize her funeral as it would wreck his illusions.

NÉGRILLION "Désirée's Baby": The black worker who is given to pretense to avoid labor and whom Armand Aubigny treats with good humor and generosity. This is an example of the beneficent affect of Désirée on her husband Armand.

NEGRO "At the 'Cadian Ball": He calls Alcée Laballière to warn him that someone is looking for him. "A Rude Awakening": The young male who comes as a messenger with the news of Lolotte's accident. "Vagabonds": At the plantation store he gives a message from Valcour. "The Locket": He accompanies a priest on a Civil War battlefield. "Charlie": The young black who fails to care for the grooming of a horse because of other duties. "The Return of Alcibiade": The carriage driver who introduces the Plochel family and describes Cloutierville to Fred Bartner. "A Night in Acadie": The old man who looks after Wat Gibson's house while the owner is playing cards. "At the 'Cadian Ball": Black musicians celebrate the end of the dance by firing their pistols in the air as was customary. "A Night in Acadie": The two fiddlers and the accordian player. "Ti Frère" (*KCM*): The accordian player.

NÉNAINE (Nanain) Creole French for godmother. Much is made of this religious and family relationship among the Catholic people of Louisiana.

NEW ORLEANS, LOUISIANA Located on the Mississippi River near the Gulf of Mexico, it is the major cultural, political, and economic center in the state. The largest city in Louisiana then and now, it was founded in 1718 by

Bienville as a French colony and named in honor of the Regent of France, Philippe duc d'Orleans. Chopin lived in New Orleans during the 1870s before moving to Cloutierville, Louisiana. The city is named in the following works and provides the major setting for several: "A No-Account Creole," "For Marse Chouchoute," "A Rude Awakening," "At the 'Cadian Ball," "The Return of Alcibiade,' "In and Out of Old Natchitoches," "At Chênière Caminada," "A Respectable Woman," "Cavanelle," "A Sentimental Soul," "Athénaïse," "Nég Créol," "A Family Affair," "The Gentleman from New Orleans," "Charlie," *At Fault,* and *The Awakening.* See American Quarter, Bayou St. John, French Quarter, Lake, Canal Street, Rampart Street, and Esplanade Street.

NEW ORLEANS CATHEDRAL   Louisiana. "In and Out of Old Natchitoches," "A Sentimental Soul," and *At Fault. See* St. Louis Cathedral.

NEW YORK CITY, NEW YORK   *The Awakening*: When Léonce goes here on business, Edna moves from the family home into a small residence nearby. "The Gentleman from New Orleans," "The Impossible Miss Meadows."

NICHOLAS, MADAME AMELIA   "The Godmother": The widow and the mother of two girls who receives late night social visits from a physician who later marries her. Tante Elodie resides in the same house as Amelia.

NICK   "The Locket": The fellow soldier of Edmond Pillier who suggests anti-Catholic and anti-French attitudes.

NIGGER-LUKE CABIN   Natchitoches Parish, Louisiana. "The Godmother": The scene of Everson's murder.

NIGGERVILLE   Natchitoches Parish. On the outskirts of Natchitoches. "The Godmother."

"NIGHT"   Translation from the French of the short story "La Nuit" by Guy de Maupassant, 1895. See translation in this volume. A frenzied account of a walk through the streets of late-night Paris, during which the narrator perceives a change—a coldness—and is driven to find life, but finds only emptiness, a chill, and possibly death.

"THE NIGHT CAME SLOWLY" (1894)   A melancholy narrator, tired of people and books, lies under a maple tree at night and meditates on nature and mystery—a contrast to the limits of organized religion.

"A NIGHT IN ACADIE" (1896)   Telèsphore Baquette, under family pressure to marry, seeks relief by going on a holiday. On the train he meets Zaïda Trodon, whom he later escorts to her cousin's. At the ball he begins to love her, and he fights André for her favor. The story concludes with the harmony of their new relationship.

NINETTE   "A Little Country Girl": The little girl whose stern guardians oppose her going to the circus. However, she does go and a destructive storm interferes with the event. She thinks that her pessimistic thoughts caused the storm as well as other dark incidents. A priest and Monsieur Perrault convince her grandparents that her psychological health would improve if they allowed her to be around younger people more often.

"A NO-ACCOUNT CREOLE" (1888, 1891)   Pledged to marry Placide, Euphrasie falls in love with Wallace Offdean. Resisting her natural impulses, she prepares for her marriage to Placide. Wallace visits her again and declares his intentions. Placide and Wallace nearly duel. In the end Placide honorably withdraws to allow Euphrasie to follow her heart.

NOAH, UNCLE   "A No-Account Creole": The old black man who has the "misery." La Chatte, as she tells of her difficulties rearing the Santien boys, compares her suffering to his.

NORA   "A Lady of Shifting Intentions" (*KCM*): She is lighting the fire when her brother Stetson comes into the room; she gives him the details of everyone's whereabouts.

NORMAL, THE   Louisiana Normal School (now Northwestern State University). A teacher training institution in Natchitoches, Louisiana. "The Godmother" and "A December Day in Dixie."

NORTH   "Aunt Lympy's Interference": Cited as a vacation place.

NUMA   "In and Out of Old Natchitoches": The favorite student of Suzanne St. Denys Godolph at the school on the Alphonse Laballière plantation.

NURSE   "Alexandre's Wonderful Experience" (*KCM*): A pretty young woman with a white cap.

NURSEMAIDS, TWO   *The Awakening*: The disagreeable and resigned black women who follow the children (other than the Pontellier children) around in their activities during the summer on Grand Isle.

O

OAKLAND   Estate of the Benoist family near St. Louis, Missouri. Oscar Chopin and Kate O'Flaherty met and fell in love here.

"O! BLESSED TAVERN" (poem, early 1899)   A playful yearning for this establishment. *See KCM* for context. Note Chopin's use of inns and similar establishments in her fiction.

OCTAVIE   "The Locket": She loves Edmond Pillier and mourns his "death" in the Civil War. "A Respectable Woman": Mrs. Baroda visits her Aunt Octavie in the city. She is obviously some years older here.

"ODALIE MISSES MASS" (1895)   In a fine dress Odalie Chotard with her family is on her way to Mass on the Assumption, but she stops to show herself to Aunt Pinky. There she discovers her untended, so she sacrifices going to Mass with her family and showing off her clothes to stay with her. Both tell stories of their past and fall asleep. Odalie is awakened by her family, but Aunt Pinky sleeps on.

ODILE   Wife of Léon and mother of Elodie, Ti Nomme, Marcéline, and Marcélette. "Regret": For two weeks she leaves her children to the care of Aurélie, her not-so-near neighbor, while she goes to a neighboring parish to tend her ill mother. Frustrated with managing her home and children during her husband's absence, she leaves in an upset state but returns happily when her mother improves.

O'DOWD, FATHER   *At Fault*: He sends a letter with Rufe Jimson to explain the particulars of Grégoire Santien's death. Thérèse Lafirme receives it for the family.

"O FAIR, SWEET SPRING" (poem, undated, published 1899)   A seasonal lyric with bird images. See *KCM* for title and line variants.

OFFDEAN, WALLACE   "A No-Account Creole": A New Orleans broker who falls in love with Euphraisie Manton when he visits the old Santien place, which his firm had bought and which her father manages. Her father takes him on a tour of the lands and tells him about his daughter. When he meets her, he recalls seeing her at Mardi Gras in New Orleans. Struck by her charm, he wins her affection from Placide Santien. Offdean is an outgoing, card-playing, and chance-taking type.

O'FLAHERTY, ELIZA FARIS (1829–1885)   Daughter of Athénaïse Charleville Faris and Wilson Faris, mother of Kate Chopin; wife of Thomas O'Flaherty (m. 1844). A genteel, charming, and outgoing personality, she received many guests at her home. In the aftermath of her husband's untimely death (1855), she grew very close to her daughter.

O'FLAHERTY, GEORGE (1840–1863)   Son of Thomas O'Flaherty from a previous marriage and half-brother of Kate Chopin. He was a favorite of Chopin's and she mourned his death from typhoid as he was returning from a Union prison camp to his Confederate unit after an exchange.

O'FLAHERTY, THOMAS (1805–1855)   Husband of Eliza Faris and father of George, Thomas, and Kate (Chopin). Born in County Galway, he arrived in St. Louis in 1825 and went into business. He prospered as a merchant and found a place in the French society of the city. He was calm, self-reliant, and generous. A staunch Catholic, he worked with the Church to aid the poor Irish. While participating in the opening of a new road for the Pacific Railroad, of which he was a founder, he was killed when a bridge collapsed under the inaugural train.

O'FLAHERTY, THOMAS, JR. (1848–1873)   Son of Eliza Faris and Thomas O'Flaherty and brother of Kate (Chopin). Killed in an accident.

"OLD AUNT PEGGY" (1892)   When the Civil War is over, Peggy declines to leave the plantation. Now over 125 years old, she has lived in the comfortably appointed cabin for many years. Her visits to the family for "sentimental" reasons are always rewarded with goods.

"OLD MIS'"   "Beyond the Bayou": The deceased mother of P'tit Maître.

"OLD NATCHITOCHES" (poem, 1898)   A reflection on time and change. *See KCM* for variants. *See* Natchitoches.

OLISSE, AUNT   "At the 'Cadian Ball": The black nurse who takes care of the babies in the *parc aux petites* and watches over coats and hats during the dancing and dining at the ball.

'LYMPIC   St. Louis, Missouri. *At Fault*: Belle Worthington and Lou Dawson attend the matinées at this theater.

OMBRIE, PAVIE   "Suzette": Michel Jardeau had once been infatuated with this young woman. Already ill, she is extremely distressed at his death.

O'MEARA, MOTHER   A member (madam) of the Sacred Heart order at the St. Louis Academy of the Sacred Heart. She taught Chopin English and encouraged her to write poems and essays for her commonplace book. A verse composition playfully commemorates "Madam" (*KCM*).

ONE-LEGGED MAN   "Juanita": Juanita marries him and provides for a cork leg. Chopin treats this person as a grotesque, which prefigures an interest of southern literature after 1920.

"ONE DAY" (poem, early 1899)   A pastoral of 17 lines with intensive flower imagery.

ORME, MILDRED   "A Shameful Affair": A summer visitor to the Kraummer farm. Her passions and her curiosities about herself are aroused by Fred Evelyn's kissing her.

ORVILLE, LOUISIANA   Rapides Parish. "A No-Account Creole": Placide Santien had a small house here which he had been improving for Euphraisie whom he hoped to marry.

OSWALD, UNCLE   "The Bênitous' Slave": The ex-slave terrified by the present and haunted by the past who longs for the security of his former bondage to the Bênitous family.

OUR LADY OF LOURDES   A Roman Catholic church at Chênière Caminada, Louisiana, it is constructed in the Gothic style and painted brown and yellow. "At Chênière Caminada": Claire brings music from the old organ and attracts the interest of Tonie Bocaze. *The Awakening*: The summer visitors at

Grand Isle attend Mass here. Edna Pontellier becomes ill during a service and has to leave the church.

OZÉINA   *See* Suzonne, Madame.

OZÈME   "Ozème's Holiday": The plantation worker who is determined to take his vacation during the busy season. However, his plans are not successful, for when he departs and stops at Aunt Tildy's, he finds her boy Sandy ill, and he brings in the cotton for her. He returns to work as if he had really done what he had planned; his fellow workers are none the wiser.

"OZÈME'S HOLIDAY" (1894)   Taking his vacation no matter what, Ozème stops along the Cane River to visit Aunt Tildy, whose son is sick. He helps her nurse him back to health, and he works the cotton fields to save them from the rains. After all of this effort, he returns from his vacation. He does not tell his fellow workers that his vacation was disrupted.

P

PADUE, BAPTISTE AND TONTINE   Parents of Bibine. "Loka": The Band of United Endeavor places Loka in their care. "Ozème's Holiday": Ozème borrows Padue's old gray mare for his vacation.

PADUE, BIBINE   *See* Bibine.

PADUE, BODÉ   Son of Baptiste and Tontine. "Ozème's Holiday": He asks about Ozème's aborted vacation plans.

PADUE, FRANÇOIS   Son of Baptiste and Tontine. "Loka": When the family returns to find the house empty, he is one of those searching for Loka and Bibine.

PADUE, JULIETTE   Daughter of Baptiste and Tontine. "Loka": She is involved in the search for Loka and Bibine.

"A PAIR OF SILK STOCKINGS" (1897)   A young widow and mother has $15. While planning to spend the money on her children's needs, she thinks of herself and older, better days. The touch of silk stockings influences her to spend the money and the day on herself. She lives intensely and fully for a short time.

PA-JEFF   "A Dresden Lady in Dixie": The old black man on the plantation who sacrifices his reputation and honor by taking the blame for a theft by a young person. In many ways he is a stereotypical character, but he is also a means of showing the relationships among Creoles, Acadians, and blacks. Chopin portrays him vividly. *See* Bedaut, Agapie.

LES PALMIERS   Natchitoches Parish near the Red River. "Charlie": The Laborde plantation where sugar is grown and where school is held for the seven Laborde daughters.

PAP   Father of Black-Gal and husband of Susan. "A Little Country Girl": He sells his plow to Dennis in order to go to the circus.

LE PARC AUX PETITS   When the Acadians held a ball, the children were placed in a common room so that they could sleep undisturbed. Houses were often poorly constructed, and their "rocking" was supposed to have helped the children go to sleep. Thus an alternative name for these balls was "fais do do."

PARDOU, PIERRE   *At Fault*: He lives at the mouth of the Red River. According to Marie Louise, Père Antoine visited Pierre as he had been ill.

PARIS, FRANCE   "A Point at Issue": Where the Faradays experiment with marriage. "Croque-Mitaine": The nursery governess is from here. "Désirée's Baby": The residence of Madame Aubigny, the black mother of Armand. "A Lady of Bayou St. John": Where Sépincourt promises to take Madame Delisle. "Lilacs": Adrienne Farival stars in the Paris opera. "Charlie": Aunt Amanda intends to take Julie and Amanda to Paris for a finishing education. *At Fault*: Thérèse Lafirme spends six months here after Fanny's death.

PARISH   Louisiana is divided into parishes instead of counties. The Roman Catholic Archdiocese of Louisiana is also divided into parishes, each headed by a pastor. Citizens of French Louisiana have an unusual loyalty to their respective parishes.

PARKERSON, JUDGE   "A Wizard from Gettysburg": The elder Bertrand Delmandé calls for him as his memory returns, but he has been dead for over 20 years.

PARKHAM, WILLIS   "An Embarrassing Position" (one-act play): The wealthy young bachelor who is a candidate for political office.

PARKINS, MR.   Father of Mrs. Bénoîte. "The Gentleman from New Orleans": His identity is mistaken as he comes to take his daughter to see her ill mother. The Parkins and Bénoîtes have been estranged, possibly over their conflicting nationalities.

PARKINS, MRS.   Mother of Millie Bénoîte. "The Gentleman from New Orleans": She is dying and yearns to see her daughter who is in Natchitoches Parish and who has been separated over a family dispute.

PASCAL, ANDRÉ   "A Night in Acadie": The rejected suitor of Zaïda Trodon who falls victim to Telèsphore Baquette's punch. He has a reputation for laziness and drunkenness, and is therefore not allowed in Jules Trodon's house.

"THE PATCH"   St. Louis, Missouri. "A Vocation and a Voice": Described as a run-down neighborhood.

PATCHLY   "A No-Account Creole": The businessman who does well on a deal in New Orleans, according to Wallace Offdean's associate, Fitch.

PAUCHÉ, ARSÈNE   Father of Azélie and Sauterelle. "Azélie": The indolent sharecropper on the Mathurin plantation for part of the year who spends the remainder of the time on Little River. *See* Grandmother (possibly his mother).

PAUCHÉ, AZÉLIE   Daughter of Arsène and sister of Sauterelle. "Azélie": An attractive Acadian girl who is devoted to her father to the point that she would steal for his perceived needs. She also uses 'Polyte's attraction to her as a means of acquiring goods for her father. Her eccentric devotion to him, her coquettish ways, and her innocent reactions to 'Polyte's advances make her a perplexing character.

PAUCHÉ, SAUTERELLE   Son of Arsène and brother of Azélie. "Azélie": Dark-eyed and full of mischief, Azélie's "little" brother peeps over the edge of the wagon on the way to Little River.

PAUL   "An Idle Fellow": The strange and visionary idler who seems to commune with the spirit of life as he walks along with the narrator.

PAUL, MONSIEUR   "Lilacs": A lover-admirer of Adrienne Farival's, whom she scorns as she does Henri.

PAXTON, LAWYER   "Madame Célestin's Divorce": The Natchitoches gentleman who is attracted to Célestin and encourages her disillusionment with her husband; he mentions divorce but to no avail. He is loquacious, businesslike, and pragmatic in a manner other than southern. His office is a plain little room opening on St. Denys Street. "Dead Men's Shoes": He reveals Gilma's inheritance to him and disposes of it according to his instructions. "Tante Cat'rinette": He is curious about how Cat'rinette came to own her property.

PAYNE, EDITHA   *See* Mobry, Editha Payne. Chopin uses her maiden name to suggest the importance of her life before marriage to the conflicts that occur when her children contemplate marriage.

PEGGY, AUNT   "Old Aunt Peggy": The freed slave who never forgets to remind her former mistress of the past. Consequently, the former owners are in bondage to the nearly 125-year-old black woman, who has never left the plantation. In one way she appears clever and conniving—able to exploit human nature.

PELOTÉ, MATHURIN   Father of Mamouche; son of Théodule Peloté and Stéphanie Galopin. "Mamouche": Apparently, he is not able to care for his son adequately—a result of Stéphanie's bad choice perhaps.

PELOTÉ, THÉODULE   Father of Mathurin; husband of Stéphanie Galopin; grandfather of Mamouche. "Mamouche": He married the love of Dr. John-Luis.

PENNSYLVANIA   "Charlie."

PENSION, THE   Grand Isle, Louisiana. *The Awakening*: The Lebruns' guest house and cottages where visitors from the French Quarter of New Orleans stay; the Pontelliers were among the guests.

PEOPLE IN THE FRENCH MARKET   "Alexandre's Wonderful Experience" (*KCM*): These include a banana vendor, a thread and needle man, a big mulatto woman with a small market basket, the sister of the banana boy with gold hoops in her ears, and a little mulatto woman.

PERDIDO STREET   New Orleans, Louisiana. A short street in the business section that runs toward the lake past Baronne Street. *The Awakening*: Arobin's law office is on Perdido—an ironic name in this case.

PERRAULT, JULES   "A Little Country Girl": The neighbor who takes Ninette to the circus and befriends her. He convinces the Bézeaus that their granddaughter needs the companionship of youth.

PERRAULT, MADAME   Wife of Jules. "A Little Country Girl": She goes to the circus with her husband; Ninette joins them and holds the baby, their only child.

PETER   "The Wood-Choppers": The black workman who passes up chopping wood for Léontine and her mother in order to move freight at Aaron's store.

PHILIBERT   ''At Chênière Caminada'': The clever workman who is repairing the hull of Tonie's lugger. He is lame and frequently drunk; at one point he staggers into Tonie.

PHILIPPE   ''Lilacs'': The old gardener at the convent who knows of Adrienne Farival's escapades as a child.

PHILOMEL   *The Awakening*: The cook at the Lebrun cottage on Grand Isle during the off-season. Her mother is a better cook.

PHILOMEL, MADAME   The music and art teacher on the Laborde plantation. ''Charlie'': Fat and old-fashioned, she studied in her youth with the Ursulines in New Orleans.

PHILOMEL'S MOTHER   *The Awakening*: The black woman who lives on Grand Isle and is said to be a better cook than her daughter.

PICAYUNE   A Spanish half real coin used in New Orleans when it was under Spanish domination. Because it was of small monetary value, the word is also used to describe something of little value or significance.

PICKANINNY   *At Fault*: The black child who delivers the message to Melicent that Cynthy is sick. A patronizing term applied by whites to black children, it may be a variation of the Portuguese word *pequenino,* which means very little.

PIERSON   *At Fault*: The young black servant who is slim and has a reputation for dancing.

PILLIER, EDMOND   ''The Locket'': The young soldier from central Louisiana who was presumed dead in the Civil War but who turns up alive.

PILLIER, JUDGE   Father of Edmund. ''The Locket'': He takes Octavie for a morning ride and encourages her to give up the mourning clothes that she wears after the news of Edmund Pillier's death.

PINKY, AUNT   ''Odalie Misses Mass'': The old black woman who lives in reveries. Because she was Odalie's old nurse, the youngster feels affection and loyalty for her. She visits the woman to show her a pretty dress and stays with her when she realizes that she is alone for the day.

PIROGUE   A small canoelike dugout and planked craft used by the Acadian to carry them through the shallow waters of the swamps and bayous. It could hold one or two people and was propelled by paddling or poling.

PLACE D'ARMES   New Orleans, Louisiana. Later renamed Jackson Square in honor of General Andrew Jackson, it fronts the Mississippi River with the Pontalba apartment buildings on either side; the St. Louis Cathedral, flanked by the Cabildo (state house) and Presbytère (priests' quarters), lies at the head. "La Belle Zoraïde." *See* French Quarter and St. Louis Cathedral.

PLACE-DU-BOIS   Natchitoches Parish, Louisiana. *At Fault*: The plantation along the Cane River owned by Jérôme and Thérèse Lafirme. The house was moved and rebuilt to accommodate the arrival of a railroad. *See* Lac du Bois. The quarters for the blacks were scattered, dividing the various fields.

PLATZFELDT, HANS   "A Shameful Affair": Mrs. Kraummer offers his services as a chauffeur to Mildred Orme, her houseguest.

PLOCHEL, ALCIBIADE   Dead son of Jean Baptiste. "The Return of Alcibiade": Fred Bartner takes the part of the son to give his senile father a moment of happiness on Christmas Day. Alcibiade had been killed in the Civil War, but his father never gave up hope.

PLOCHEL, JEAN BAPTISTE   Father of Alcibiade. "The Return of Alcibiade": Now senile and confused, he keeps waiting for his son's return from the Civil War, although he had long ago received news of the young man's death in battle. When Fred Bartner acts as his son one Christmas, the old man dies peacefully. *See* Esmée.

PLYMDALE   An imaginary American university town. "A Point at Issue."

PLYMDALE UNIVERSITY   "A Point at Issue": Charles Faraday teaches mathematics here.

"A POINT AT ISSUE" (1889)   Charles Faraday and Eleanor Gail plan to marry. However, they decide that marriage should not interfere with their individual development. Eleanor goes to Paris to complete her education by learning French. Charles joins her at the end of the year. His jealousy is aroused when he sees her in a carriage with a gentleman. She is somewhat concerned about Kitty Beaton's hospitality to him in her absence. However, nearly all concerns are solved when he is presented a portrait of Eleanor by herself and the artist, the gentleman in the carriage.

POLDORF   "Wiser than a God": The pianist who is short and heavy. Paula Von Stoltz thought his weight to have come from his "inordinate consumption of beer."

POLICEMAN "The Blind Man": He calms the disturbance of the children upset by the blindman.

POLISSON "A Turkey Hunt": The yard boy who goes up the bayou looking for the lost turkeys.

"POLLY" (1902) An assistant bookkeeper, Polly looks forward to her fiancé George receiving a good job in St. Joseph. Each day she waits anxiously for her mail. One day a letter arrives from Uncle Ben with a gift of $100. His conditions are that it be spent. In one afternoon she spends it and causes a great uproar when the packages arrive. Her uncle promises another gift when she goes to St. Joseph. That evening she hears that "Ferguson's going to open up in St. Jo."

"POLYDORE" (1895) Polydore, whose mother had died, lives with his god-mother, Mamzelle Adélaïde, who assumed responsibility for him. Not wanting to work one day, he stays in bed, feigning illness. The work of the plantation goes on without him, and Adélaïde, performing one of his chores, falls ill with a fever from the heat. Polydore is consumed with guilt and confesses. The occasion becomes the instrument of realizing their mutual affection.

POLYDORE "Polydore": After the death of his mother, his godmother Adélaïde becomes his guardian, a person whom he comes to love when he realizes her affection for him. He lives in the garret of the plantation house, from which he can see his former home, a cabin high on the hill now occupied by blacks. His father has a reputation for being slothful and indolent. The absence and often the irresponsibility of fathers are themes that recur in Chopin's works.

'POLYTE "Azélie": The young Acadian fellow who is the manager of Mr. Mathurin's plantation store. He falls in love with Azélie Pauché to the point where he can exercise little judgement. At first enraged at her thefts, he gives her the articles she needs so long as she benignly allows him to fondle her. Finally, he leaves his job to accompany her to Little River.

POMPEY "The Lilies": The black boy who is a waiter for Mr. Billy. First, he ridicules Marie Louise, and then, having encouraged his employer's anger, he works to get back in his favor.

PONTELLIER, EDNA Sister of Janet and Margaret; mother of Etienne and Raoul; wife of Léonce. *The Awakening*: A Presbyterian who grew up in Kentucky and Mississippi, she is "an American woman, with a small infusion of French which seemed to had been lost in dilution." At 28, she has yellowish brown hair and eyes. Her body is long, lean, and symmetrical with "a graceful severity of poise and movement." A handsome woman, she has quick eyes and a frankness of facial expression. Unlike many of the Creole women, she is detached to some extent from her children, not given to the exchange of confidences, and unaccustomed to outward expressions of affection. Her interests include music, art, and reading. Her frequent sleeping and crying spells indicate that she is undergoing a personal crisis. On Grand Isle Adèle Ratignolle recognizes her vulnerability, and Robert Lebrun without malice begins to exploit it. She becomes clearly disillusioned with her husband and marriage, and she begins to discover her own capacity for passion. In New Orleans she makes decisions to try to put herself in control of her own life. Edna rebels against both custom and her marital situation. Although she has grown to love Robert, she is able to have a sexual relationship with Alcée Arobin, a man whom she does not love. Frustrated by the difficulties and perplexities of her newly discovered life, she returns to Grand Isle on a winter day, enters the waters of the Gulf of Mexico, and swims to her death. It is probable that when she went to the island she did not intend to commit suicide, but once there the overwhelming nature of her circumstance affects her, and in the rolling waters with ponderous sky overhead, she yields to it.

PONTELLIER, ETIENNE   Son of Edna and Léonce. *The Awakening*: The four-year-old boy who has a naughty temperament and spends time in Iberville.

PONTELLIER, GRANDMOTHER   Mother of Léonce. *The Awakening*: The Pontellier children visit her often at Iberville. She seems to have the warmth that one finds in Adèle Ratignolle.

PONTELLIER, LÉONCE   Father of Etienne and Raoul and husband of Edna. *The Awakening*: An established Creole businessman in New Orleans, he marries outside of his Catholic faith and French nationality. Tradition and its attendant social responsibilities are important to him. He sees himself in his family relationships as lord and master, a concept of the Napoleonic Code in practice throughout Louisiana. Léonce courted Edna with ardor and devotion, but his relationship to her became more understood and understated after their marriage. She and the children are very important to his emotional and psychological well-being. He frequently expresses his affection through gifts—which are also reminders of his authority. When Edna begins to do things that alarm and displease him, he acts not only to inquire into the cause but to prevent any damage to the family's reputation. Léonce is in many ways quite ordinary for his time and social class with his interest in family, business, society, and cards. His frequent absences and nearly constant influence contribute to his being more a force and less of a character.

PONTELLIER, RAOUL   Son of Edna and Léonce. *The Awakening*: The five-year-old boy who is ill on Grand Isle. *See* Pontellier, Etienne.

PORCHER, FRANCES An assistant editor at the *Mirror* under W. M. Reedy. She had a strong interest in being a writer, but she was careful to observe feminine custom. When *The Awakening* appeared, she gave it a negative review in the *Mirror*.

POSTMASTER "For Marse Chouchoute": He reads the charge of duty as mail carrier to Chouchoute.

POUPONNE "Cavanelle": The old mulatto woman who serves and works for Cavanelle and his sister. She was known for preferring to receive low wages, playing the lottery, and believing in voodoo. *The Awakening*: Madame Pouponne is possibly the same person some years later or earlier. She is a mulatto of a respectable family who rents rooms.

POUSETTE "Athénaïse": The friendly and forgetful black servant who works in the house in New Orleans where Athénaïse is staying.

POUSSIN, JOE "Vagabonds": Valcour apparently tries to kiss Joe's wife, and he fires a shotgun at the transgressor.

POUSSIN, MADAME Wife of Joe. "Vagabonds": Apparently she is an ugly woman, and the narrator upbraids Valcour for trying to kiss her.

PRIEST "A Vocation and a Voice": The orphan boy on a winter trip south serves Mass for him in his Louisiana parish. The priest is interested in the youngster's spiritual well-being, especially since he likes serving Mass. "The Locket": He tends victims on a Civil War battlefield. "A Little Country Girl": He offers the Bézeaus advice on Ninette's despondency.

PRINTY, AUNT "The Lilies": Mr. Billy employs her as a cook. Uncle Jonah turns over her cream.

PROTEUS BALL New Orleans, Louisiana. "A No-Account Creole": An annual ball—invitation only—held during the Mardi Gras season by the Krewe of Proteus, a social organization of gentlemen. *See* Mardi Gras.

PRUDENCE "Mamouche": The black cook in the home of Dr. John-Luis.

PRYTANIA STREET New Orleans, Louisiana. Runs from Canal Street through the American Quarter (now Garden District). "A No-Account Creole": Fitch boarded a Prytania Street car. "Cavanelle": Reference to the streetcar line. "A Matter of Prejudice": Henri Carambeau married "an American girl from Prytania Street."

"PSYCHE'S LAMENT" (poem, about 1890)   Uses dark and light in lamenting lost love. Closes with "O Night come back to me." *See The Awakening* and "A Respectable Woman."

P'TIT MAÎTRE   "Beyond the Bayou": In his youth he was wounded in a military skirmish, which so shocked La Folle that she stayed isolated on one side of the bayou for years. Now in middle age, he is the master of the plantation and the father of Chéri, whose accident brings La Folle back.

P'TIT PAUL   "Croque-Mitaine": The young child who learns about the ogre.

PUGGY   "Odalie Misses Mass": The black woman who ordinarily sits with Aunt Pinky, but who on the Assumption leaves her to attend Mass.

PULLMAN CAR   A sleeping car complete with beds, on passenger trains. Rail travel was a relatively new phenomenon in Chopin's Louisiana.

PURGATORY MARY   "Nég Créol": She prays "for the shades in Purgatory."

PUSH & PRODEM, MESSRS.   "Miss McEnders": Furnishers of material and clothes.

Q

QUADRILLE   A popular dance consisting of five or six ''squares'' of four couples who danced to music in 6/8 or 2/4 time.

QUADROON   A person with one-quarter black ancestry. In the color caste system of social rank in Louisiana, an octaroon (one-eighth black ancestry) generally had a higher social status than a quadroon.

QUADROON NURSE   *The Awakening*: She is responsible for the care of Raoul and Etienne Pontellier and is always at a distance behind them as they pursue their activities at home in New Orleans and on vacation at Grand Isle. On one occasion she is described as having a ''far-away, meditative air.''

QUARTIER FRANÇAIS   *See* French Quarter.

R

RACELL "Suzette": He lives across the Red River. The doctor, who was called to attend his sick child, crossed the river just before Michel Jardeau.

RAMPART STREET New Orleans, Louisiana. Originally the inland rampart of the city. "At Chênière Caminada": Claire Duvigné lives on this street at the edge of the French Quarter. *See* French Quarter.

RANDALL "The Unexpected": Despite separation and repeated illnesses, he loves Dorothea.

RAPIDES PARISH, LOUISIANA South of Natchitoches and west of Avoyelles. "A Night in Acadie": Telèsphore Baquette tells Zaïda Trodon that he has lived here in his own place since 1892.

RATIGNOLLE, MADAME ADÈLE Wife of Alphonse. *The Awakening*: As the image of the Creole "mother-woman," she has four children from her seven years of marriage. Mother-women "idolized their children, worshipped their husbands, and esteemed it a holy privilege to efface themselves as individuals and grow wings as ministering angels." However, as strong an image as she is and as fervent a foil to Edna Pontellier, she is a rich character whose home exudes an atmosphere of music and lively conversation. She and Alphonse are well wed and well suited for each other. Physically, she is a women of mature beauty, and psychologically, she has the authority of both station and experience. What she sees in Edna offers no fear for herself, only fear for Edna and the memory of her own adjustments and compromises.

RATIGNOLLE, MONSIEUR ALPHONSE   Husband of Adèle. *The Awakening*: The good-natured pharmacist who treats his wife with devotion. The two appear as ideal complements in a marriage. Thin and tall, he "swayed like a reed in the wind when he danced."

RAUL   "A Horse Story" (*KCM*): The cattledriver who reports the death of the pony Ti Démon on Bonham Road. For possible connection, *see* Driver.

RAYMOND   Husband of Kitty. "Tante Cat'rinette": He is in financial straits and his wife is ill. Cat'rinette, who once worked for his father-in-law, saves him. "A Horse Story" (*KCM*): He owns a mule.

"THE RECOVERY" (1896)   After 15 years of blindness, Jane's sight is restored. Her suitor Robert had been faithful to her for a long time. But her new sight brings the problems of reconciling her illusions fostered over the years and the reality of herself and Robert. The disappointment over the loss of youth is crushing.

RED-FACED MAN   "Mamouche": The crude and insensitive man who, upon reading the notices advertising a reward for the capture of the person who caused Dr. John-Luis difficulties, seizes Mamouche and brings him to the doctor.

RED RIVER   Runs from the northwestern part of Louisiana to the Tunica hills where it empties into the Mississippi River. In Chopin's time it was a navigable river important to the towns and plantations along its route. "A No-Account Creole": The Santien place is on this river. "Athénaïse": She disembarks from the St. Louis and Shreveport packet on the river to catch a southbound Mississippi river steamer. "Suzette": Michel Jardeau drowns here. *At Fault*: Hosmer's wife Fanny drowns in this river, the *deus ex machina* device ending the novel. "A Night in Acadie."

RED RIVER PARISH, LOUISIANA   Located northwest of Natchitoches Parish. "Tante Cat'rinette": Eusèbe, "a free mulatto," from this parish, passes on the news that Kitty is calling for her.

REDEMPTORIST'S ROCK CHURCH   St. Louis, Missouri. *At Fault*: Belle Worthington attends this Catholic church.

REEDY, WILLIAM MARION   The editor of the *Mirror* in St. Louis who published avant garde fiction like de Maupassant's stories and built a reputation as an unprovincial critic. He admired Chopin from his first contact with her work in *Bayou Folk* and invited her to submit fiction for publication. She respected him over the years despite his failure to appreciate fully her accomplishment in *The Awakening*. *See* Porcher, Frances.

"A REFLECTION" (1899)   The narrator observes life from the roadside as the masses move by. There is a comfort in the contemplation of this activity.

RÉGIME, OLD   The term used by the citizens of New Orleans to refer to the Spanish Colonial period (1766–1803).

"REGRET" (1894)   Aurélie, a satisfied spinster of 50 years, becomes charged with the responsibility of Odile's children for two weeks. After some struggling, she acquires a motherly efficiency. When Odile returns, the children are exhilarated, but she is saddened by the silence. She weeps with regret for a life she refused years ago.

REISZ, MADEMOISELLE   *The Awakening*: She summers at Grand Isle and lives in New Orleans. A musician of some note and sensitivity, she consents to play for Edna Pontellier; one of the pieces is from Chopin. She becomes a kind of alter ego for Edna, who seeks inspiration, counsel, and support from her. In her way she is mysterious and oracular, a key to the theme of self-knowledge and determination that Chopin weaves into this novel.

'RELIUS   Son of Aunt Halifax. "Dead Men's Shoes": He seems often to be present and in the way.

"A RESPECTABLE WOMAN" (1894)   Provoked at her husband's inviting Gouvernail to visit the plantation, Mrs. Baroda registers her disapproval. On meeting him, she finds him dull. However, a chance encounter one evening awakens a response to him. Afterward, she avoids seeing him during his stay. When her husband brings up the possibility of a return visit, she repeatedly rejects it. Then suddenly, she proposes his visiting and promises that she "shall be very nice to him."

"THE RETURN OF ALCIBIADE" (1892)   On a business trip Fred Bartner comes to the Plochel plantation on Christmas morning as he needs a repair to the buggy. The old master, "mad" since the loss of his son in the Civil War, thinks he is the son returned. His granddaughter Esmée convinces Fred to feign Alcibiade's identity to make the old man happy. Her grandfather dies peacefully and the young man falls in love with Esmée.

RICH MAN   "The Blind Man": He dies preparing for his summer holiday journey.

RICHARDS "The Story of an Hour": The friend of the Mallards who carries the message of her husband's alleged death to Louise.

RICHMOND "A Family Affair": The overseer of Madame Solisainte's plantation.

RIGOLET A French variation describing a small channel or trench, perhaps the offshoot of a bayou as in the case of the rigolet de Bon-Dieu.

"RIPE FIGS" (1892) Babette's godmother promises her a visit to her cousins on Bayou Lafourche when the figs are ripe. When the season comes, she goes to see them with the message that the aunts will meet when the chrysanthemums bloom.

ROBERT "The Recovery": Jane's suitor who waits for her during the many years of her blindness.

ROCK SPRINGS, MISSOURI "Juanita": The village, a summer resort in the Ozarks, where Juanita and her mother own a store.

RODNEY, BERT *At Fault*: He seems to attend matinée performances at the theater to meet ladies, especially when his family is out of town. There he meets Mrs. Dawson, who flirts with him; later he calls on her. Mr. Dawson discovers the arrangement and shoots him.

RODNEY, MRS. Wife of Bert. *At Fault*: Aware of the cause of her husband's being shot and the resulting disfigurement, she is "utterly prostrated" and "refuses to see her most intimate friends."

ROME, ITALY "Charlie."

ROSALIE "Lilacs": The neighbor of Adrienne Farival's who is Sophie's confidant of sorts.

ROSE "A No-Account Creole": The black woman on the old Santien place who gets La Chatte to talk about the Santien boys.

"THE ROSES" (poem, 1898) Depicts an unconsoling moment when even roses fail to help. Probably the poem alludes to the deaths of Chopin's brother and husband, both of whom died in December, the month of the poem's composition. *See KCM* for variant lines.

ROYAL STREET New Orleans, Louisiana. One of the streets connecting Canal Street and Esplanade Street in the French Quarter. "In and Out of Old Natchitoches": Maman Chavan has a small house on a narrow street between

Royal and Chartres streets. "La Belle Zoraïde": The heroine is described as being "as charming and as dainty as the finest lady of la Rue Royale."

RUBEN, UNCLE   "Charlie": The black butler who directs and carves in the Laborde dining room.

RUBY, AUNT   "Regret": Mamzelle Aurélie's black cook who is always one step ahead of the children—she had many.

"A RUDE AWAKENING" (1891)   Lolotte, who has been caring for the younger children, accepts the responsibility forsaken by her father. One day the wagon and the mules get away from her control and she is nearly killed. Joe Duplan rescues her, cares for her, and—to teach the father a lesson—hides her. A reunion is arranged, and the father is shamed into accepting his responsibilities.

RUE RIVOLI   Paris, France. "A Point at Issue": The street in Paris where Eleanor Faraday has a room.

RYDON, ABNER   "The Going Away of Liza": Strong, impulsive, and critical, he lives apart from others psychologically and geographically. His wife leaves him only to return later.

RYDON, MOTHER   "The Going Away of Liza": The mother of Abner who though a solid and stoic type shows her heart ultimately.

S

SABINE PARISH   Louisiana. The Sabine River forms its western border with Texas; Natchitoches Parish the eastern. "In Sabine": Bud Aiken, after his futile attempts at making a living, settles here with his Acadian wife.

SACRED HEART CONVENT   St. Louis, Missouri. Chopin studied under the French-founded order of nuns here. *At Fault*: Belle Worthington's 12-year-old daughter is being educated at this institution.

SAHARA DESERT   "A Point at Issue."

SAINT PHILLIPPE   Located on the Mississippi River in the Missouri-Illinois region of the old Louisiana territory. "The Maid of Saint Phillippe": The log-cabin village being evacuated before the English advance.

SALAMBRE, MLLE   "Miss McEnders": The seamstress whose moral reputation is tarnished. However, when challenged, she informs Georgie about the "skeletons in her own closet."

SAM   "The Gentleman from New Orleans": The black worker who is in the immediate area of the Bénoîte house.

SAMBITE   "Loka": Loka recalls that this Choctaw is given to revelry and a certain amount of violence.

SAMPSON   *At Fault*: The young black servant who makes "insinuating" advances toward Melicent Hosmer. He makes the fire for the Hosmers and gathers produce from the garden.

SANDY   Grandson of Aunt Tildy. "Ozème's Holiday": His illness disrupts the harvest, and Ozème interrupts his vacation to help out until he improves.

SANS-CHAGRIN   "The Maid of Saint Phillippe": The owner of a tavern in the village of Saint Phillippe.

SANS-CHAGRIN'S TAVERN   Saint Phillippe, Louisiana territory. "The Maid of Saint Phillippe": A group of men are gathered on the gallery here discussing the British being ready to possess their ceded territory at last.

SANTIEN, GRÉGOIRE   Brother of Hector and Placide. "In Sabine": The high-spirited and nobly inclined gentleman who rescues 'Tite Reine from her cruel husband, Bud Aiken. Grégoire stops at their Sabine Parish farm on his way to Texas from his home in Natchitoches Parish. The youngest Santien is like others in his region who would go to Texas to release their frustrations. *At Fault*: The shooting of Joçint and his failed love affair with Melicent Hosmer cause his flight to Texas, where after his stop at the Aiken place, he is killed over a racial slur in Cornstalk. He is a favorite nephew of Thérèse Lafirme's, and the community about Place-du-Bois responds to his death as if he had been her son. "A No-Account Creole": Grégoire, like his brothers, had gone his own way after the loss of the old Santien place to creditors.

SANTIEN, HECTOR   Brother of Grégoire and Placide. "In and Out of Old Natchitoches": Later identified in New Orleans as Deroustan the gambler, he is often in the company of a distant cousin, Suzanne St. Denys Godolph. His dual identity and his restraint in his relationship with Suzanne reflect the responsibility that he has to the name of his old Creole family. "A No-Account Creole": Like his brothers, he is landless and on his own.

SANTIEN, JULES   Father of Hector, Grégoire, and Placide. "A No-Account Creole": He could not repair and restore the Santien plantation to its pre-Civil War condition and prosperity. *At Fault*: He dies four years before the time of this novel. In both works Chopin seems to suggest that he is broken and weakened since the Civil War.

SANTIEN, LUCIEN   Father of Jules. "A No-Account Creole": He has 100 slaves, 1,000 acres of plantation land, and wealth before the Civil War. "Ma'ame Pélagie": He is in conversation with Monsieur Lafirme. *At Fault*: He is mentioned as a gourmet.

SANTIEN, MADAME   *At Fault*: Grégoire tells Melicent at the McFarlane grave that his mother had gone to Paris four years ago when his father Jules died. Thérèse Lafirme refers to her departure as irresponsible, almost criminal, and appears to lay Grégoire's death at her feet. The abandonment of children—three sons here—appears as a motif in a considerable part of Chopin's fiction.

SANTIEN PLACE ("the old Santien place")   On the Red River, Natchitoches Parish, Lousisiana. "A No-Account Creole": Lucien Santien farmed this plantation's 1,000 acres with 100 slaves. It was damaged severely during the Civil War, and his son Jules could not restore it. His three sons inherited the estate, but were burdened with inheritance taxes and could do no better. Harding & Offdean, New Orleans creditors, bought the plantation and assumed its debts.

SANTIEN, PLACIDE   Brother of Hector (the eldest) and Grégoire. "A No-Account Creole": He breaks his engagement to Euphraisie Manton to allow her to marry Wallace Offdean, with whom she falls in love. He acts the part of the proud Creole despite his disappointment. *At Fault*: Placide and Grégoire try to manage the plantation for a year after their father fails, but they fail as well.

SATAN   "A Dresden Lady in Dixie": A character in Pa-Jeff's story of conscience.

SAUTIER, EMILE   "A December Day in Dixie": The manager of a saloon near the railroad tracks. He drinks in the evenings, arrives home late, and does not conserve his supplies. Having lost an eye, he is indifferent to fate.

SAUTIER INFANT   Son of Emile. "A December Day in Dixie": The child falls into an old unused cistern, but the fall is broken by tree branches. After two hours in this lizard- and snake-infested place, he is saved.

SAUTIER, MADAME   Wife of Emile. "A December Day in Dixie": Young, fat, and dirty, she wears a black-white "Nubia" about her head. Her time is divided between kitchen and child.

SAUTIER'S SALOON   Cypress Junction, Louisiana. "A December Day in Dixie": Located on the railroad line taken by the Natchitoches train, this saloon offers food, company, and a view of both the community and the cotton fields.

SCHUYLER, WILLIAM   The friend and observer of Chopin's who wrote an oft-quoted sketch of her for *The Writer* in August 1894. However, he made no public comment about *The Awakening*. He taught high school in St. Louis, and was also a writer, critic, and composer.

SCUDDER, HORACE E.   Editor of the *Atlantic*. He encouraged Chopin to begin writing a novel in early 1897.

SENTIMENTAL RELATIVE   ''The White Eagle'': The person who places the white eagle by the unnamed woman's grave.

''A SENTIMENTAL SERENADE'' (poem, ca. 1893)   A love lyric with images of breeze and star.

''A SENTIMENTAL SOUL'' (1894)   Fleurette falls in love with Lacodie, a neighboring locksmith who would come to her store daily for the paper. When he fails to drop in one day, she misses him. And when she discovers his illness, she visits him. All the while her conscience troubles her because he is married. When he dies, she cannot forget him. But after his widow marries, she is free to love him in his death.

SÉPINCOURT   ''A Lady of Bayou St. John'': He tries to woo Madame Delisle with promises of Paris while her husband is away fighting with the Confederate forces. However, he is a puzzled suitor when the lady, hearing of her husband's death, rejects him and devotes her life to her dead mate.

SERAPHINE   ''Boulôt and Boulotte'': The child who with others waits for the return of the twins from town.

SÉVÉRIN   ''Ozème's Holiday'': Ozème borrows a harness from him. ''Aunt Lympy's Interference'': He is able to get along while Lympy is away.

SÉVÉRIN, NÉG   ''The Return of Alcibiade'': Jean Baptiste Plochel, becoming confused, recalls that Robert McFarlane wished to buy this slave. Nég Sévérin is either Sévérin or Sévérin's father.

SÉVÉRIN'S BOY   ''A Turkey Hunt'': The lad who carries the message about the three missing turkeys.

''A SHAMEFUL AFFAIR'' (1891)   Mildred Orme, a summer visitor at the Kraummer farm, encounters a young man while she is enjoying the landscape. They are attracted to each other, and their repeated kisses reveal to her something about her own passions. When she discovers that the fellow is Fred Evelyn, a family friend, she is even more embarrassed over the affair.

SHE   ''Two Summers and Two Souls'': The woman who at first rejects her lover, but later writes to him seeking his affection. Chopin is frequently interested in ideas in a direct way, and she experiments with vague characters and places as fictional vehicles.

SHE   "The White Eagle": The nameless woman who grew up and died emotionally attached to a cast-iron white eagle.

SHELL ROAD   Runs New Orleans, Louisiana to Lake Pontchartrain. *The Awakening*: Edna Pontellier accompanies Arobin on a carriage ride to the lake along this road.

SHELTON, FLORENCE   "The Impossible Miss Meadows": The visitor of high social standing. It worries Mildred Hyleigh that she will find Far Niente disorderly.

SHEPHERD, SI   "Elizabeth Stock's One Story": A character in the failed story by Elizabeth Stock.

SHREVEPORT, LOUISIANA   Caddo Parish. A trade and agricultural center for northwestern Louisiana in the nineteenth century. "A No-Account Creole": Fitch travels here from New Orleans for Harding & Offdean. "The Return of Alcibiade": The Texas & Pacific railroad joined New Orleans and Shreveport. "Dead Men's Shoes": Lawyer Paxton returns from here to the news of Mr. Gamiche's death. "The Gentlemen from New Orleans": Cited in a generalization regarding visitors from the cities.

SIEGFRIED   "Mrs. Mobry's Reason": Sigmund refers to his playing a pipe beneath a tree in town. It is a reference to a performer in a visiting opera.

DE SIERGE, MA TANTE   "Lilacs": She and Julie form a happy memory of home for Adrienne Farival.

SIGMUND   Cousin of Naomi. "Mrs. Mobry's Reason": The medical student who is in love with Naomi. Considering the psychological theme of the story, one can easily observe the allusion to Freud in his name.

SINEY, AUNT   "Polydore": The black cook at Adélaïde's home.

SINN, DR.   "Wiser than a God": The physician who visits Mrs. Von Stoltz on the night of her death. His carriage before the door alerts Paula that a crisis is at hand.

SISTER OF FLAGMAN   "Caline": She lives in a cottage near the French Quarter in New Orleans and employs Caline for domestic tasks.

SISTER OF ADÉLAÏDE   "Polydore": She is married and takes care of Adélaïde during her illness.

SLOCUM, JOE   "Charlie": He is mistakenly recognized as approaching the Laborde home with Charlie. "The Wood-Choppers": His plantation with its gear and livestock has just been sold.

SLOCUM PLACE   Natchitoches Parish, Louisiana. "The Wood-Choppers": George Willet purchases this plantation about six miles below Léontine's cabin near the Cane River.

SMITH   "Polly": The grocer in Filmore who is part of the confusion at the crowded McQuade home.

SMITH, SI   "The Going Away of Liza": One of the station gang at Bludgitt Station, Missouri.

SNECKBAUER, MR.   "The Gentleman from New Orleans": Dapper, wide awake, and affable, he comes from New Orleans in a handsome, chauffeured carriage drawn by two fine horses. Earlier his identity had been attributed in error to Mr. Parkins. He has an engagement with Mr. Bénoîte, who is expecting his arrival.

SOCOES   Grapes from the muscadine vine.

SOHMEIR, MR.   "Wiser than a God": It is his recommendation that the Brainards hire Paula Von Stoltz to play the piano for a social event.

SOLISAINTE, MADAME FÉLICIE   "A Family Affair": The old, fat, selfish, and spirited woman who learns through a hard lesson to stand literally on her feet again. Her sister's daughter, Bosey Brantonniere, applies pressure on her to control her own life more effectively and redistributes, much to her aunt's fury, the family inheritance that she had appropriated only to herself.

SOLISTAN   "A Horse Story" (*KCM*): The 23-year-old farmer who is concerned about the riderless pony he has come across and finds Herminia at the Labatier place. He later marries her.

"SOLITUDE"   Translation from the French of the short story "Solitude" by Guy de Maupassant 1895. See translation in this volume. On an evening walk in Paris, one gentleman addresses another on the nature of being alone, even when in the intimate company of a woman. A motif of madness runs throughout. *See* Night.

SOMMERS, MRS.   "A Pair of Silk Stockings": The young widow who is the mother of Janie, Mag, and the boys. With $15 to spend, she is caught between the needs of her children and the needs of herself. The touch and feel of silk spurs an awakening of her sensibilities and herself.

"THE SONG EVERLASTING" (poem, ca. 1893)   A love poem with images of flowers, bees, and birds. Uses refrain "Awake love."

SOPHIE, TANTE   "Ozème's Holiday": Ozème intended to visit her on his holiday.

SOPHIE   "Lilacs": An old character who runs the household, part of her Paris neighborhood, and, to an extent, her employer, Adrienne Farival.

SOPHIE   Sister of Ernst and granddaughter of Papa Konrad. "With the Violin": The inquisitive and loving child whose sensibilities and perceptions charm her grandfather.

SOPHRONIE   Sister of Thomas "Buddie" Bénoîte. "The Gentlemen from New Orleans": There is no mention of her husband, but she is married, perhaps a widow. Her personality is vivacious, and she is interested in the handsome visitor, Mr. Sneckbauer, from New Orleans. When her brother is away, she "manages" the house.

SOSTHÈNE   "A Dresden Lady in Dixie": He carries the mail to the Valtour plantation.

SOUTH, THE   *At Fault*: Hosmer cites the hard yet attractive aspects of living here. "The Unexpected": Healing warmth of the South.

SPAIN   "Wiser than a God" and "The Maid of Saint Phillippe."

SPERRIT (SPIRIT)   "A Dresden Lady in Dixie": Pa-Jeff uses this allegorical character in his story of conscience.

ST. ANNE   "Ozème's Holiday": A family on whom Ozème intended to call during his travels.

ST. CHARLES AVENUE   New Orleans, Louisiana. A grand thoroughfare extending from Canal Street through the American Quarter toward Jefferson and Carrollton. "A Matter of Prejudice": Madame Carambeau drives out this avenue to her son's on a Christmas morning. "Alexandre's Wonderful Experience" (*KCM*): The doctor who is looking for an antique chest lives here.

ST. CHARLES HOTEL   New Orleans, Louisiana. An opulent hotel on St. Charles Avenue near Canal Street—the American side. "Athénaïse": Sylvie had nursed a foreign lady of distinction here some years before.

ST. DENIS STREET   Natchitoches, Louisiana. "The Bênitous' Slave": Oswald carries fruit to his mistress on this street. "Madame Célestin's Divorce": Lawyer Paxton has his office here.

ST. JOSEPH, MISSOURI   "Polly": The site of an expansion by a St. Louis, Missouri, department store.

ST. LANDRY PARISH   Louisiana. Located between Evangeline and Point Coupée parishes. "A Night in Acadie."

ST. LAZARE   Paris, France. "Lilacs": Probably a mental asylum.

ST. LOUIS, MISSOURI   Kate Chopin was born here in 1850. Her early and adolescent years were also spent in this city. From 1870 to 1884 she lived in New Orleans and then Natchitoches, Louisiana. She returned to St. Louis, where she died in 1904. It is important to realize the substantial cultural and economic life shared by St. Louis and New Orleans. "The Maid of Saint Phillippe": Laclede's village is referred to as St. Louis. "Miss Witherwell's Mistake": Home of Hiram Witherwell. "Miss McEnders": Home of the McEnder family. "Ozème's Holiday": His suit had come from here. "Her Letters": The husband tosses his wife's letters from a St. Louis bridge over the Mississippi River. "Elizabeth Stock's One Story": Miss Stock dies at the city hospital. "Polly": Polly goes shopping here. *At Fault*: David Hosmer and Fanny Larimore's native city serves as a contrast to the French and southern environment around Natchitoches, Louisiana.

ST. LOUIS ACADEMY OF THE SACRED HEART   Chopin and Katherine Garesché studied here through the 1860s with an interruption during the Civil War. The Sacred Heart order that sponsored the school was founded in France, and accordingly, the curriculum had a distinct intellectual character. The order is one of the few then whose nuns kept their family name.

ST. LOUIS CATHEDRAL (the cathedral, New Orleans Cathedral)   New Orleans, Louisiana. The major Roman Catholic church, a minor basilica, in the state. It fronts the Place d'Armes and looks out toward the Mississippi River from its French Quarter location. "In and Out of Old Natchitoches": Suzanne St. Denys Godolph attends Sunday Mass and Vespers here. "A Matter of Prejudice": Madame Carambeau breaks tradition by not attending Mass on Christmas at the French Cathedral and going to St. Patrick's, an American church. "La Belle Zoraïde": Madame Delarivière intends for Zoraïde to be married from the Cathedral. "Aunt Lympy's Interference": The curé recommended a French priest at the Cathedral to Melitte as a confessor. "Alexandre's Wonderful Experience" (*KCM*): Alexandre dreams of being married at the Cathedral. *The*

Awakening: Father Fochel of the Cathedral attempts to explain indulgences unsuccessfully to the lady in black. *See* New Orleans Cathedral.

ST. LOUIS EXPOSITION   St. Louis, Missouri. A city fair prior to the 1903–1904 Louisiana Purchase Exposition. *At Fault*: Chopin describes the many visitors, atmosphere, and the art gallery.

ST. PATRICK'S CHURCH   New Orleans, Louisiana. "A Matter of Prejudice": The Roman Catholic church on Camp Street that drew its congregation from the American Quarter. Madame Carambeau of the French Quarter attends Mass here on a Christmas morning.

ST. PHILIP STREET   New Orleans, Louisiana. "At Chênière Caminada": Tonie Bocaze meets Madame Lebrun and her mother here on a cold day. "Nég Créol": Chicot, bent under the weight of a gunny-bag, disappears in this direction.

STERLING, CAPTAIN   "A Maid of Saint Phillippe": The English commander who comes to take possession of the lands west of the Alleghenies in 1765.

STETSON   Brother of Bess and Nora. "A Lady of Shifting Intentions" (*KCM*): Arriving home, he inquires about the household and leaves the room. Bess and Beverly speak of Will, probably a more familiar name for Stetson.

STOCK, ELIZABETH   "Elizabeth Stock's One Story": She died of a lung disease at the age of 38 after being discharged as postmistress, an event that caused her to withdraw her sister's son Danny from school and apprentice him to a grocer. Her story is an epitaph.

STONE, MARGARET M. B.   Novelist from St. Louis. She founded the Modern Novel Club in 1885. Chopin observes her determination and spirit of reform and describes her as "a woman who accepts life as a tragedy and has braced herself to meet it with a smile on her lips" (*KCM*).

STONELIFT, MISSOURI   A village on the railroad near St. Louis. "Elizabeth Stock's One Story": Where she had been postmistress for six years; it had fewer than 100 houses, including stores, churches, post office, and the mansion on the hill.

"THE STORM: A SEQUEL TO 'AT THE 'CADIAN BALL' " (1898).   While Bobinôt and his son are away from home, Alcée Laballière comes by their home as a storm is about to break. During the rain, he and

Bobinôt's wife Calixta recall their romance and succumb to each other's desires. When the weather clears, Alcée rides away, Bobinôt returns, and they all lead their lives as if nothing had happened.

"THE STORY OF AN HOUR" (1894)   Louise Mallard hears news of the death of her husband in a train accident. She retreats to her room where she experiences an unconventional response: joy and a feeling of freedom. However, when her husband arrives home alive, she sees him and collapses—dead from the "joy that kills."

STRAIGHT-BACKED YOUNG FELLOW   "Suzette": The object of Suzette's romantic intentions.

STUART, RUTH McENERY   A Louisiana-Arkansas writer whom Chopin met and enjoyed. She appreciated Stuart's "Carlotta's Intended."

SUBLET, ARCHIE   "A Gentleman of Bayou Têche": The son of the visiting artist at the Hallet plantation who is rescued from drowning by Evariste Anatole Bonamour.

SUBLET, MR.   "A Gentleman of Bayou Têche": The artist who is a visitor at the Hallet plantation. He is interested in making a sketch of Evariste Bonamour, an Acadian. Chopin suggests a certain antipathy to local color in the reluctance of Bonamour to be treated as less than a person.

"SUICIDE"   Translation from the French of the short story "Suicides" by Guy de Maupassant, 1895. See translation in this volume. A framed story in which the narrator reads a letter written by a suicide victim. It reveals the ennui of life, the images of the past raised by an old letter, and the hopelessness of the future—solitude and infirmity.

SULPHUR SPRINGS, MISSOURI   A village on the Mississippi River at Glaise Creek, southwest of St. Louis. *See* The Cedars.

SUMTER, FORT   Near Charleston, South Carolina. "Ma'ame Pélagie": Reference to the opening cannonade of the Civil War here.

SUSAN   Mother of Black-Gal and Joe and wife of Pap. "The Godmother": The black servant who goes with her family to the circus.

SUSAN   "A Family Affair": The black field worker whom Madame Solisainte had been using as a cook; Bosey replaces her when she takes over the running of the house.

SUSIE, OLD LAME *The Awakening*: The cook at Madame Pontellier's home in Iberville.

SUZANNE, 'DAME "After the Winter": She cuts roses on her place for Easter and notices Monsieur Michel's arrival in church.

SUZE Niece of Uncle Hiram. *At Fault*: A black servant at Place-du-Bois.

"SUZETTE" (1897) Suzette rejects the affection of Michel Jardeau, who later drowns in the Red River. This coquette is bothered less by the news of his death than the failure of a young fellow on a cattle drive to notice her in a nearby window.

SUZETTE "Suzette": The coquette who rejects the affection of Michel Jardeau. She becomes interested in a cattledriver who does not notice her when he passes by. The young lady is more affected by this moment than by Jardeau's death.

SUZIMA Once Susan. "A Vocation and a Voice": The gypsy who befriends and sexually initiates an orphan boy who later leaves for a monastery. However, he eventually returns to her. Abused by her companion, she is a warm and loving person whose humanity is touched by the boy.

SUZONNE, MADAME Possibly Ozéina's mother. "At the 'Cadian Ball": She disapproves of Calixta's behavior and comments that were Ozéina to do similarly, she would be sent home.

SYLVESTER *At Fault*: The worker at the lumber mill near Place-du-Bois who is supposed to be on guard there on Halloween night.

SYLVIE "Athénaïse": Her Dauphine Street rooming house is where Athénaïse stays while in New Orleans. Sylvie is a quadroon in her fifties. Her sense of social place provides that only blacks are allowed to call her madame.

SYLVIE "The Storm": The black maid who helps Calixta.

SYMOND "The Godmother" and "Ti Démon": The storeowner who runs a regular card game and owns a donkey.

SYMOND'S STORE Natchitoches Parish, Louisiana. "The Godmother": Scene of a regular card game. "Ti Démon": Aristides Bonneau diverts Ti Démon from his shopping to a social hour here.

T

"TANTE CAT'RINETTE" (1894)   Tante Cat'rinette, who had been given freedom and property by her former master, becomes a hermit as she guards her condemned house. When she hears that Kitty, the daughter of the master, is ill and needs her, she goes to her. When she discovers their poor financial situation, she offers her money (providing it be legally secured) and her personal service. Her decision to help, she insists, comes about as the result of a vision.

TAVIE, AUNT   "The Locket": In her sadness Octavie thinks of her old sad aunt whom "some youthful affliction had robbed of earthly compensation while leaving her in possession of youth's illusions."

TEACHER AT LOUISIANA NORMAL SCHOOL   "The Godmother": The Kansas blonde who is attracted to Gabriel Lucaze and to Delonce, whom she sees more regularly. Gabriel ultimately breaks his relationship with her as a result of his guilt in Everson's death.

TENNIS GIRL   "A Mental Suggestion": The visitor at a resort whom Chopin uses as a satirical device.

TENOR OF THE FRENCH OPERA   *The Awakening*: There is gossip about his having received "letters which should never have been written."

TEXANS   "Désirée's Baby": The heroine, Désirée, is thought to be a castaway from a group of Texans passing near the Valmondé plantation.

TEXAS   References to this state are largely to its eastern section bordering northwestern Louisiana. Chopin's attitude toward this region is that it is an uncivilized frontier, a contrast to the civility of the French parishes of Louisiana. *At Fault*: Grégoire Santien, in a depression over his broken engagement, goes to Texas to let out his emotions; he is killed in Cornstalk. "In Sabine": Grégoire stops at the Aiken place before crossing the Sabine River into Texas. "Regret": Odile's husband, Léon, is in Texas "a million miles away." "A Horse Story" (*KCM*): Solistan comments that Raul had driven cattle into Texas last month and found Ti Démon's dead body on the Bonham Road.

TEXAS ROAD   Route through northwestern Louisiana to Texas, near Natchitoches and Cloutierville. "In Sabine": Grégoire Santien does not follow this route; rather he moves circuitously to the Sabine River. *See* Bonham Road.

"THERE'S MUSIC ENOUGH" (poem, 1898)   A light spring lyric. *See CW* for variant titles and versions.

THÉRÈSE, SISTER   "Lilacs": The nun who is detailed by the Mother Superior to look after Adrienne Farival's needs during her visit to the convent.

"TI DÉMON" (1899)   Plaisance earned the nickname Ti Démon one Saturday when he had been fooled by his friend Aristides Bonneau into playing cards past the hour of his regular dinner with Marianne. That evening, when he found Aristides with her, he assaulted them both. Marianne married neither one, and despite this being his only violent act, he earned a bad reputation.

TI DÉMON   "A Horse Story" (*KCM*): Chopin personifies this pony as a sensitive being, bothered by exclusion from attention and affection. When his owner, Herminia, marries, he runs away and is killed. Chopin uses names for many animals in her fiction, especially horses.

TI DÉMON (Plaisance)   "Ti Démon": Unluckily nicknamed, he is tricked and in the end loses his girl. His attack on Aristides belies his true nature of gentility, but gives proof for his malicious name. He becomes a misunderstood outcast. This story follows "A Horse Story" by eight months; both are concerned with alienation. *See* above.

"TI FRÈRE" (1896, *KCM*)   Ti Frère, tired of working in the cotton patch, injures his foot with an axe. Azémia witnesses the accident and provides aid. He insists on her calling him by his name, Joe, in a rude way and she leaves. Later he makes up for his insult with a gift of peaches, but she keeps her distance. On Saturday, he fights Bud Aiken at Nat Bower's cabin. Although he wins, his injury worsens and confines him to his home. Azémia returns to nurse him, and they discover a different dimension to their relationship.

TI FRÉRE (JOE) "Ti Frère" (*KCM*): He injures his foot with an axe and later fights Bud Aiken before collapsing from the wound. He lives with a widower brother-in-law and a disagreeable cousin. Azémia comes to help nurse him, but her attraction to him exceeds that of a nurse for her patient.

TIGNON A bandana once required by law to be wrapped about the head of a slave woman moving freely on the streets of New Orleans. Over the years it became a customary headdress for black women.

TILDY Grandchild of Uncle Wisdom. "Madame Martel's Christmas Eve": She accompanies her grandparents to the railroad station to meet her mother. They are blacks and show deference to Madame Martel.

TILDY, AUNT Grandmother of Tildy. "Ozème's Holiday": The old black domestic who once worked where Ozème lives.

TINA, M'AME "At the 'Cadian Ball": Reference is made to her cow.

TINETTE "Charlie": According to Nannouche, her baby had died in the past week.

TI NOMME Brother of Elodie, Marcéline, and Marcélette and son of Odile. "Regret": He stays in the care of Aurélie during his mother's absence.

TISANE (TISANNE) Popular in New Orleans, this tea was made from herbs and often used for medicinal purposes.

'TIT-EDOUARD "A No-Account Creole": He exchanges gossip while waiting for the post office to open. *See* Blount, Judge and Abner, Uncle.

'TITE REINE Daughter of Baptiste Choupic and wife of Bud Aiken. "In Sabine": Once a lovely Acadian maiden whose name means Little Queen, she is abused over a period of time to the extent that her appearance and personality reflect her torments. Grégoire Santien stops at the Aiken farm in Sabine Parish, and seeing her condition, rescues her from both her husband and her hostile environment.

"TO 'BILLY' WITH A BOX OF CIGARS" (poem, 1895) A witty Christmas greeting. *See CW* for title variation.

"TO BLANCHE" (poem, 1895) A Christmas sentiment.

"TO CARRIE B." (poem, 1895) Centers on personal experience and closes with humor: "from gentlemen of high degree/I always flee." For earlier titles, *see CW*.

TOILE-CIRÉE   The French word for oil cloth or American cloth.

TOLVILLE   "Cavanelle": The opera singer who probably appears at the French Opera in New Orleans.

"TO HENRY ONE EVENING" (poem, 1898)   On the consolation of friendship.

"TO HIDER SCHULER" (poem, 1895)   A Christmas greeting. *See CW* for variant versions.

"TO MRS. R." (poem, 1896)   A friendly sentiment, it includes the line "We talk as women talk," a reference to playing music and creating a "spell" with it; and "the street/where people meet"—all relevant themes and images in *The Awakening*. *See CW* for a variant title.

"TO THE FRIEND OF MY YOUTH: TO KITTY" (poem, possibly 1900)   Uses images of lilacs and rose as agents of memory. *See* Garesché, Katherine.

TOUSSAINT OF KASKASKIA   "The Maid of Saint Phillippe": The elder citizen who leaves Saint Philippe for the village that grows to become St. Louis, Missouri.

TOUSSAINT, TOUS-SAINT EVE   All Saints Day was not only a religious feast day, it was also a major social event in New Orleans, where a civil holiday was declared. The eve of All Saints or Halloween was an important occasion for the practitioners of voodoo. This November holiday involved dark and mysterious activities on the evening before, but the day itself is marked by reunions at the family graves in the cemeteries. *At Fault*: Joçint does his wicked adventuring on Halloween night.

TOZIER   *At Fault*: Rufe Jimson tries to explain to his friend Tozier what happened to Grégoire Santien in Cornstalk, Texas.

TRAGEDIAN, A.   *The Awakening*: A picture of this actor aroused Edna Pontellier's passions when she was an adolescent.

TRANQUILINE   "Love on the Bon-Dieu": Azenor's black cook who at his direction intercepts Azélie with food after her communion fast. She is almost a mother figure with her spirited care of Azenor.

TRÉZINIE.   Daughter of the blacksmith. "After the Winter": One of the children who pick flowers for Easter from Monsieur Michel's retreat.

TRODON BABY   Daughter of Mentine and Jules and sister of 'tit Jules. "A Visit to Avoyelles": Chopin uses the children to emphasize the established nature of Mentine's life.

TRODON, JULES   Husband of Mentine and father of Jules and a baby. "A Visit to Avoyelles": He lives near Marksville in a three-room home with a gallery. He seems busy with running a small farm and supporting his family. "A Night in Acadie": His cousin Zaïda Trodon visits him.

TRODON, MENTINE   Wife of Jules and mother of Jules and a baby. "A Visit to Avoyelles": Doudouce goes to visit her in an attempt to recapture the happiness of an old love. Now married seven years, she has borne two children and works on the farm. Her figure is lost and her skin is brown and rough. Her voice is shrill from calling to children and dogs. However, there is still a quality that makes her attractive to Doudouce. "A Night in Acadie": She appears as Madame Trodon.

TRODON, 'TIT JULES   Son of Mentine and Jules. "A Visit to Avoyelles": Doudouce offers him a small pony during the noon meal conversation.

TRODON, ZAÏDA   Cousin of Jules Trodon. "A Night in Acadie": Fleeing from her parents to marry a young man, she encounters Telèsphore Baquette, who changes her plans to include him. She lives near Bayou de Glaize. Zaïda is "neither tall nor short, nor stout nor slender, nor . . . beautiful . . . nor . . . plain." But two men fight over her.

"A TURKEY HUNT" (1892)   When three turkeys are missing from the flock, nearly everyone searches for them, but without success. However, Artemise, who was waiting on the houseguest, discovers the turkeys as she attempts to hide herself to avoid hunting for them.

"TWO PORTRAITS" (1895)   Alberta the wanton enjoys the pleasures of the sensual life and possesses not only a beautiful body but a knife. Alberta the nun moves from sensual experience to spiritual reality. She has visions of the eternal life in Christ and possesses the power of curing the afflicted.

"TWO SUMMERS AND TWO SOULS" (1895)   A man (He) begins to love a woman (She) during a five-week visit in the country. She is confused and sends him away. In his absence, she realizes her love for him and writes him to return. When he receives the request, he pauses to think of the pain of separation and his current situation, but he drops everything to go to her.

U

"UNDER MY LATTICE" (poem, 1895)   Muses on the longevity of life in the form of a bird's song.

"THE UNEXPECTED" (1895)   Randall and Dorothea are to marry, but circumstances require him to be away for a month. However, his illness prevents his return, and when he does, his appearance is quite disfigured. She recoils and rescinds her promise to marry him—despite his fortune which he says is hers.

UNION DEPÔT   St. Louis, Missouri. *At Fault*: The remarried Hosmer and Fanny depart in a Pullman car from here to the good-byes of the Worthingtons and Dawsons.

UNKNOWN QUESTIONER   "The Locket": The soldier in a Confederate unit who inquires about the locket. Later, he steals the locket, and then is killed in battle. The story turns on the discovery and the account of how he has possession of the locket. The anti-Catholic and anti-French attitudes of Edmond's messmate complement his being in the dark shadows and suggest the atmosphere of evil.

URSULINES   The Ursuline Convent, probably the Seminary. New Orleans, Louisiana. School for girls established by the Ursuline nuns in 1727. "Charlie": Madame Philomel, who teaches music and the arts on the Laborde plantation, studied here in her youth. Charlie attends the Seminary for a period of time as well.

UTICA, NEW YORK   *At Fault*: Johanna has relatives in this city.

V

"VAGABONDS" (1895)   The narrator is called to meet a poor traveling man who often passes near the plantation. They speak of local gossip and he goes on to Alexandria, where he had heard of a job. She muses on his life and his perplexities as she walks.

VALCOUR   "Vagabonds": A ne'er-do-well relative of the narrator's, and one who goes from place to place. There is a value in his experience: "to get close to the black night and lose oneself in its silence and mystery."

VALMÊT, LÉANDRE   Brother of Ma'ame Pélagie and Pauline and father of La Petite. "Ma'ame Pélagie": He returns after some years to the society of his sisters when they decide to leave the past and face the present.

VALMÊT, PAULINE   Sister of Pélagie and Léandre. "Ma'ame Pélagie": For many years she and her older sister have lived among the ruins of their home which was ravaged by the Civil War. The longer they keep the hope of rebuilding the great home, the more they are in isolation. When Léandre's child visits, the contrast between their static life and the vital life of the youngster awakens Pauline.

VALMÊT, PÉLAGIE   Sister of Pauline and Léandre. "Ma'ame Pélagie": The strong woman who lives with her younger sister and yearns to rebuild Valmêt plantation from its ruins. For years they live spare lives, but her brother's child changes their plans. And they begin to enter life more fully, as people once again return to their company and their new but modest home. Chopin embraces in Pélagie the power not only of youth but of the present.

VALMÊT, LA PETITE   Daughter of Léandre. "Ma'ame Pélagie": When she visits her aunts Pélagie and Pauline in the little cabin next to the ruins of Valmêt, she awakens first Pauline's thirst for life. Then Pauline influences her sister to change her mind about rebuilding the plantation. La Petite is a symbol of life, the vitality of the present, and the promise of the future. Chopin frequently uses children as catalysts in her fiction.

VALMÊT, PHILIPPE   Father of Pauline, Pélagie, and Léandre. "Ma'ame Pélagie": He built Valmêt plantation before the Civil War.

VALMÊT PLACE   Natchitoches Parish. Louisiana. "Ma'ame Pélagie": Philippe Valmêt's red brick mansion on the Côte Joyeuse near Natchitoches that was sacked and burned during the Civil War.

VALMONDÉ, MADAME   "Step-mother" of Désirée. "Désirée's Baby": The warm, tender, and responsible chatelaine who regards Désirée as "a beneficent Providence . . . the child of her affection, seeing that she was without child of the flesh." A knowledgeable woman, she notices the Negroid features of Désirée's child and says nothing. When Armand responds violently to the discovery, she tells Désirée to come home with her child. Madame Valmondé is a protocharacter of the mother-woman whom Chopin creates in Madame Ratignolle of *The Awakening*.

VALMONDÉ, MONSIEUR   "Désirée's Baby": Although his adopted daughter Désirée is his idol, he is quite concerned about her proposed marriage to Armand Aubigny. He "grew practical and wanted things well considered: that is, the girl's obscure origin." Despite being lightly sketched, Monsieur Valmondé has the kindness one finds in Monsieur Ratignolle of *The Awakening*.

VALMONDÉ PLANTATION   Natchitoches Parish. Louisiana. "Désirée's Baby": Located just above Coton Maïs's ferry on the Red River and near L'Abri plantation, its gates are on the road connecting the ferry with the Texas Road. Désirée is found abandoned as an infant at the stone pillar gateway.

VANDERVOORT'S STORE   St. Louis, Missouri. *At Fault*: Melicent Hosmer meets Belle Worthington here, where she discusses Thérèse and Hosmer publicly.

VALSIN   "Regret": The mulatto who drives Odile to her mother's in his mule cart.

VALTOUR, MADAME   Wife of Albert. "A Dresden Lady in Dixie": The chatelaine who is upset over a missing china figure of a lady, mostly because of its sentimental value. "A Night in Acadie": She has several charming and accomplished daughters. However, in the previous story she intimates that she had a daughter who died.

VALTOUR, MONSIEUR ALBERT   "A Dresden Lady in Dixie": Pa-Jeff "confesses" to him about Satan while the family is at dinner.

VALTOUR, OLD MARSE   Father of Albert. "A Dresden Lady in Dixie": Pa-Jeff had served him well during the Civil War campaigns.

VANCE, WALLACE   Elizabeth Stock's One Story": The postal patron who admires Elizabeth Stock, the postmistress.

VAN WYCKE, MRS.   *At Fault*: A St. Louis resident who is one of Melicent Hosmer's friends and fellow bridge players. This lady cheated at cards.

VAUDRY, CAPTAIN ALEXIS   "The Maid of Saint Phillippe": The French Army officer who urges Marianne to return with him to La Rochelle, France. He is anxious to marry her.

VELCOURS   "Ozème's Holiday": Ozème intends to visit this family on his time away from the plantation.

VERA CRUZ, MEXICO   *The Awakening*: Robert Lebrun enters Mexico through this port city.

VERANDA   Usually a roofed and open porch on a home where people congregated to dispel the heat, and engage in reading, sewing, or conversation.

VERCHETTE, ARMAND "CHOUCHOUTE"   "For Marse Chouchoute": The illegitimate Acadian boy who learns responsibility at the cost of the death of his black friend, Wash. Chouchoute is hired to carry the mail to the train station, but he stops for a party one day, and Wash, who tries to save his job by getting the mail to the train on time, falls from his horse to his death. Brotherly love is a persistent theme in Chopin's fiction.

VERCHETTE, MADAME   Mother of Armand. "For Marse Chouchoute": Wash and the other people of Cloutierville love her very much. And she is anxious for the happiness and success of her son despite her fears.

VERDON, MARSE   *At Fault*: The blacksmith who is treated to drinks by Grammont, the storeowner.

VERDON, VICTORIA RICHELET   Grandmother of Victoire Verdon Charleville and ancestor of Chopin's. She owned a keelboat line that operated on the Mississippi between New Orleans and St. Louis.

VERNON PARISH   Louisiana. Located below Natchitoches and west of Rapides Parish on the Texas border. "In Sabine": Aiken is planning to move to this parish to try his luck anew.

VERSAILLES, FRANCE   "Maid of Saint Phillippe."

"A VERY FINE FIDDDLE" (1891)   Old Cleophas plays a fiddle given him by a late Italian friend, often to quiet the children. Fifine threatens to smash it. One day she sells it for a surprising amount of moeny and a replacement, but the fiddle is not the same to Cleophas, and he never plays it again.

VESPERS   The sixth canonical hour in the Roman Catholic liturgy that is said or sung in the late afternoon and is traditionally announced by a bell.

VICTOIRE, COUSIN   "Ozème's Holiday": Ozème has intentions of calling on this relative.

VIEUMAITE   Father of Kitty. "Tante Cat'rinette": The old master who gave Cat'rinette $1,000. He lives powerfully as an influence in her memory.

VINY   "A Dresden Lady in Dixie": The black housemaid in the home of Madame Valtour. Pa-Jeff uses her and her sassiness in his fiction about the "Dresden Lady."

VIRGINIA   "A Lady of Bayou St. John": Gustave Delisle is killed here during the Civil War.

"A VISIT TO AVOYELLES" (1892)   Often Doudouce hears news of the fallen condition of his old love, Mentine. He puts aside his present duties to travel to her in a nearby parish and, if possible, to help her. He barely knows her when he sees her. After dining with her, Jules, and the little boy (to whom he offers a pony), he departs crestfallen as Mentine gazes toward her husband entering the fields.

"A VOCATION AND A VOICE" (1896)   An orphan boy in search of love and security finds consolation in Suzima, a gypsy. She initiates the boy sexually. He stands in marked contrast to her scowling companion Gutro. As they travel together, he encounters a priest who influences his thinking. So he enters a monastery and becomes known as Brother Ludovic. But one day Suzima passes near the fence he has built on the monastery grounds, and he leaves to join her.

VOLSEY, MADAME PIERRE FRANÇOIS DE   Subject of a story told by Madame Charleville to Chopin about a lady of social position who behaved scandalously, so much so that her husband obtained a divorce, the first granted in the city of St. Louis. *See At Fault.*

VON STOLTZ, MR.   Father of Paula. "Wiser than a God": Although he is dead, he still maintains a significant presence through his wife's memories of their being in Leipsic when Paula was young and when he played the piano.

VON STOLTZ, MRS.   Mother of Paula. "Wiser than a God": She constantly objects to Paula's playing the piano at parties, for she considers them obstructions to her musical career. She has a "querulous invalid voice." This native of Austria dies while Paula plays for a party at the Brainards.

VON STOLTZ, PAULA   "Wiser than a God": An untypical heroine for her time, Paula chooses a career in classical music over the tradition of marriage following courtship. Even the deaths of her parents do not weaken her from pursuing "the purpose of my life." Her self-determination is less a rejection of love than an affirmation of the power of music in her life.

W

WALLACE, VANCE "Elizabeth Stock's One Story": The patient admirer of Elizabeth Stock who is always waiting for her.

WALTON, FIRMAN "Charlie": The native of New Orleans who seems an attractive and intelligent businessman. Charlie shoots him by accident on the plantation. However, he pays some attention to Charlie during her school days in the city, for he holds no rancor over the incident. Later, he marries her sister Julia.

WASH "For Marse Chouchoute": The slightly deformed black boy who sacrifices his life in the aid he offers his friend Chouchoute. He dies after falling from a horse as he galloped to meet the mail train, a responsibility of Chouchoute's. The parallel of Jim in Mark Twain's *Huckleberry Finn* offers an interesting perspective on race relations and the theme of brotherly love.

WEST ILLINOIS "The Maid of Saint Phillippe": The territory ceded to Spain.

"THE WHITE EAGLE" (1900) A little girl grew up in the shadow of a white iron eagle. As she matures, she takes it with her from place to place. She does not marry and she grows old, but the eagle is always among her belongings. When she dies, it becomes her tombstone.

WHITE MAID   "A Matter of Prejudice": She answers the door at the Henry Carambeau residence. White domestic servants are unusual in Chopin's Louisiana fiction. In antebellum Louisiana, blacks were perceived to have more value as workers than Irish immigrants.

WHITEMAN, DR. "The Impossible Miss Meadows": The physician who gives Miss Meadows a letter of introduction when she moves.

"WHITE OAKS" (poem, 1898)   A poem on the power of nature as a soothing agent. See *KCM* for variants and context.

WIDOW NICHOLAS   "The Godmother": She is having a romance with the doctor.

WIFE   "Her Letters": Her sentimentality in keeping her lover's letters causes her husband's suicide.

WIFE OF THE CONSUL   *The Awakening*: Gossip has it that Alcée Arobin had an affair with her.

WIFE OF SYLVANO   *The Awakening*: *See* Francisco.

WIGGS, MISS   *The Awakening*: A Tuesday visitor at the Pontellier home.

WILKINS   Son of Dicey. "A Gentleman of Bayou Têche": The black servant who waits on the dining room table at Hallet plantation. He is concerned that he not serve social inferiors.

WILL   *See* Stetson.

WILLET, MR. GEORGE   "The Wood-Choppers": The new landowner who startles, aids, and then marries Léontine. He had bought the Slocum place which was about six miles from Léontine's cabin and near the Laborde plantation.

WILLIAM   "The Impossible Miss Meadows": The coach driver at Far Niente.

WILLIAM, UNCLE   "Elizabeth Stock's One Story": Elizabeth Stock's uncle who is both her literary and general advisor.

WILLIAMS, BUCK   "A Wizard from Gettysburg": The black laborer who has been recently digging the cistern. Bertrand and his grandfather recover his shovel to dig for the fortune.

WILLIAMS, LUKE   "A No-Account Creole": Uncle Abner cites this plantation owner in his painting story. Judge Blount mentions his having a bull with a broken leg.

WILSON, ROLAND   "Miss Witherwell's Mistake": The former fiancé of Mildred Witherwell's who is reunited with her when she discovers him working in the office of the Boredomville *Battery*. An attractive and responsible young gentleman, he becomes the editor in chief.

WINN PARISH   Louisiana. Borders upper eastern Natchitoches Parish. "In Sabine": Bud Aiken lived here, but he was unsuccessful and moved on. "The Gentleman from New Orleans": Mr. Parkins comes from here to bring his daughter Millie Bénôite to the bedside of her ailing mother.

WISCONSIN LAKES   "The Impossible Miss Meadows": Location of the Hyleigh summer home. *See* Far Niente.

WISDOM, UNCLE   Grandfather of Tildy. "Madame Martel's Christmas Eve": The old black man out walking with his wife and grandchild who gives Madame Martel the right of way.

"WISER THAN A GOD" (1889)   Paula Von Stoltz has been reared by her Austrian parents to develop her talent as a pianist. Despite the deaths of her parents, she follows a career in music. Although she loves George Brainard, she does not accept his proposal of marriage. However, when she returns to Europe, her music professor, who is also in love with her, still pursues her.

"WITH A VIOLET-WOOD PAPER KNIFE" (poem, early 1899)   A quatrain in the romantic tradition of honoring out-of-the-way blossoms. *See KCM* for title variant.

"WITH THE VIOLIN" (1889)   Papa Konrad tells his grandchildren a story about himself. Some years before when he was cold, hungry, and in despair, a young violinist whom he had heard playing in the next room called on him and gave him hope. The very next day this violinist, now the conductor of the opera, is to come for Christmas dinner.

WITHERWELL, FRANCES   Sister of Hiram. "Miss Witherwell's Mistake": The weekly columnist for the Boredomville *Battery* who is an "exact and punctilious" woman. She writes articles with titles such as "The Wintering of Canaries" and "A Word to Mothers." She enjoys her niece's disrupted love life, but is happy with the promise of Mildred and Roland's reunion. Chopin points up the folly of this type of female writer.

WITHERWELL, HIRAM   Brother of Frances. "Miss Witherwell's Mistake": The sagacious gentleman who leaves Boredomville for St. Louis to work as a merchant when he detects signs of "commercial paralysis" in the town. His letter to Frances introduces Mildred.

WITHERWELL, MILDRED   Daughter of Hiram. "Miss Witherwell's Mistake": Engaged to Roland Wilson, the young woman is distraught when their relationship is dissolved. She goes to her aunt's home in Boredomville. There she finds Roland working, and they reestablish their relationshp under the influence of Frances Witherwell.

"A WIZARD FROM GETTYSBURG" (1891)   Young Bertrand Delmandé, recalled from college because of a family crisis, discovers a wounded old man at the edge of the plantation. He tends his wound and brings him home. The old man discerns that there is trouble and inquires about its nature. He then shows Bertrand a spot on the grounds where he should dig. A box is unearthed. The old man reenters the house, drops the box of gold on the table, and announces his identity as Bertrand's grandfather, who had been long thought dead in the Civil War.

WOMEN'S REFORM CLUB   St. Louis, Missouri. "Miss McEnders": Issues before this group include the single tax, the dignity of labor, and the moral condition of the St. Louis factory girls.

"THE WOOD-CHOPPERS" (1901)   On a rainy day there is no wood for the fire at Léontine and her mother's home. The workers did not come to chop it, so Léontine takes an axe to chop it in the foul weather. Mr. Willet sees her, helps her over her objections, and begins to call on her. In the spring, he marries her. The axe is an item of honor in his house.

WOODHULL, VICTORIA CLAFFLIN   Sister of Mrs. Tennessee Bartels. She fought for women's suffrage and urged the independence of women.

WOODLAND PARK   In Chopin's time a park in the suburbs of St. Louis, Missouri. "A Vocation and a Voice": A boy, later known as Brother Ludovic, confuses this location with Adams Avenue.

WOODSON   *At Fault*: The worker at the lumber mill near Place-du-Bois who refuses to be out on Halloween watching and guarding the mill.

WORTHINGTON, MR. LORENZO   Husband of Belle. *At Fault*: The custom house employee with a literary and intellectual avocation. In one of his conversations he indicates his interest in tracing the history of religions. Works by Ruskin, Schopenhauer, and Emerson are included among his "hoards" of books. He has a less than positive opinion of women.

WORTHINGTON, MRS. LORENZO (BELLE)   *At Fault*: The shallow friend of Fanny Larimore's who is more concerned about her hair and clothing than almost any other interest. She is given to attending the matinee at the theater with her friends. And she has no regard for her husband's books.

WORTHINGTON, LUCILLA   Daughter of Lorenzo and Belle. *At Fault*: The subdued 12 year old who is ordinarily in the care of an aunt. a nun of the Sacred Heart order.

X

XAVIER, CÉSAR FRANÇOIS (CHICOT; NÉG; MARINGOUIN) "Nég Créol": The black man who refuses to admit, even in the face of personal tragedy, that his illusions of grandeur are broken. He identifies with the old master's family the Boisdurés, and he is devoted to Aglaé, the last of them. When she dies, he cannot bring himself to recognize her passing.

XENOPHORE "Charlie": The youthful field hand who plays with Charlie.

Y

YALE UNIVERSITY   New Haven, Connecticut. "Wiser than a God": George Brainard might have studied at this institution.

YELLOW (YALLAH) TOM   "Odalie Misses Mass": In a reverie Aunt Pinky recalls this suitor and the old master.

YOSEMITE (NATIONAL PARK)   California. *At Fault*: Melicent Hosmer intended to visit this site on her proposed western tour.

"YOU AND I" (poem, ca. 1893)   A memory verse involving love and youth with images of spring and night. *See CW* for the two versions.

YOUNG GENTLEMAN   *The Awakening*: The visitor with whom the adolescent Edna (Pontellier) is infatuated. He is engaged to a young lady on a neighboring plantation.

YOUNG LADIES' SEMINARY   New Orleans, Louisiana. "Charlie": Charlie attended classes here as a boarding student; it is probably the same as the Ursuline Convent. *See* Ursulines.

Z

ZANDRINE "Désirée's Baby": The "yellow nurse woman" Madame Valmondé gazes upon as she perceives the mutually shared Negroid features of the Aubigny infant and his nurse. Moving her "turbaned head majestically," Zandrine responds to Désirée. Always detached and on the fringe of the scene, she is carrying the infant on the gallery when Désirée removes him from her arms and heads for the swamp. Zandrine serves as a device for comparison and as a black alter ego to the idealized Désirée.

ZIDORE, MADAME Grandmother of Lalie. "Love on the Bon-Dieu": The local outcast the community seems to have forgotten in the cottage at the edge of the swamp. Azenor suggests a "spiritual" dimension to her personality as he muses on her communing with the moon. "Suzette": She carries the news of Michel Jardeau's drowning to Suzette and the community. She appears younger and more active.

ZORAÏDE "La Belle Zoraïde": The young mulattress who is enjoined from marrying her black lover Mézor by Madame Delarivière. Her child is given away and Mézor is sold (*see* Griffe Girl). These events cause this beautiful, nearly light, woman to go mad. She carries a doll around as a substitute for her child. The story emphasizes the evils of slavery but also the importance of choice.

Kate Chopin's Translations

＆

Monsieur Pierre

＆

Adrien Vely

It was night, and intensely cold. Anne-Marie, all wrapped in her shawl, was hurrying with rapid strides toward the village. She had been engaged in sewing at a neighboring chateau, and was now hastening to reach home before the hour of dinner, knowing as she did, that her husband would not willingly wait.

Suddenly she was met by a young soldier, who, having recognized her, stopped at once.

"Good evening, Anne-Marie?"

"Good evening, Monsieur Pierre."

"How pale you are," he said, "and you must be frozen! Have you been working again at the Chateau?"

"Yes, and I had forgotten the hour. I fear that it is late."

"And fear, above all, to be scolded, maltreated! Poor Anne-Marie."

"You are mistaken, I assure you, Monsieur Pierre. I shall be neither scolded nor maltreated."

"I am not mistaken, Anne-Marie. I know that your husband repays your care and devotion with hard words. I know that you toil like a slave to support your child, forgetful of self, whilst he muddles himself with drink."

"Oh, Monsieur Pierre! Believe, me, you are wrong."

"Come now! He beats you—the wretch! Do not deny it. I know that he has beaten you."

"Monsieur Pierre, you are cruel. Well, yes; all that you say is true. But is it right for you to accuse my husband to me?"

"How can I help it, Anne-Marie? I suffer so in knowing your unhappiness. You are so gentle, so courageous. I suffer so in being powerless to help you;

you whom I love so well. For I do love you, Anne-Marie. I love you to distraction."

"M. Pierre!" cried the young woman, affrighted, "hush—I must not listen to you. I implore you to say no more." She retreated to a neighboring tree, against which she leaned, shivering from head to foot.

"Yes, I know," said Pierre, "everything separates us, and I should not have spoken—but that was more than I could do. I have kept this secret closed so long in my heart, suffering in silence. Oh, I repeat it. I adore you. But you are troubled—and how you tremble. Are you angry with me? Have I offended you? Why do you not answer? You are weeping. Ah no! There is a smile through your tears! Oh, Anne-Marie, that would be too much happiness—I cannot believe that you love me."

"M. Pierre, I beg of you!" murmured the young woman faintly.

"Ah! you do love me. I feel it—I see it. Why do you try to hide it? You may yet be happy since we love each other."

"Monsieur Pierre," replied Anne-Marie gravely, "Well, yes, I love you and with all my heart. I love you because you are kind and noble; because you have always shown an interest and affection for me. But I am married and I am honest. After what I have told you, we must never see each other again."

"You are right, Anne-Marie. It is better so—that we should never meet again."

"Monsieur Pierre, did you not hear the sound of a footstep?"

"No; it is only the wind blowing the fallen leaves."

"I must make haste; it is late. From today, we are strangers. Good-by."

"Good-by, Anne-Marie."

It was the night following. A freezing night. Pierre, enveloped in his large, hooded cloak had mounted guard at the powder-mill just beyond the town. Suddenly a man advanced toward him.

"Qui vive?" called Pierre.

"How? You do not know François, the husband of your good friend?"

"Halt or I fire!"

"Fire on me? Come now! But if you killed me you could never marry Anne-Marie."

"Wretch!"

"Oh, abuse me if you want. I have you in my power and I defy you to fire on me. I heard you both last night. It was charming—it was touching! Truly, I was moved to tears, and I pitied you both from my soul. What an immense favor to you two if I should disappear now—if I should die. No more obstacles, my good friends. A bullet in the head and that would end it."

"My duty is to fire on you!"

"Your duty! Now if you fired on me, my fine fellow, do you think Anne-Marie would believe you did it from duty? Would she be willing to marry you under such conditions? With a single motion you could, you ought to put an end to me. But that motion you will not make. And I have come expressly to tell you this. Kill me, and Anne-Marie is lost to you forever. Spare me and you forfeit your honor—your honor of a soldier, to which you hold more than life. What do you say to this little revenge? Is it not well thought out? But this is only the beginning. I have some pleasant surprises of the same nature, in reserve. I shall see you again.''

And while Pierre stood immovable, dumb with rage, and powerless, the scoundrel retreated whistling.

He then hastened, as was his custom, to the ale-house, and in an hour's time was stupefied with drink.

Then there came to him a drunken, ferocious whim.

He started in the direction of his house, and once there, entered the room where Anne-Marie was sleeping, and brutally laying hold of her, dragged her from her bed.

"What is the matter?" cried the trembling woman still half-asleep.

"Dress yourself."

"But why?" she asked timidly. "It is not yet morning."

"Will you dress yourself?" and he advanced upon her, enraged, with uplifted arm.

Poor Anne-Marie, seeing that it was useless to resist and knowing that he would beat her rather than abandon his purpose, dressed herself hurriedly.

Then he seized her violently by the wrist, dragging her after him into the street.

"Oh, where are you taking me?" she moaned.

"Where am I taking you? You wish to know? I am taking you to a tender rendezvous, my sweet one. I thought you might find the time long away from your lover, Pierre; that you dreamed of him perhaps. So I concluded it would be a charity to unite you both.''

"François, have pity! What do you mean to do? Oh, this is terrible! Let me return.''

"No, no." cried the wretch, hurrying her violently over the road. "He is sad out there alone. You must go and keep him company—go and distract him. Come on.''

When they reached the powder-mill, it was midnight and the silhouette of the sentinel stood out somber and immovable.

"Qui vive?''

"Come, do not get excited. See how kind I am; I bring you your good friend. I am amiable.''

"Halt or I fire!''

"Oh, no, my brave fellow; you would not kill me in face of your sweetheart—you—''

A shot resounded through the plain and François fell in a senseless heap, muttering a last imprecation. Anne-Marie had fainted away.

The report brought the Sergeant of the Post at once to the spot.

"What has happened?" he cried.

"Why," replied the sentinel, "I had just relieved my comrade, Pierre, and had taken his watch, when a man approached me with threats. I cried, 'Qui-vive, halt!' He continued to advance; then I obeyed orders and fired. I believe that he has his deserts."

A Divorce Case

Guy de Maupassant

"Messers. President and Judges," spoke Madame Cassel's lawyer, "the case which I am entrusted to defend belongs to the province of medicine more than to that of justice and savors rather of pathology than the right of law. At first view, the facts appear simple enough.

"A young man, rich, possessing a noble and exalted soul and a generous heart, falls in love with a girl, more than beautiful—adorable, charming, good, as affectionate as she is lovely, and he marries her. For a while he conducts himself toward her as an attentive and devoted husband. Then at once he begins to neglect her, is rude in his behavior toward her, and seems to feel for her an insurmountable repulsion or irresistible disgust. One day he even strikes her. Not only without reason, but without the shadow of a pretext.

"I shall not describe to you gentlemen, the erratic and incomprehensible conduct of this man. I shall not picture the abominable life of these two beings and the horrible sufferings of this young woman. To convince you, it will be sufficient to read to you certain fragments of a journal written daily by this unfortunate man, this poor lunatic. For it is a lunatic with whom we have to deal. The case is all the more curious, the more interesting, as it recalls in many instances that of the unhappy prince but lately deceased. The eccentric king who reigned platonically over Bavaria. I should call this case one of poetic lunacy. Let me briefly remind you of what has been told of this singular prince. In the heart of the most magnificent portions of his kingdom, he constructed veritable fairy palaces. The natural beauty of the landscape did not satisfy him. He imagined and created fictitious horizons, obtained by means of theatrical artifice, dissolving views, painted forests, in which the leaves upon the trees were of precious stones. There were Alps, glaciers, steppes, sandy deserts burnt by the sun; and at night under the rays of the real moon glimmered lakes, lighted from beneath by fantastic, electric appliances. Upon these lakes floated swans, while an orchestra composed of the foremost performers of the world lulled with poetic fantasies the soul of this royal lunatic. This man was chaste—he was a virgin. He never loved but a dream—his divine dream.

"One night he was accompanied in his barque by a young woman, very beautiful and a great artist, and he entreated her to sing. She sang, intoxicated herself by the bewitching scenery, the soft mild air, the perfume of flowers and by the ecstasy of this young and beautiful prince. She sang as women do who are moved by love. Beside herself she fell upon his heart, her lips seeking his. But he hurled her into the lake and seizing the oars rowed toward the shore, without the slightest concern as to her possible fate. We find ourselves, gentlemen, confronted by a case singularly similar. I shall content myself with reading passages from the journal which was discovered in drawer of the secretary.

" 'How sad is everything, how hideous; always the same, always odious. How I long for a world more beautiful, more noble, more pure. How meager would be the imagination of their God—if their God existed—or if he had not created other things beside. Always the wood—little wood, streams which resemble streams, plains like unto other plains; all the same, all monotonous. And man! man? What a horrible animal, wicked, proud and repugnant. . . .

" 'To love—to love distractedly without seeing the object of one's love! For, to see is to understand and to understand is to despise. To drink one's self drunk with love as with wine—drink, drink, drink, night and day!

" 'I think I have made a discovery. She was in her whole being something ideal which seems not to belong to this earth, and which gives substance to my dream. Ah! my dream, how unreal are its pictures! She is blond, a light blond, with hair of inexpressible shades. Her eyes are blue! Blue eyes alone carry away my soul. All that in woman reaches the depths of my heart, appears in the eyes, and in the eyes.

" 'Oh, mystery! What mystery in the eye! the whole universe is in it, since it sees and reflects the visible world. It contains the universe, things and kings, forests and oceans, men and hearts and stars and all things—all. It sees, gathers, and holds. But there is more in it. There is the man who thinks, the man who loves, the man who laughs, the man who suffers! Oh, look at the blue eyes of women those which are deep as the sea, changeable as the sky; so soft, so soft; soft as the zephyrs, soft as music, soft as kisses, and so clear, so transparent that through them we may see the soul; the blue soul which colors them, animates them, defies them. Yes, the soul has the color of the glance. The blue soul is pregnant with dreams; it has gathered its azure from the billows and the ether.

" 'The eye! think of it, the eye! It drinks visible life to nourish thought. It drinks in the world, color, movement, books, pictures, all that is beautiful and all that is ugly and with these it forms ideas. And when it rests upon us, it imparts a sensation of happiness which is not of this earth. It reveals that which is hidden from us; it makes us comprehend that the reality of our dream is but miserable dust.

" 'I love her also for her walk. The poet says, that even when a bird walks we feel that it has wings. When she passes me, I feel that she is of another race than that of ordinary women, some more ethereal, more divine.

" 'I marry her tomorrow. I am afraid . . . I am afraid of so many things.

" 'Two beasts, two dogs, two wolves, two foxes, roaming the woods, encounter each other. One is male, the other female. They couple. They couple from a bestial instinct which forces them to continue the race, their race, whose form, shape, bristles, movements, habits they have. All brutes do the same without knowing why. . . .

"We also . . . ."

" 'That is what I did in marrying her. I obeyed that imbecile passion which thrusts us toward women.

" 'She is my wife. So long as I ideally desired her, she was for me the intangible dream about to be realized. From the very second in which I held her in my arms, she became a creature which nature has used to betray our hopes.

" 'Has she betrayed them? No. And yet, I am tired of her. So tired as to be unable to touch her even so slightly with my hand or my lips, but my heart is stirred by an inexplicable disgust. Not, perhaps a disgust for her, but a more far-reaching one; greater, more despicable. A disgust for the embrace of love, so vile that it has become for all refined beings a shameful act to be concealed, which is mentioned only in a whisper and with a blush.

" 'I can no longer endure to have my wife approach me, appealing to me with her smile, her glances, and her arms. I can stand it no longer. I formerly believed that her kiss could transport me to heaven. One day she was suffering with a passing fever, and I detected in her respiration the light, subtle, almost intangible breath of human corruption. Oh! flesh! seductive and living ordure, putrefaction which moves, thinks, speaks, which looks and which laughs—in which nourishment ferments . . . and which is pink, pretty, tempting, treacherous as the soul.

" 'Why is it that flowers alone smell so good, the large flowers, brilliant or pale, whose tones and whose colors stir my heart as trouble my eyes. They are so beautiful. Oh so fine a structure—so variegated and so sensual, unfolding like organs. More tempting than the mouth; and deep, with turned lips, indented, fleshy, powdered with a life which in each produces a different perfume.

" 'They alone in the world reproduce themselves without soil to their inviolate race; diffusing about them the divine incense of their love, the odorant heat of their caresses, the essence of their incomparable bodies. These bodies endowed with every grace and elegance; of all shapes, which have the coquetry of all colors, and the intoxicating seduction of all the perfumes.

" 'I love flowers; not as flowers, but as delicious and material beings. I pass my days and nights in the hot houses where I hide them as women are hidden in harems. Who, besides myself knows the carnal, ideal, superhuman sweetness, the maddening charm, the tremulous ecstasy of their tenderness. And the delicate, rare, fine, unctuous, kisses of the admirable flowers on the pink flesh, on the red flesh, on the white flesh—dipping miraculously.

" 'I have hot houses to which no one penetrates but myself and the ones who have them in charge.

" 'There I enter as to steal into a place of secret pleasure. In the high glass gallery I pass between two masses of corollas, closed, half open, or fading which slant upward from the ground to the roof. They send me their first kiss.

" 'These flowers which adorn this vestibule of my mysterious passions are my servants and not my favorites. They salute me as I pass, with their changing brilliancy and their fresh exhalations. They are *mignonnes*, coquettish, ranged upon eight rows to right and left and press so closely together that they seem like two gardens extending to my feet. My heart palpitates, my eye illumines at beholding them. The blood courses through my veins, my soul is exalted, and my hands already quiver with desire to touch them. I pass on. There are three closed doors at the end of this high gallery. I may choose. I have three harems.

" 'But I enter oftenest among the orchids, my slumbering favorites. Their chamber is low, suffocating. The warm damp air moistens the skin, seizes the throat, and makes the fingers tremble. They come, these strange girls from marshy, burning and unwholesome lands. They are captivating as sirens, fatal as poison, deliciously bizarre, enervating, frightful. There are some which re-semble butterflies with enormous wings, slender extremities and eyes! For they have eyes, they look at me, they see me, these prodigious, marvellous beings— fairies, children of a sacred world—unpalpable air and warm light—that mother of the world. Yes, they have wings and eyes and color that no painter can portray. They have all the charms, the graces, the shapes that can be dreamed of. They spread their flanks, odorant and transparent, open for love and more tempting than all women's flesh. The incomparable shapes of their tiny bodies throw the swooning soul into a paradise of visions and ideal voluptuousness. They quiver upon their stems as if about to fly. Will they fly and come to me? No. It is my heart that floats above them like a mystical male being tortured with love.

" 'No intrusive insect may disturb them. We are alone, they and I, in the bright prison house which I have made for them. I contemplate them with admiration—with adoration, one after the other.

" 'How plump they are, how deep and rosy with a rose tint which moistens the lips with desire. How I love them! The borders of their chalices are curled, paler than their throats, and within hides the corolla. Mysterious mouth, capti-vating, sweet under the tongue, showing and unveiling the delicate organs, the admirable and sacred organs of these small divine creatures which smell sweet and do not talk.

" 'At times I have a passion for one of them which endures as long as its existence. Sometimes days—sometimes nights. It is then removed from the common gallery and enclosed in a miniature cabinet of glass, where murmurs the running of a thin stream over a bed of tropical verdure from the isles of the great Pacific. I stay near it, ardent, feverish and tormented; anticipating its approaching death and watching it fade whilst I possess it, inspire it, drink, gather its short life in an inexpressible caress.' "

When he had finished the reading of these fragments, the lawyer said: "Decency, gentlemen, prevents me from disclosing to you further the strange avowals of this insane, shameless idealist. The few fragments which I had submitted, will, I think, help you to appreciate this case of mental disease, less rare than one would suppose in our epoch of hysterical devotion and corrupt decadence.

"I feel that my client has better claim than most women to a divorce, considering the exceptional situation in which she is placed by this strange sensual perversion of her husband."

ॐ

Mad?

ॐ

Guy de Maupassant

Is this madness that possesses me, or only jealousy? I do not know; but I have suffered inexpressibly. I have committed an insane action, a wildly insane action. But fiercest jealousy; overmastering love, betrayed and scorned; the abominable tortures which I have endured, are these not sufficient motives for crime without being adjudged really criminal at heart or in mind?

Oh! I have suffered, suffered continually, acutely, fearfully. I loved that woman with frenzied transport . . . and yet, that is not true. No, no, no. She possessed me, overpowered and bound me up soul and body. I was, I am her thing, her toy. I belong to her smile, to her lips, to the curves of her body and the contours of her face; her whole exterior being that holds me a panting struggling captive. But she, the woman [who] inhabits that body, I hate, despise, and loathe. Because she is perfidious, bestial, unclean. She is the woman of perdition; the animal false and sensual without a soul, ignoring the bliss of free and wholesome thought. She is the human beast, less than that: she is but a morsel of soft round flesh which harbors Infamy.

The first days of our union were strange and delicious ones. Within her ever open arms I exhausted myself in a frenzy of insatiable desire. Her eyes filled me with thirst that I opened my lips to quench. At noon they were gray; tinged with green at nightfall, and blue in the morning. I am not mad. I swear that they possessed these colors. During the hours of love they were blue, (black and blue)—the pupils restless and enormous. From between her trembling lips would escape the tip of her tongue, rosy and moist which quivered like that of a reptile; and beneath heavy and languid lids gleamed that ardent swooning glance which maddened me. Straining her in my arms, I gazed into her eyes and shivered, moved as well by the necessity to kill this beast as by the need to possess her unceasingly.

When she walked across my room, the sound of her every footfall awakened a turmoil in my whole being: and when she began to remove her garments, letting them fall about her to the floor, and emerging infamous and radiant, I felt in every member a fainting ignoble but infinitely delicious.

One day I perceived that she was tired of me, I saw it in her eyes at waking. Each morning, bending over her, I awaited that first glance. I awaited it full of rage, of hate, contempt for that slumbering brute whose slave I was. But when the pale blue of her iris—that liquid blue like water—revealed itself still languid from recent caresses, it scorched me like a quick flame fretting my passion.

That day when she opened her eyes, I detected an indifferent and sullen gleam which betrayed no desire.

Oh! I saw it, I knew it, scented and understood it at once. So all was over, over for good; every hour, every second convinced me of it. When I invited her with my arms, with my lips, she would turn impatiently from me murmuring: "Shall I never know peace? You are odious! Leave me."

Then I was jealous, but jealous as a dog; a trickster, suspicious, dissimulating. I knew well that she would recommence ere long; that another than I would come and reinflame her senses.

I was frantically jealous; but I am not mad; certainly not.

I waited, oh! I was crafty, she could not deceive me; but she stayed cold, unmoved. She sometimes said: "Men disgust me." It was true.

Then I grew jealous of herself; jealous of her indifference; of her solitude; of her nights. Jealous of her gestures, of her thoughts that I felt were always infamous; jealous of all that I guessed. And when upon awaking she sometimes had that soft, languid look which used to follow our passionate nights, as if some concupiscence had visited her soul and stirred her senses, suffocating rage seized me; trembling indignation; a desire to strangle her. I wanted to drag her down upon my knee, and with my fingers about her throat force her to confess the shameful secret of her heart.

One night I saw that she was happy. I felt that a new passion possessed her. I was sure of it, indubitably certain. She palpitated as after our embraces. Her eyes glowed, her hands were warm, all her vibrating body exhaled that vapor of love which had been the source of my infatuation.

I feigned ignorance, but my attention enveloped her as might a net.

However, I discovered nothing. I waited a week, a month, a whole season. She expanded in the function of some mystical passion. She seemed in the bliss of some intangible caress.

And suddenly I guessed it. I am not mad. I swear it, I am not mad.

How shall I tell it, so as to be understood? How to express this abominable and implausible thing? This is how I discovered it. One night as she entered the room after a long ride, she fell into a low chair opposite me. Her cheeks were glowing, her bosom heaving, and her limbs seemed to fail her. She was in love.

I could not be mistaken. Desperate, and unwilling to contemplate her longer I turned to the window and saw a groom leading by a bridle toward the stable her big prancing saddle horse. She also followed with her eyes the fiery brute. When he had disappeared, she suddenly fell asleep. I lay all night thinking, and I seemed to penetrate mysteries which I had never before suspected. Who will ever sound to its depth the perversion of woman's sensuality? Who will understand their incomprehensible caprices and the gratification of their bizarre fancies?

Each morning at daybreak she started out upon her gallop over woods and plains, and each time she reentered languid as if from the ecstacies of love.

I had finally understood. I was jealous of that nervous galloping horse; jealous of the wind that caressed her face as she went her swift course; jealous of the leaves that kissed in passing her delicate ears; of the grains of sunlight that filtered upon her brow through the tree branches; I was jealous of the saddle, pressed against her thigh.

It was all this that enraptured her, and brought her back to me listless and almost insensible. I resolved to revenge myself. I grew gentle and full of attention toward her. Each morning I held out my hands, helping her to dismount after her reckless ride; the furious animal would turn upon me; and she would pat his curled neck, kiss his quivering nostrils without afterward wiping her lips. The perfume of heated body—as after the warmth of the bed—mingled with the acrid animal smell of the beast. I awaited my day and hour. Every morning she traversed the same path that led through a small birch wood to the forest.

I went out before daybreak, carrying a rope with me, and my pistols in my bosom, as if going to a duel. I hurried to the middle path that she loved to travel, and there stretched the rope between two trees; concealing myself in the bushes. With my ear pressed to the ground I could hear the horse's distant gallop. Then I saw him still far off beneath the vaulted branches of the avenue, but tearing madly toward me. Oh I had not deceived myself, it was this! She seemed transported with bliss; her cheeks were flaming, her eyes glowed and her nerves, from the swift motion agitating them, were vibrant with brutal, unmingled pleasure.

The animal hurled himself against the snare which I had prepared for him, and rolled to the ground his forelegs broken. I received his rider in my arms. I have the strength to carry an ox. When I had laid her upon the ground. I approached him. He was looking at us. Then as he attempted to bite me, I placed the muzzle of my pistol to his ear and killed him, like a man.

But I myself staggered, my face cut by two lashes of a riding whip. As she menaced me anew, I sent my remaining ball into her abdomen.

Tell me, am I mad?

It?

Guy de Maupassant

MY DEAR FRIEND: I understand that you cannot believe it. You think I have lost my senses? Well, perhaps I have, partially, but not for reasons which you suppose.

My ideas and convictions on the subject of matrimony have suffered no change. I still consider legal mating a folly. More than ever do I feel incapable of confining my love to one woman. I long for a thousand arms, a thousand lips, that I might hold in one embrace a very host of those beings at once so charming and so insignificant.

And still I shall marry.

Let me add that I have but the slightest acquaintance with my wife of tomorrow; I have seen her but four or five times all told; yet she is not disagreeable to me, and that is sufficient. She is small, stout, and blonde. Day after tomorrow I shall be wishing that she were tall, dark and slender! She is not rich; she belongs to the bourgeoisie; a young girl such as we find by the wholesale, without special traits or talents, and without apparent faults.

Then why do I marry, you ask. I hardly dare confess to you the strange, unaccountable reason which drives me to this stupid act.

I marry in order not to be alone! I hardly know how to make myself understood. You surely will pity and despise me, so utterly miserable is my state of mind.

I wish to be no longer alone at night. I wish to feel a human being near me— next to me; a being who can talk—say something, no matter what. I want to be able to disturb her slumber; ask a question at random and abruptly; any senseless question, in order to hear a voice; to feel that my home is inhabited; to feel a soul awake, a reason at work; to see, upon suddenly lighting my candle, a human figure at my side—because—(oh, the shame of it!)—because I am afraid when I am alone!

I know that you do not yet understand me. I fear no danger. I could kill a malicious intruder without a tremor. I am not afraid of spirits; I do not believe in the supernatural. I am not afraid of the dead, for I believe in the complete annihilation of every being who passes away. I am afraid of myself! I am afraid of fear; afraid of madness; afraid of that horrible sensation of incomprehensible terror!

You will laugh; but, oh! it is fearful—uncontrollable! I am afraid of the walls, the furniture, familiar objects which for me seem instinct with animal life. I fear, above all, the confusion of my thoughts, of my clouded reason, which eludes me, dissipated by some mysterious, hidden anguish.

I feel at first a vague uneasiness which traverses my soul and sends a shiver along the flesh. I look about me. Nothing! And I want something! What? Something comprehensible, since I am afraid simply because I do not understand my fear.

I speak, and I am afraid of my voice. I walk; I am afraid of the unknown behind the door; behind the curtain; in the closet; under the bed. And yet I know there is nothing there. I turn suddenly, fearing that which is back of me, though there is nothing, and I know it.

My agitation grows and my terror increases. I shut myself up in my room, plunge into bed and hide myself beneath the sheets, cowering, desperate at the thought that my candle remains lighted and I shall have to extinguish it! Is it not frightful that I should be so—I who formerly did not know what fear meant?

It began last year in a singular way. It was a rainy day in autumn. Dinner was over and my servant gone, and I asked myself what I should do next. For a while I tramped about my room. I was tired; depressed without cause; unable to work or even to read. A fine rain clouded the windowpanes. An incomprehensible sadness and melancholy penetrated my whole being, bringing with it a desire to weep, to speak to some one—any one—in order to dispel the heaviness of thought.

I felt alone. My lodging had never seemed so empty. A feeling of solitude—poignant, infinite—enveloped me. I could not remain seated, and found no relief in walking. Perhaps I was feverish, for I noticed my hands, which I held clasped behind me while I walked, felt hot against each other. Suddenly a cold chill passed along my back. I thought the dampness of the outer air had penetrated within doors, and the idea came to me to light a fire. I did so. It was the first of the season. Then I seated myself again, watching the flames. But to remain quiet was impossible. I felt that I must move about; go somewhere; find a friend.

I went out in search of companionship, but not one of the comrades whom I sought was at home. It was dreary everywhere. The wet pavements glistened. The tepid rain was chilling; an impalpable moisture filled the streets, clouding the gas jets.

I walked with a dragging step, always seeking someone with whom to converse. In the several cafés which I entered, from the Madeleine to the Faubourg Poissoniére, were seated dejected-looking creatures, seemingly without energy enough to consume the refreshments before them.

About midnight I turned my steps toward home. I was quite calm but very tired. My conciérge, who always retires before 11, opened the door for me at once, contrary to his usual custom; and I thought, "There! Some other lodger must have entered just before me."

When quitting my room I always turn the key twice in the lock. I found the door simply pushed to, and that surprised me; but I supposed that my letters had been brought in during the evening.

I entered. The fire was still burning and even partly illuminated the room. I picked up a candle to go and light it at the fireplace, when, in glancing ahead of me, I perceived someone seated in my armchair warming his feet, with his back toward me. I was not afraid; oh! not the least in the world. One of my friends had come to see me; that was all. The conciérge, following my instructions, had said that I would soon be back and had offered the use of his key. This explained the circumstance of the door being open for me at once, and of my own door standing ajar. My friend—of whom I could only see the back of his head—had fallen asleep before my fire while waiting for me, and I advanced to awaken him. I could see perfectly that one arm hung down on the right side; his feet were crossed; and the position of his head—inclined a little to the left— indicated slumber. I wondered who it might be. The room was quite dim. I reached out my hand to touch his shoulder. There was no one there! The chair was empty!

Heavens! What a shock! I recoiled as if in the face of some terrible danger. I turned, feeling that there was someone behind me, but spun quickly around, forced by an imperative necessity, to look at the chair again. And so I stayed, panting with fright, ready to drop.

But with the return of my usual sangfroid my reason came back to me. "I have had an hallucination, that is all," I thought. And thought travels swiftly in such moments. I had had an hallucination; that was an incontestable fact. My mind had remained lucid, logical. The trouble was, therefore, not with the brain. The eyes alone had been deceived and had deceived the intellect. The eyes had beheld a vision; one of those visions which lead simple folk to believe in miracles. It was a nervous accident to the optical apparatus—nothing more; a little congestion, perhaps.

I lighted my candle. In stooping toward the fire I noticed that I trembled; and in drawing myself up with a start, it seemed as if someone had touched me on the back. I was surely not composed. I took a few turns through the room; spoke aloud; sang a refrain below my breath.

Having closed the door, double bolting it, I felt somewhat reassured. At all events, no one could enter. I seated myself and reflected long upon my singular adventure. Then I went to bed and blew out the light.

I lay on my back quietly enough for a while; then, obeying an imperative necessity to look about the room, I turned on my side. There were only a few embers left in the grate, and their dim glow fully lighted the feet of the armchair. I thought I saw the man seated in it, and hastily struck a match. I had been mistaken; I saw nothing. However, I arose and went and hid the chair behind my bed. Again, in the obscurity, I tried to sleep. But, losing consciousness, the whole scene of the evening came back to me in a vivid dream. I awoke with a start, and, having relighted my candle, sat up in bed without even trying to sleep. Twice, however, for a few seconds, sleep over-powered me, and twice the vision reappeared. I thought I had gone mad. But with the approach of day reason seemed to return to me, and I slept peace-fully till noon.

Now it was over and done for, I thought. I had had a fever—a nightmare. I had been ill, in short. Nevertheless, I felt rather foolish and ashamed.

The whole of that day I was very gay—dined at the cabaret and went to the play in the evening.

But, returning home, a strange uneasiness seized [me] upon nearing the house. I was afraid of seeing it again. No, not afraid of it; not afraid of its presence, in which I did not believe. I feared the hallucination—the fright of it.

For an hour I walked back and forth before the house. But realizing the folly of my conduct, I entered at last. I was breathless and could scarcely mount the stairs. Ten minutes longer I lingered upon the landing before my apartment. Then with a sudden impulse of courage, a steeling of the will, I thrust the key in the lock, opened the door, candle in hand, and gave a rapid, terrified glance toward the fireplace. I saw nothing. Ah! what a relief! What comfort! What a joy! I moved about the room with a careless, forced unconcern. I turned with sudden starts. The obscurity of the corners disconcerted me. I slept poorly, awakened incessantly by imaginary noises. But I did not see it. No, that was ended.

Since that day I am afraid when alone at night. I feel it there, near me, about me—the vision. It did not reappear. Oh, no! And, besides, what could it matter since I do not believe in it—since I know it is nothing? It frets me, however, because I think of it incessantly. A hand slung at the right side; the head inclined toward the left like that of a man who sleeps. But, in God's name, enough! I want no longer to think of it.

Yet what means this persistence—this obsession? Its feet were quite near the fire! It haunts me! This is senseless, but so it is. Who? It? I know that it does not exist—that it is nothing. It exists only in my apprehension—in my dread—in my anguish! Enough of this!

But reason as I can, steel myself as I will, I cannot longer remain alone at home, because it is there. I shall not see it again. I know that is ended. But it is there all the same, in my thought. It remains invisible. That does not hinder its being there. It is behind doors, shut up in closets, under the bed, in all the obscure corners, in all the shadows. I feel it behind me. I turn, certain, however, that I shall not see it. It is still none the less behind me.

This is at once stupid and atrocious. What would you? I cannot help it.

But if there were two of us at home I feel—yes, I surely feel—that it would no longer be there! For it is there because I am alone; solely because I am alone.

Solitude

Guy de Maupassant

It was after a jovial ''stag'' dinner that one of the party, a friend of long standing, proposed to me to accompany him in a walk up the Avenue of the Champs Elysées.

We strolled very leisurely under the trees that were but beginning to put forth leaves. No sound could be heard save the confused and continued rumble of Paris. A cool breeze was blowing, and a legion of stars besprinkled the black heavens like powdered gold.

''I know not why it is,'' began my companion, ''but here, at night, I breathe more freely than anywhere else. Here, my thoughts seem to expand, and there comes to me at times a sort of spiritual illumination, like a promise of the revelation of hidden things.''

At intervals shadowy couples flitted by us. Upon a bench which we passed a man and woman were seated, and so closely interlaced in each other's arms to give the impression of a single dark figure.

''Poor things!'' muttered my friend, ''they inspire me with profound pity, seeking like the rest of us—like all creatures—to escape the isolation of self.''

''For a long time'' he continued, ''I have endured the anguish of having discovered and understood the solitude in which I live. And I know that nothing can end it; nothing! Whatever we may do or attempt, despite the embraces and transports of love, the hunger of the lips, we are always alone.

''I have dragged you out tonight in the vain hope of a moment's escape from the horrible solitude which overpowers me. But what is the use! I speak and you answer me, and still each of us is alone; side by side but alone.

''You may think me a little mad, but since I have realized the solitude of my being I feel as if I were sinking day by day into some boundless subterranean depths, with no one near me, no other living soul to clasp my outstretched, groping hands. There are noises, there are voices and cries in the darkness. I strive to reach them, but I can never discover whence they come, in the darkness, in this life which engulfs me.

"Others besides myself have known this atrocious suffering. Musset disclosed something of it when he wrote:

"Who comes? Who calls? No one!
    I am alone. It is the hour which sounds.
O, Solitude! O, Poverty!"

"But with Musset it was a mood, not an abiding horror as with me. He was a poet who peopled life with phantoms and dreams. He was never really alone as I am.

"And Flaubert—Gustave Flaubert—one of the unhappiest because one of the most lucid of men, says despondingly: 'We are all in a desert where no one person understands another.'

"No, we do not understand one another, try as we may. Do you know what is happening yonder among those stars flung like grains of fire across the heavens? Do you know any better what passes within the soul of another man? We know less of it, because thought is unfathomable.

"Can you conceive of anything more fearful than this incessant contact with beings whom we are unable to penetrate? I never feel more alone than when I have opened my heart to some friend. He is there before me. I see his bright eyes fixed upon me. But do I know the soul behind them? What does he think as he listens to me? He hates me, perhaps, or despises or mocks me. He judges, scoffs, condemns me; thinks me commonplace or stupid. How can I know what he thinks? How know whether he cares for me as I for him? What a mystery is the unfathomed thought of a human being; the hidden, free thought that we can neither know nor lead nor direct nor subdue! And I, myself, desire as I may, to open all the portals of my soul, the wish is vain. I still keep in the very depths that sanctuary self where no other soul penetrates.

"Do you think me mad? Are you asking yourself, 'what ails him tonight?' Oh, if some day you could come and say to me. 'I understand you,' it would make me happy for a moment perhaps.

"It is, above all, women who make me sensible of my solitude. Horrors! How I have suffered through them! Because they, oftener than men, have deceived me with the illusion that I am not alone.

"You must have known delicious moments spent in the company of some being whose charm of feature, whose hair, whose glances were maddening. But after each embrace the isolation grows, and how poignant it is. And after the rapturous union which must, it would seem, blend two souls into one being, how, more than ever before do you feel yourself alone—alone!

"And yet, after all, there is nothing better in the world than to spend an evening beside a well-beloved woman, without speaking, almost completely happy, through the single sensation of her presence. Let us not ask for more.

"As for me, now that I have closed my soul, my thoughts, my beliefs, my loves remain closed within it. Knowing myself condemned to hideous solitude, I keep my opinions. What are opinions to me! What are strife and pleasure and beliefs! Why should I be interested in what I cannot share with another! My invisible thought remains unsolved. Do you understand?"

We had ascended the long avenue as far as l'Arc de Triomphe de l'Etoile, and we descended to la Place de la Concorde—for he had said all this slowly— this and much more which I have forgotten—the granite obelisk stood before us, its long Egyptian profile lost amid the stars. He stopped and suddenly extended an arm toward the exiled monument.

"There," he said, "we are all like that stone." And he quitted me without a further word.

Was he drunk? Was he mad? Was he wise? I do not know. Sometimes I think he was right. Sometimes it seems to me that he had lost his mind.

Night

Guy de Maupassant

I love the night passionately; with an instinctive, profound, invincible love; as one loves his country or his mistress. I love it with all my senses: with those which inhale it; with my eyes which behold it; with my ears that bend to its silence: with my whole body, which the darkness enfolds.

The lark sings in the sunlight; in the blue warm ether of bright mornings. The owl skulks through the night, an inky spot in darkest space; rejoicing, drunk with somber immensity, he utters his vibrant sinister cry.

The day worries me, it is noisy and brutal. I rise in the morning unwillingly and dress myself with disgust. I go out, dissatisfied, and every step, every moment, gesture, every word and thought fatigues me as if I were bearing a weighty burden.

But when the sun goes down, an incomprehensible delight possesses me, rouses, reanimates me. I become like another being, younger, stronger, more joyous and more alert. I watch the great, soft darkness deepen as it descends. It floods the city like an impenetrable wave, hiding, effacing everything; destroying colors and forms, enveloping houses, monuments, people, in an imperceptible embrace.

It is then that I want to scream out with pleasure like a screech owl; I want to run along the roofs like a cat; and an impetuous and overmastering desire to love kindles in my veins.

I go and walk about; now along the shadowy faubourgs, again in the neighboring woods of Paris, where I hear prowling about, my brothers the poachers and my sisters the animals.

That which we love too violently ends by killing us. But how shall I explain what has happened to me? How can I make it understood that I could relate it? I do not know. I only know that it is so. That is all.

Well, then, yesterday—was it yesterday? Yes, no doubt; unless it was before that. Some other day, some other month, some other year. I do not know. It must, however, have been yesterday, for the day has not risen since, nor the sun appeared. But how long has the night lasted? Who can say? Who will ever know?

Yesterday, then, I went out as I do every evening after my dinner. The night was warm, soft and beautiful. In descending toward the boulevards, I gazed overhead at the black stream studded with stars, outlined in the heavens by the rooftops. It seemed a veritable running river of stars. Everything shone clear in the lambent air, from the planets to the gas jets. The darkness was made luminous by the fires burning above and through the city. How inspiring is the glorious night, by contrast with the day of vivid sunlight!

The cafés on the boulevard were ablaze. There were people laughing, drinking, moving about. I entered a theater. What theater? I do not know. The glare within saddened me, and I went away, depressed by the shock of the brutal light reflected upon the gilded balcony, by the factitious sparkle of the huge crystal lustre, by the dreariness of this false, crude brightness. I gained the Champs Elysées, where the café-concerts glowed amid the foliage. The *marronniers*, reflecting a yellow light, were like phosphorescent trees; and the electric globes like pale, radiant moons, like little moons fallen from the sky, like monster pearls in whose mysterious effluence the gas jets and garlands of colored lights looked pale and hideous.

I stopped beneath l'Arc de Triomphe, to contemplate the long, beautiful avenue reaching out toward Paris between two lines of fire and the stars! The unknown stars, flung at hazard in immeasurable space, tracing their fantastic designs, making us dream, making us think!

I entered the Bois de Boulogne and stayed there long, long. A strange shivering had taken hold of me; an unlooked for and powerful emotion; a mental exaltation that touched upon madness.

I walked long, long, and then retraced my steps. What time was it when I repassed beneath l'Arc de Triomphe? I do not know. The city was falling asleep, and great black clouds were slowly overspreading the heavens.

For the first time, I felt that something new and strange was about to take place. It seemed to me that it had grown cold; that the air thickened; that the night—my well-beloved night—oppressed me heavily. The avenue was deserted now. Only two sergents de ville were walking before the fiacre stand. And along the way, dimly lighted by the gas jets that seemed dying, a line of vegetable wagons was moving toward the markets. They were going slowly, laden with carrots, turnips, and cabbages. The drivers were asleep; the horses walked with measured paces following the wagon that went before; all silently on the wooden pavement. Under each flare of gas light, the carrots shone out red, the turnips shone white, the cabbages shone green; and they passed one behind the other—those red wagons, red as fire, white as silver, green as emeralds. I followed them, and turning into la rue Royale, regained the boulevards. No more brilliant cafés; no one was there; there were only a few belated people who hurried along. I had never seen Paris so deserted, so dead. I looked at my watch; it was two o'clock.

An inward force drove me. I went on as far as the Bastille. There I noticed that I had never seen a night so gloomy; for I could not even distinguiush *le colonne de Julliet* with its gilded Génie lost in the impenetrable obscurity. A smirky volume of clouds had submerged the stars and seemed to be lowering upon the earth to annihilate it.

I returned. There was no one to be seen. At Place du Chateau d'Eau, however, a drunkard jostled me, then vanished in the darkness. I stood listening for a while to his uneven, resounding footfalls. On I went. Far up the Faubourg Montmartre, a fiacre passed by, going toward the Seine. I hailed it. The driver did not answer. A woman was prowling near la rue Drouot. "Monsieur, listen, please!" I hurried by, to elude her extended hand. Then nothing more. Before the Vaudeville, a ragpicker was rummaging in the gutter; his little lantern grazing the surface. I asked him the hour. "Do I know?" he grumbled, "I have no watch."

Suddenly I perceived that the gas lights had been extinguished. I knew that at this season they extinguished them before day, for economy's sake; but the day was yet so far away!

"To the markets!" I thought. "There at least I shall find life." I started, but could not distinguish the way. I advanced slowly as one walks through a dense wood, recognizing the streets only by counting them.

Before the Credit Lyonnais, a dog growled. I turned into la rue Grammont. I lost myself, wandering around till I came upon La Bourse, which I recognized by the iron railing that surrounded it. Paris slept with a profound, frightful slumber. In the distance could be heard the rumble of a fiacre, a single fiacre, the one perhaps which had passed me a while before. I attempted to reach it, following the sound of its wheels across the black deserted streets; black thick as death.

Again I lost myself. Where was I? What a folly to extinguish the lights so early! No one was stirring; not a belated soul, not a prowler, not a mewling, amorous cat. Nothing. Where, then, were the sergents de ville? I asked myself. "I shall call. They will come." I cried out. No one answered.

I called still louder. My voice escaped without echo, feeble, smothered by the night, the impenetrable night.

"Help, help, help!" I howled. My frenzied cries remained unanswered. What time could it be? I drew forth my watch but I found no matches. I listened to its soft tic-toc with a strange satisfaction. It seemed alive. I was less alone. What a mystery! I began to walk like a blind man, feeling the walls with my cane;

and at every instant I lifted my gaze overhead, hoping to discover some sign of approaching day. But only blackness met me; a blackness more profound than that which enveloped the city.

What time could it be? I seemed to have been walking for countless hours; for my legs failed me; I panted; I suffered horribly with hunger.

I decided to ring at the first porte-cochère, and pulled the brass knob. The ring echoed sorrowfully through the house. It sounded strange, as if its vibrations had been alone in the house. I waited. No response came. I rang again; still I waited. Nothing!

I was afraid! I ran to the adjoining dwelling and twenty times in succession I pulled the bell of the passage in which the concierge must have been asleep. But he did not awaken, and I went on, ringing the bells with all my strength, striking with my cane, with my hands and feet against all the doors so obstinately closed.

I perceived suddenly that I had approached the market. It was deserted, without sound or movement. Not a wagon there, not a man, not a box of vegetables or flowers. It was empty, abandoned, dead!

A horrible fright possessed me. What was the matter? Oh!, my God! What was the matter?

I started again. But the hour! I must know it. Who would tell me the hour? No clocks sounded in tower or monument.

"I shall open the glass of my watch," I thought, "and feel the needles with my fingers." I drew out my watch. It had stopped. Nothing, nothing. Not a quiver throughout the city, not a gleam, no faintest sound in the air. Nothing! nothing more! Not even the distant rumble of the fiacre. Nothing more!

I was on the quay and an icy coldness ascended from the river.

Was the Seine still running?

I wanted to know. I found the steps and descended. I could not hear the current boiling beneath the arches of the bridge. . . . More steps . . . then sand . . . slime . . . then water. I submerged my arm . . . it ran . . . it ran . . . cold . . . cold . . . cold . . . almost freezing . . . almost dead.

And I felt plainly that I would never have the strength to retrace my steps . . . and that I would die there . . . I also, of hunger of fatigue of cold.

Suicide

Guy de Maupassant

Almost daily we read in the newspapers the account of a suicide, the causes of which remain unknown. We at once imagine and search for a love drama. We suspect money trouble. Failing to discover the definite reasons for the act, we are content to dismiss it as "another mystery."

A letter discovered upon the table of a suicide has fallen into my hands. It was written during the last night and lay beside a loaded revolver. It is interesting, as it reveals nothing of the great catastrophes which we invariably seek as motives for such acts of despair. But it discloses the slow succession of life's little miseries; the fatal disorganization of a solitary existence left without illusions. It gives a reason for tragic endings which only the nervous and hypersensitive can fully comprehend. The letter reads:

It is midnight. When I shall have finished this letter I shall kill myself. Let me endeavor to tell my reasons for doing so; not for the benefit of those who will read these lines, but for myself; to reenforce my failing courage, to impress upon myself the real necessity of the act which, in any event, could be but deferred.

My parents were simple people who believed and taught me to believe with unquestioning faith. The dream endured long; in fact shreds of it have but just vanished.

For the past few years a singular phenomenon has been at work in me. All the splendors of life seem to have faded out of my existence. The significance of life has revealed itself to me in its brutal reality. The mere significance of love has disgusted me, even with poetic tenderness.

We are the everlasting playthings of stupid and engaging illusions—forever renewed.

So, in growing old, I have become sensible to the misery of all things; of the inutility of effort, the vanity of endeavor. Tonight, after dinner, a new and stronger light has revealed to me the absolute nothingness of life.

Formerly, I was cheerful and easily pleased, the women passing by pleased me. The sights on the streets, my abiding place, whatever it might be, and I was even interested in the shape of my garments. But the constant recurrence of such sights, the repetition of events has ended by filling my being with lassitude and ennui, as might happen for the spectator frequenting the same theater night after night. For thirty years I have arisen every morning at the same hour; I have eaten in the same restaurant at the same hour, the same dishes!

I attempted to travel, but the isolation which we experience in strange lands frightened me. I felt so small, so alone upon the earth, that I hurriedly retraced my steps homeward. But there, the mere look of my furniture, standing for thirty years at the same place, the odor of my room (for every apartment takes with time its own peculiar odor) these things filled me each night with the nausea of custom and the blackest melancholy.

Things repeat themselves incessantly and stressingly. Even the manner in which I introduce the key into the lock at retiring, the place where I always find my matches, the first glimpse of my apartment, caught in the flare of the match, all these give me the desire to jump through the window, and to have done once and for all with the monotonous happenings, which we can never escape.

While shaving, each day, I feel an immediate desire to cut my throat, and the sight of my face with its lathered cheeks, always the same that I see in the little glass, impels me to weep with sadness.

I cannot even bear to see the people whom I formerly met with pleasure. So well do I know them, what they are going to say and what I shall answer; so often have I perceived the fixed mold of their thought and the form of their reasoning. The brain is like a circus ring in which a wretched, imprisoned horse turns, turns incessantly. Despite our efforts, our evasions, our makeshifts, the limit is narrow and encircling with no single outlet opening upon the unknown. We must turn, turn always about the same ideas, the same joys, the same habits, the same beliefs, the same disgusts.

The fog was horrible tonight. It enveloped the boulevard, where dim gas jets resembled smoking candles. A heavier burden than usual seemed to weigh upon me. Perhaps my digestion was bad.

For a good digestion is everything in life; it lends inspiration to the artist, stirs the pulses of youth, clears the brain of the thinker; and besides, it enables one to eat much and well, which is a great blessing. A feeble stomach leads to skepticism, to incredulity, engenders hideous dreams and even a desire for death. I have noticed this. I would perhaps not kill myself if I had digested well tonight.

When I had seated myself in the armchair, which I have occupied for thirty years, I cast my eyes about me and I was seized by a distress so horrible that I thought I was going mad.

I sought some means to escape from myself. The thought of occupation overcome me as more odious than inaction. Thus it occurred to me to put order among my papers. The need of doing so has long been present with me, for I have thrown, for the past thirty years, all my letters and accounts pell-mell in the same receptacle. And though such confusion has often troubled me, I undergo such a moral and physical disgust at the mere thought of arranging anything that I have never had the courage to attempt the odious work.

But tonight I seated myself before my secretary and opened it, meaning to make a choice among my old papers of those which I wished to destroy.

Oh, if you value your life, never disturb the resting place of your old correspondence or if you are led by accident to do so, seize those letters by handsful and without a glance that might awaken remembrance, cast them into the flames; crush their very ashes into an invisible powder, else you are lost—as I have been lost for the past hour.

The first letters which I read did not interest me. They were of recent date and from living men whom I often meet. But suddenly the sight of an envelope addressed in large, bold characters made me tremble. It was from my dearest friend, the companion and confidant of my youth, and he appeared to me so vividly, with his kind smile and his hand extended toward me, that a shiver pierced me to the very bones.

Yes, yes, the dead return, for I saw him! Our memory is a more perfect world than the universe; it restores to life that which has ceased to exist! I moaned for very anguish, as I read with tremulous hand and misty glance the words that he had written me.

As we ascend a stream, thus I retraced the course of my life. I encountered people long forgotten. In my mother's letters I found the old servants, the form and features of the old home, the little trifling details to which the minds of children cling. I saw again all the old toilets of my mother changing with the fashions which she followed; the different coiffures which she successively adopted. She haunted me more than all in a silk dress of quaint design, and I recalled a speech which she had made to me one day when wearing that dress: "Robert, my child, if you do not hold yourself straight, you will be a hunchback all your life."

Suddenly opening another drawer, I found myself confronted by my love souvenirs—a ball slipper, a torn handkerchief, even a garter, locks of hair and dried flowers. Recalling the tender romances of my past life—the heroines, who are white-haired today—plunged me in the profoundest melancholy.

Oh! the youthful brows with their curling, golden tresses; the caressing hands; the glance which speaks; the throbbing pulse; the smile which promises the lips, the lips which promise rapture!

Gathering those old tokens of past tenderness, I covered them with frenzied kisses; and in my soul, ravaged by recollection, I saw again each loved one, and I suffered an anguish more cruel than the fabled tortures of hell.

A last letter remained. It was my own, dicated by my writing master.

"My darling little mama," it read, "I am seven years old today. It is the age of reason, which enables me to say that I thank you for having given me life.

"Your little son who adores you, ROBERT."

It was over. I had reached the source. And brusquely I turned to face the days that were left for me. I saw old age, hideous, solitary; approaching infirmities; no one near me; the end, the end, the end.

My revolver is there on the table. . . . I have loaded it. . . . Never read your old letters.

And it is thus that many a man kills himself, in whose life we may seek in vain to discover great sorrows.

For Sale

Guy de Maupassant

Oh! the intoxication of being abroad at sunrise, walking along the edge of a calm sea, through dewy fields! An intoxication that penetrates you through and through; with every breath of the soft air; with such buffet of the velvety wind; with all the glory of light that the eye gathers!

Why do we cherish the memory—keen, delicious, poignant—the memory of certain moments of fondness for the earth! The memory of a sensation, fleeting, exquisite—whether the glimpse of a landscape caught in a turn of the room— the sight of a lily along the riverside—as we sometimes carry with us the recollection of a beautiful complaisant woman. Among other days I remember one. I was going along the coast of the Brittany sea, toward Point Finistère. I was walking rapidly without thinking of anything—along the edge of the water, in the environs of Quimperlé, that most delightful portion of Brittany. It was one of those mornings in Spring that make one feel younger by twenty years, that rekindle one's hopes and give back the dreams of early youth. I was walking along a path hardly [traveled], between the water and the fields. The wheat was motionless and the waves were almost still. There was the delicious odor of ripe fields and the salt scent of the sea intermingled. I went on, thinking of nothing, simply pursuing my journey begun a fortnight [before] along the Brittany coast. I felt strong, buoyant, happy; I went on. I thought of nothing. Why should one think in such moments of profound, physical joy; the joy of the animal that runs through the grass and that floats through the blue ether in the sun?

From afar I heard the sound of a religious chant—a procession presently [?], for it was Sunday. But as I turned a little promontory, I stopped, motionless, ravished. Five large fishing boats appeared, filled with people—men, women, and children, going to the Pardon of Plouneven. They were skirting the shore slowly, hardly moved by the gentle breeze that puffed the brown sails at intervals—and dying away let them fall again flapping along the masts. The heavy barques glided lazily filled with these people, all singing. The men, wearing their large hats, stood upright. Their powerful voices, the shrill notes of the women and children like discordant fifes mingled in violent religious clamor. The passengers of all five boats chanted the same canticle of which the monotonous rhythm mounted in the still air. And the five boats went one behind the other; close to one another. They passed before me and as they dipped farther and farther into the distance, I heard the song grow fainter and die away.

Then I started dreaming of delicious things—as very young people dream; in a puerile, naïve fashion. How fast that age of illusions passes! the only happy period of existence; when we are never alone, never sad, morose, desolate; when we carry within us the divine faculty—to lose ourselves in hopes. What a fairyland is this hallucination of vagabond thought; in which everything happens. How beautiful is life seen beneath the golden ponds of dreams? Alas! that is all past and done for. I began to dream. Of what? of everything that we expect, of everything that we desire—fortune, glory, love. And I walked with long strides, caressing with my hand as I went, the blond heads of the wheat which bent beneath my fingers tickled my flesh as if I had touched human hair.

Rounding a little promontory, I discovered at the far end of a narrow strip of shore, a white house built on three terraces, which descended to the water. Why did the sight of that house cause me to quiver with pleasure. Do I know? Oftentimes in traveling thus we discover little corners of earth that we seem to have known for a long time; so familiar are they, with such sweet intimacy do they greet us. How seductive was the soft line of the horizon, the disposition of the trees, the color of the sand!

Oh! the beautiful house, high up on the terrace. Large fruit trees, like giant steps, had grown along the embankments that descended toward the water. Each terrace wearing like a gold crown upon its summit a long bouquet of Spanish genets in bloom. I stopped, enchanted with this dwelling. How I should have loved to own it, to live in it always! As I approached the door, my heart beating with desire, I perceived on one of the pillars of the fence a large sign: "For Sale."

I felt a shock of pleasure as if it had been offered to me; as if it had been given to me. Why? I do not know!

"For Sale." Thus it hardly belonged to anyone. It could be mine—anybody's. Why this joy, this sensation of profound, inexplicable contentment! How could I pay for it? Never mind, it was for sale. The bird in the cage belongs to its master; the bird in the air is mine, since it is none other's.

And I entered the garden. Oh the charming garden with its rising terraces, its trellises with long arms like crucified martyrs; its tufts of golden genets, and two old fig trees at the end of each terrace.

When I had reached the last one, I looked at the horizon. The beach rounded, sandy, extended at my feet; separated from the high sea by three rocks, heavy and brown, which enclosed the entrance and must have broken the waves when the sea was high. On the farther point were two enormous stones, one standing, the other lying in the grass. They were like two married people—estranged, struck motionless by some witchcraft, and they seemed to be looking—looking always at the little house which they had seen built, which they would see crumble and vanish away—the little house for sale!

I rang the bell as if I had been ringing at home. A woman came and opened the door; a little old woman wearing a black dress and a white cap, who resembled a would-be nun. It seemed to me that I knew this woman also. I said to her: "You are not a Breton?" She answered: "No, sir, I am from Lorraine," adding, "Do you come to visit the house?"

"Why, yes, of course," and I entered. I felt as if I recognized everything; the walls, the furniture. I was almost surprised not to find my canes in the vestibule. I entered the parlor, a pretty room covered with matting. It looked out at the sea by three large windows. On the mantle were some China vases and a large photograph of a woman. I went toward it, persuaded that I should also recognize her. And I did know her, though I was persuaded that I had never seen her before. It was she, she herself; the one whom I expected, whom I desired, whom I called; whose images haunted my dream. She; the one whom we seek for everywhere, always; the one whom we shall see presently in the street, whom we shall find in the country lanes under the red parasol that we see moving across the wheat. The one who must already have arrived in the hotel which I reach; in the train which I entered, in the salon whose door opens before me. It was she; surely, indubitably she! I knew her by her eyes that looked into mine; by her hair rolled à l'anglaise; by her mouth above all, by that smile which I had known long ago.

I asked: "Who is this woman?" The bonne with the nun's head replied dryly "It is Madame."

"Is it your mistress?" I pursued. She answered with her hard, devout air, "Oh! no, sir."

I sat down and said bluntly: "Tell me all about it." She remained stupefied, silent. I insisted: "She is the owner of this home, then?"

"Oh! no, sir."

"To whom then does this house belong?"

"To my master, Monsieur Tournelle."

I pointed to the photograph. "And this woman, who is she?"

"It is Madame."

"The wife of your master?"

"Oh! no, sir."

"His mistress, then?" The nun did not reply, I resumed, bitten by a vague jealousy, by a smothered rage against the man who had found this woman.

"Where are they now?"

The bonne murmured: "Monsieur is in Paris. As for Madame, I do not know." I quivered.

"Ah! they are no longer together?"

"No sir."

I grew crafty and said with a serious voice: "Tell me what happened. I might probably render some service to your master. I know this woman, she is a bad one." The old servant looked at me, and encouraged by my seeming sincerity [she] grew confident.

"Oh! sir, she made my master very miserable. He became acquainted with her in Italy, and he brought her back with him as though he had married her. She sang very well. It was pitiful to see how much he loved her. They traveled last year through this country and they found this house which had been built by a lunatic—a real lunatic who wised to install himself two miles from the village. Madame wanted to buy it at once, to live in it with my master; and he bought the house to please her. They lived in it all last summer sir, and nearly all winter. And then one morning at breakfast time, my master called me: 'Césarine,' he said, 'has Madame come in?' 'Why no, sir,' I told him. He waited all day. My master was like one demented. We searched everywhere; we did not find her; she was gone sir; we never discovered where nor how."

Oh! what rapture seized me! I felt like embracing the old bonne, like taking her by the waist and making her dance in the parlor. Ah! she had gone, she had run away, she had quitted him, tired, disgusted with him! How glad I was! The old woman resumed: "Monsieur almost died of grief, and returned to Paris leaving me and my husband behind to sell the house. The price is 20,000 francs." But I was not listening! I was thinking of her! And suddenly it seemed to me that I had but to start out to find her; that she must have returned this spring to see the house, the pretty house that she would have loved so well without him.

I threw ten francs in the old woman's hands. I seized the photograph and fled with it, blindly kissing the sweet face as I went.

I regained the road and walked on, always looking at her! What rapture to know that she was free, that she had run away! Surely I would find her today or tomorrow; this week or the next, since she left him. She had left him because my hour had come!

She was free somewhere in the world! I had only to find her since I knew her.

And all the while I caressed the bending heads of the ripe wheat. I drank deep the salt [air] that swelled my bosom, I felt the sun kissing my face. I went on, on; wild with happiness; drunk with hope. I went on, sure that I would soon find her and bring her back to live with me in the pretty house that was for sale. How pleased she would be this time!

Father Amable

Guy de Maupassant

The sky, moist and gray, seemed to weigh upon the vast brown plain. The stagnant evening air was thick and heavy with the scent of autumn; that sad odor of the damp, naked earth, of fallen leaves and dead grasses. Peasants were still scattered through the fields at work; awaiting the sound of the Angelus which would recall them to their homes whose thatched roofs could be seen through the distant stripped branches of trees that sheltered the apple orchards.

A little child sat at the edge of a road upon some women's garments spread there. He sat with legs wide apart, playing with a potato that kept falling into his lap. Five women with bent figures and slow rhythmic movement were planting bits of cabbage in the neighboring plain, in the long deep furrow which the plow had just turned.

A man who passed, whip in hand, and his feet encased in wooden shoes, stopped before the child, picked it up and kissed it. One of the women upon perceiving him, straightened herself and approached him. She was a large, reddish girl with thick waist and hips and broad shoulders; a tall Normand with yellow hair and sanguine complexion. She addressed him abruptly: "That's you, Césaire, what news?"

"Nothing, nothing, always the same story."

"He won't give in?"

"Not an inch."

"What are you going to do?"

"Do I know?"

"Go see the curé, I tell you."

"I'm willing enough."

"Go now, while you are about it."

"All right, I'll go."

They looked at each other. He was still holding the child in his arms. He kissed it once more and set it down.

On the horizon between farms, a man could be seen pushing a plow. The horse, the plow, the man, passed slowly against the dull evening sky. The woman resumed: "But what does your father say?"

"He says he won't have it, just that."

"Why won't he?"

The young fellow indicated with a gesture the child which he had just set down, and with a glance the man who was pushing the plow in the distance, and he said: "Because it is his."

The girl shrugged her shoulders and remarked angrily: "Pardi! Everyone knows it is Victor's child. What of it? I know I went wrong. Am I the only one? My mother did the same before me, and yours too, before she married your father. Who hasn't in the country? It was Victor because he took me in the barn when I was sleeping; that's the truth. Then afterward when I wasn't asleep. I would have married him if he hadn't been a farm hand. Am I worth less for that?"

The man said simply: "For me, I want you just as you are, child or no child. It is only my father that objects. I'll try to bring him around."

"Go see the curé right away," she suggested.

"I'm going." And he started off with his heavy, peasant's tramp, while the girl, with arms akimbo, returned to planting her cabbages.

In spite of his old deaf father, Amable Houlbrèque, Césaire wanted to marry Céleste Lévesque who had had a child with Victor Lecoq, simple hired hand upon her parents' farm, and who had been dismissed for that reason. The hierarchy of caste is unknown in the fields, and by industry and acquisition the valet may become the equal of his former master.

As Césaire Houlbrèque plodded along, whip in hand, his heavy sabots gummed with earth, he abandoned himself to reflection. He certainly wanted to marry Céleste Lévesque, even with her child, because she seemed indispensable to him. He could not have told why, but he knew it. He had only to look at her to be convinced of it, to feel moved, stupefied with contentment. It even gave him pleasure to embrace Victor's child because it was hers. And as he thought this he looked with dislike upon the distant figure of the man pushing his plow along the horizon.

But father Amable would not hear of the marriage. He opposed it with the stubbornness of the deaf; with furious persistence. Césaire might bellow as much as he liked into the old man's ear—the ear that could still catch a few sounds: "We'll take good care of you, father. I tell you she's a good girl; a fine, saving girl." But no argument could move father Amable.

One hope remained to Césaire. His father was afraid of the curé because of his death which he felt approaching. He had no fear of God, the devil, hell or purgatory, of which he could form no conception. But he feared the priest, who prefigured death and burial, as one might dread a physician through horror of medicine. For eight days Céleste, who knew this weakness of father Amable, had urged Césaire to go in search of the curé. But Césaire hesitated because he himself had no great love for the black gown which to him meant a hand ever extended for alms or the *pain bénit*. He had decided, however, and he was going along toward the parsonage, thinking of the manner in which he would present his case.

L'abbé Raffin, a little, thin, vivacious priest, never shaved, sat warming his feet before the kitchen fire while he waited for his dinner. He turned his head as the peasant entered.

"Why, Césaire, what brings you here?" he asked.

"I've come to talk with you, sir." The man stood timidly, holding his cap in one hand and his whip in the other.

"Well, go ahead," said the priest. Césaire looked uneasily at the servant, an old woman who dragged her feet while she went about setting the table for her master before the fire. He stammered: "It's . . . it's a kind of confession, you see." Then l'abbé Raffin closely scanned his peasant, and noticed the fellow's air of embarrassment, his shifting glances.

"Maria," he ordered, "go to your room for five minutes while I speak with Césaire." The woman looked sullenly toward Césaire and went away grumbling. The peasant still hesitated; looked down at his *sabots*, twisted his cap, and, upon further urging from the priest, blurted out: "You see, I want to marry Céleste Lévesque."

"Well, my boy, who prevents you?"

"It's my father who won't hear [of] it."

"Your father?"

"Yes, sir, my father."

"What does he say?"

"He says that she has had a child."

"She is not the first to whom that has happened since the days of mother Eve."

"A child with Victor, Victor Lecoq, the valet of Anthime Loisel."

"Ah! So, he won't hear of it!"

"Not more than a donkey that won't budge; asking your pardon."

"What have you told him?"

"I tell him she's a good girl—a clean and saving girl."

"And he won't listen! I see, and you want me to speak to him. But what can I say to your father?"

"What you say in your sermons, sir, to make them shell out the pennies."

In the mind of the peasant, all the efforts of religion were directed toward loosening men's purse strings; toward emptying their pockets to fill the coffers of heaven. Paradise seemed to him to be a huge commercial concern employing the priests to advance its business to the detriment of the country folk. He knew well that the priests rendered great service to the very poor, to the sick, the dying: that they assisted, consoled, sustained, but all that meant money in exchange for white satin—beautiful, gleaming silver with which to buy sacraments, masses, advice and probation, forgiveness of sins, and indulgences, purgatory, and heaven according to the income and the generosity of the sinner.

L'abbé Raffin who knew his man, and who never got angry, began to laugh.

"Well, yes, I shall tell him my little story—but you, my boy, you will come to church to the sermon."

Houlbrèque held out his hand to him: "On the faith of a poor man! If you do that for me, I promise."

"Nay well—when do you want me to see your father?"

"The sooner the better—tonight if you can—"

"In a half-hour then, after supper."

"In a half-hour."

"Agreed—good-bye, my boy."

"Good-bye, M'sieur l'Curé; thank you kindly."

"Don't mention it." And Césaire Houlbrèque returned home, his heart relieved of a great weight.

He held in lease a little farm—very small—for they were not rich, he and his father. Although Césaire was a good workman, they lived a pinched life, alone with a servant of fifteen who tended the chickens, milked the cows, and churned the butter. But they found neither sufficient land nor beasts of burden to earn him then the bare amenities.

The old man no longer worked. Sad, as the deaf days are, stupefied with pains, he went through the fields, leaning on his stick, and looking at men and beasts with a hard, mistrustful eye. Sometimes he sat on the edge of a ditch and stayed there, without moving, for hours, thinking vaguely of the things which had occupied him all his life—the price of eggs, and grain, thinking of the sun and the rain which makes or mars the crops. And moved by the rheumatism, his old limbs still absorbed the humidity of the soil, as they had absorbed for seventy years the vapor of the walls of his lone hut, with its damp straight roof.

He returned at the close of day, taking his place at the end of the table in the kitchen. And when they had placed before him the earthen pot containing his soup, he enclosed it in his hurt fingers, which seemed to have retained the rounded form of the vessel, and he warmed his hands, winter and summer, before beginning to eat, in order to lose nothing—neither a particle of heat that came from the fire—which cost dearly—and neither a drop of soup in which there was fat and salt, nor a crumb of bread which came from the wheat.

After that he climbed a ladder to the attic where he had his straw mattress—while the son slept below, in the depths of a sort of niche near the chimney. The little servant shut himself up in a kind of can—a black hole which formerly served to store potatoes.

Césaire and his father rarely conversed. Only from time to time when there was question of selling a crop or buying a calf, the young man took the advice

of his father, and forming a speaking trumpet of his two hands, he bellowed out
his reasons; and father Amable approved or controlled them in a slow hollow
voice that issued from the depths of his stomach.

So, one night, Césaire approaching him as though there were question of a
horse or a heifer, now communicated at the top of his lungs, his intention of
marrying Céleste Lévesque.

Then the father grew angry—why? Through insanity? Not at all. The virtue
of a girl is of little importance in the fields. But his avarice, his profound ferocious
intent to save had revolted at the idea that his son could rear a child which was
not his own. He now realized all at once, in a second, all the soups which the
youngster would eat before being able to be useful on the farm; he had calculated
all the pounds of bread, all the measures of cider, which this urchin would
consume before his fourteenth year, and a wild rage broke loose in him toward
Césaire who had not thought of all that.

And he replied with the force of an unused voice: "Have you lost your senses?"
Wherefore, Césaire proceeded to enumerate his reasons, to rehearse the qualities
of Céleste, to prove that she would earn a hundred more times the cost of the
child. But the old man doubted her merits, whilst he could not doubt the existence
of the little one; and he repeated incessantly without further explanation: "I
won't have it; I won't have—as long as I live, it won't be." So for the past
three months the matter rested there, neither yielding, but resuming once a week
at least the same discussion, using the same arguments, the same words, gestures,
and the same irritability.

Then it was that Céleste had advised Césaire to go and ask the assistance of
their curé.

In entering his home, the peasant found his father already at table, since his
visit to the parsonage had delayed him.

They dined in silence, face to face, eating a little butter on their bread after
the soup, and drinking a glass of cider; then they stayed motionless on their
chairs, hardly lighted by the candle which the little servant had brought to wash
the spoons, wipe the glasses, and trim beforehand the crusts for the early breakfast.

A knock sounded on the door which opened at once; and the priest appeared.
The old man ran from his moving eyes, and sensing danger, he was inclined to
climb his ladder, when the abbé Raffin placed his hand on his shoulder, and
[shouted] against his temple: "I want to talk to you, father Amable!" Césaire
had disappeared, profiting by the door which had remained open. He would not
stay to listen, so frightened was he—he did not wish his hopes to crumble before
any obstinate refusal of his father; he preferred to hear at one blow, the truth,
good or bad—later; and he went away in the darkness.

It was a night without moon, without stars, one of those hazy nights when
the air seems gray with humidity. A vague odor of apples floated near the yard,
for it was the season when the ripest were gathered. The mouths, when Césaire
passed along their walls, breathed through their narrow windows the warm odor

of living animals asleep on the [manure], and he heard near the stables the tramping of horses standing and the noise of their jaws, pulling and chewing the hay from the racks. He went ahead thinking of Céleste in that simple mind in which ideas were hardly more than images born directly of objects, the thoughts of love, formulated themselves but by the [picture?] of a large reddish girl, standing in a hollow road, and laughing with her hands on her hips.

It was thus he had perceived her the day upon which the desire for her was awakened. He knew her however since infancy, but never as that morning had he noticed her. He had chatted some moments, then he went away, and in walking kept repeating: "Cristi! she's a fine girl all the same. It's a pity she went away with Victor." Until night he thought of her and the day also.

When he saw her again, he felt something tickling the bottom of his throat, as if a feather had been thrust into his heart [or] to his chest; and after that, anytime he found himself near her, he was surprised at that tickling which always recommenced.

In three weeks he decided to marry her, so greatly did she please him. He could not tell whence came the power over him, but he expressed it in these words: "I am pleased by her." As if he had carried within him the desire for the girl like some power of hell. He did not bother about her fault. So much the worse after all; that did not spoil her, and he felt no ill will toward Victor— himself.

But if the curé had not concurred, what then? He did not dare to think of it, so much did this selfishness torture him.

He had revisited the parsonage and had seated himself near the little wooden fence (barrière) to await the return of the priest.

He had been there an hour perhaps when he heard steps on the road, and he soon distinguished, though the night was so dark, the still blackened shadow of the *soutane* [cassock]. He arose, his legs [shaking?] not daring to talk—to guess.

The priest saw him and said gaily: "Well, my boy, it's all right."

Césaire stammered, "It's all right! us!"

"Yes my boy, but not without trouble. What an old [dolt] your father is!"

The peasant kept repeating, "Yes but I."

"But yes, come tomorrow to decide about the publication of the banns."

He never had seized the hand of his curé—he pressed it, shook it, [bruised it] in stammering: "True?..true? . . . true . . . for '*vers* l'curé? Faith of an honest man, you will see me Sunday at your sermon."

II

The wedding took place about the middle of December. It was simple, the couple being not rich. Césaire, dressed all in new clothes, was ready at 8 o'clock in the morning to go get his fiancée and conduct her to the mairie [mayor's office]; but as it was too early, he seated himself before the kitchen table and awaited members of the family and friends who were coming to get him. For a week it had been snowing, and the brown earth, the earth already pregnant with the autumn sowing, had become livid, asleep beneath a sheet of ice. It was cold in the huts covered with their white bonnets; and the round apple trees in the yard seemed in bloom, powdered like the beautiful birth of their flowering.

That day, the great northern clouds, the gray clouds, misty clouds had disappeared, and the blue sky spread over the white earth upon which the rising sun shown silvery reflections.

Césaire looked before him through the window, without thinking of anything— happy. The door opened. Two women entered, peasants in their Sunday clothes, the aunt and cousin of the groom, and their men, his cousins, and a neighbor. They seated themselves on chairs and they stayed silent and motionless, the women on one side of the kitchen, the men on the other, seized with sudden timidity, with that sad embarrassment which takes hold of people milled for a ceremony. Presently one of the cousins asked, "Isn't it time?" Césaire replied, "I think it is."

"Come let us start," said another. They arose. Then Césaire, whom uneasiness was invading, climbed the ladder to the loft to see if his father was ready. The old man, usually an early riser, had not yet appeared. His son found him in his straw mattress, rolled in his quilt, his eyes open and looking mean. He cried in his ear: "Come, father, get up—here is the hour of the wedding."

The deaf man murmured with a suffering voice: "I can't, I have a chill that has frozen my back—I can't move." The young man, cast down, looked at him, detecting his arm, "Come father, free yourself."

"Oh, I can't."

"Here let me help you." And he leaned toward the old fellow, unrolled his cover, took him by the arm, took him by the arms and lifted him. But father Amable began to groan, "How! how! how! What pain! How, how, Oh, I can't! My back is knotted—must be some cold air that came in from that d—n roof." Césaire understood that he would not succeed, and furious for the first time in his life with his father, he cried this: "Well you'll have no dinner since we are to have our meal at 'Polyte's inn. That will teach you to be stubborn!" And he descended the ladder, and started off followed by his relatives and invited guests. The men had rolled their trousers so as not to stain them with the snow; the women held their skirts high showing their ankles, their gray worsted stockings, their boney shanks straight as broom sticks. And all went balancing on their legs, one behind the other, one behind the other, without talking, slowly out of prudence to not leave the road, disappeared into the white cloth—uniform— uninterrupted by the snows.

In approaching the farms they perceived one or two persons waiting to join them. And the procession lengthened incessantly (surfautait?) following the rims, the contours of the road, [and] looked like a living chaplet of black beads undulating through the white country.

Before the door of the bride a numerous group tramped about awaiting the groom. They exclaimed when he appeared; and presently Céleste came out of the room, attired in a blue dress, her shoulders covered with a little red shawl and her head blooming with orange blossoms.

But each one asked Césaire. "Where is your father?" He replied with embarrassment: "He can't stir today, with rheumatism." And the farmers shook their heads with an incredulous [waggish] air.

They started toward the maire. Behind the young couple, a peasant carried Victor's child; as if there were questions of a baptism; and the peasants, two by two, now arm in arm, went through the snow with the motions of boats at sea.

After the mayor had joined the fiancés in the little mission, in full house, the curé afterward united them in the modest little house of God. He blessed their union promising them fecundity, and he preached of matrimonial virtues—the same and simple virtues of the folk—work, counsel, fidelity, while the child with cold was bawling behind its mother's back.

As soon as the couple reappeared in the threshold of the church, gun shots broke forth in the ditch of the graveyard. There could be seen but the mouth of the cannon which issued rapid shouts of smoke; then a head appeared regarding the procession. It was Victor Lecoq, celebrating the marriage of his first friend; [wishing] her happiness and expressing his fond wishes with the explosions of powder. He had reunited some friends—five or six laborers for his musketry [shots]. It was thought that he acted very well.

The repast was held at the inn of 'Polyte Cacheprune. Twenty covers had been set in the large hall when dinner was served on market days, and the enormous leg of mutton turning on the spit, the chickens glistening in their juice, the chitterlings, frying in the bright fire, filled the house with a thick odor, with the smoke of coals, freely sprinkled with [fat], the very powerful odor of country food.

They seated themselves at noon; and at once the soup was poured into the plates. The faces were already anointed; mouths opened to cry out jests, eyes twinkled with mischievousness. They were going to amuse themselves, party!

The door opened and father Amable appeared. He looked wicked, furious, and he dragged himself on his crutches (batons) groaning at every step to indicate his suffering.

They ceased talking at his appearance, but elderly father Malivoire, his neighbor, a big jovial fellow who knew everybody's business, began to howl as Césaire did in making a speaking tube of his hands: "Hi, old wide awake, what a nose you must have to smell 'Polyte's kitchen from your house." A curious laugh burst forth. Malivoire, excited by success continued: "For pain, there is nothing to equal a [dressing] of Andouille! It keeps the stomach warm with a glass of (trois-six)." The men shrieked, pounded the table with their fists, turned to the side to laugh, bending and raising their bodies as if working a pump. The women chuckled like hens, the servants doubled up along the walls. Only father Amable did not laugh, and waited without a word for them to make a place for him. They placed him in the middle of the table opposite his daughter-in-law, and the moment he was seated, he began to eat. It was his son who said after all, he had to take his share. At every ladleful of soup that fell into his stomach, at each mouthful of bread or meat crushed between his gums, at every glass of cider and wine that trickled down his throat, he felt as if he were regaining some of his property, getting back some of his money which these gluttons were downing; to save a part of his belongings, in short. And he ate in the obstinate silence of a miser who hides pennies, with the sober timerity which he formerly brought to his previous labors.

But suddenly he perceived at the foot of the table Céleste's child on a woman's lap, and his eyes never left it. He continued to eat, with his regard fixed on the little one, whom the woman fed at times with a bit of *fricot* [stew] that she mashed. And the old fellow suffered more from those few mouthfuls sucked by that larva than all that the others swallowed.

The repast lasted till night. The sick one went home. Césaire lifted father Amable. "Come father, we have to walk," said he and he put the two sticks into his hands. Céleste took her child in her arms and then went away slowly through the pale light that the snow lightened. The old deaf man, three-quarters tipsy, made cross by drunkenness, obstinately held back. Several times even he seated himself with the idea that his daughter-in-law might catch cold, and he groaned, without saying a word, uttering a long suffering complaint.

When they had reached home, he climbed at once to his loft while Césaire arranged a bed for the child near the deep niche where he was to sleep with his wife. But as they did not sleep at once, they heard for a long time the old man tossing about in his straw bed and he even spoke aloud several times, whether dreaming or letting escape his thought through his mouth, despite himself; without being able to withhold it, unless claimed of a fixed idea.

When he descended next morning, he perceived his daughter-in-law going about the work. She cried to him: "Come father, hurry up; here is some good soup," and she sat down at the end of the table the round black earthen pot full of steaming liquor. He seated himself without answering, took the [hot] bowl, warmed his hands after his habit; and as it was very cold, he even pressed it against his chest to try to have a little of the warmth of the boiling water enter into his old body shifted by the many winters.

After, he sought his sticks and went away into the frozen country until noon— till the dinner hour, for he had seen installed in a large soap box Céleste's little one who still slept.

He took no part in anything. He lived in the hut as family, but he had the appearance of not belonging there, of interesting himself with working, of looking upon these people, his son, the woman, the child as strangers whom he did not know, to whom he never spoke.

The winter went by. It was long and severe. Then the first spring days started the grains; and the peasants, anew, like laboring ants, spent their days in the fields, working from dawn to night, under the [wind] and the rain along the brown furrows that mothered the bread of men.

The year started well for the newly married. The crops grew briskly; there were no late frosts; and the blooming apple trees let fall upon the grass their red and white snow which promised for the winter an abundance of fruit.

Césaire worked hard, arose early and went to bed late to [save] the expense of a hired man.

His wife sometimes said to him: "You will do yourself harm." He answered, "Truly not—I am [up] to it." One night, however, he entered so fatigued that he went to bed without supper. He arose at the usual hour the next day, but he could not eat, despite the fast of the day before; and he had to come in in the middle of the afternoon to rest again. During the night he began to cough; he tossed feverishly on his straw mattress, his forehead burning, his tongue dry, drained by an ardent throat. He went however back to his fields till evening, but the mid-day they had to call a physician who found him very sick, with pleurisy.

And he did not leave the obscure niche which served him for a bed. They could hear him coughing, gasping, moving in the depths of the hole. To see him, to give him drugs, to apply poultices, they had to bring a candle to the entrance. They could see then his sunken face soiled with his big beard, beneath a thick lace work of spider webs which floated and hung in mid-air. And the hands of the sick man seemed dead on the gray sheets.

Céleste nursed him with an uneasy activity, made him drink the remedies, applied poultices, and went through the house; while father Amable stayed at the edge of his loft, watching from afar the somber hole, where his son lay agonizing. He did not approach for hatred of the woman, skulking like a jealous dog. Six days went by; then one morning when Céleste, who slept now on the floor on two bundles of loose straw, went to see if her husband was better, she no longer heard his quick breathing even from his deep bed. She asked, "Well, Césaire how did you fare the night?" He did not answer. She stretched forth her hand to touch him and encountered the icy flesh of his face. She uttered a great cry of a woman terrified. He was dead.

At the cry the old deaf man appeared at the top of his ladder; and as he saw Céleste rush out of doors in search of help, he descended quickly, felt in turn his son's face, and suddenly understanding, went to fasten the door to prevent the woman entering and taking possession of his dwelling, since his son was no longer alive. Then he seated himself on a chair before the dead. The neighbors arrived, called, pounded. He did not hear them. One of them broke the window frame and entered the room. Others followed; the door was reopened; and Céleste reappeared wiping all her tears, her cheeks swollen and red. Then father Amable, vanquished, said not a word but went again to the loft.

The funeral was next day; and after the ceremony the father and daughter-in-law found themselves alone on the farm with the child.

It was the hour of dinner. She lit the fire, prepared the soup, set the plates on the table, while the old man seated on a chair, waited without seeming to look at her. When the repast was ready, she called in his ear: "Come, father, you must eat." He came, took his place at the end of his table, emptied his bowl, chewed his bread covered with butter, drank two glasses of cider, and went away.

It was one of those mild days, one of those beneficient days when life ferments, palpitates, blossoms over the surface of the earth—father Amable followed a little footpath through the fields. He looked at the young wheat and oats and thought that his child was underground now, his poor child. He went along with his [pace] out step, dragging his legs and limping. And as he was all alone on the plain, all alone under the blue sky, amid the glowing crops, alone with the larks that he saw floating overhead, without hearing their light song, he began to weep in walking.

Then he seated himself beside a pool and stayed there till night, watching the little birds that came to drink; and as night fell he returned, ate his supper without saying a word, and climbed to his loft.

And his life continued as of yore. Nothing ha[d] changed except that his son Césaire slept in the cemetery.

What should the old man do? He could no longer work, he was only fit to eat the soups that his daughter-in-law made him. And he ate them in silence, night and morning, watching with a furious eye the little one who ate also, facing him on the other side of the table. Then he went out, roamed about the country like a vagabond, went and hid himself behind barns to sleep an hour or two, as if he dreaded to be seen, and he reentered at the approach of night.

But great preoccupations began to haunt the spirit of Céleste. The land needed a man who would watch and work them. It was necessary for someone to be there, always about the fields, not only a simple hireling, but a real cultivator, a master, who knew the business and took an interest in the farm. A woman too could not farm the culture, follow the price of grain, direct the sale and purchase of beasts. These ideas entered her head, simple, practical ideas that she realized during the night. She could not marry before a year, and it was necessary, immediately to save the pressing interests.

A single man could withdraw her from trouble. Victor Lecoq, the father of her child. He was close, understood farming, he would ride here with a little money in his pocket, an excellent farmer. She knew it, having known him at work with her parents.

So one morning seeing his pony on the road with a load of manure, she went out to meet him. When he saw her, he stopped his horses and she said as if she had seen him the day before: "Good day, Victor, are things well with you?"

He replied: "I am well, and you?"

"Oh, Victor, it would be well if I were not alone at home; that bothers me on account of the land."

Then they talked a long time, leaning on the wheel of the heavy wagon. The man at times scratched his forehead under his cap and reflected. While she, with red cheeks, spoke with ardor, told her reasons, her intentions, her prospect for the future—at last he murmured: "Yes, perhaps you are right." She opened her hand like a peasant who concludes a bargain, and asked: "It's settled?" He pressed her extended hand. "Settled."

"It goes for Sunday, then?"

"For Friday."

"Then good-bye, Victor."

"Good-bye, Madame Houlbrèque."

III

That Sunday was the village feast, the annual feast and festival which is called "Assembly" in Normandy. For eight days, there had been coming along the roads, with slow steps, sorry-looking horses, gray and red, foreign-looking vehicles in which lodged roaming families who frequent fairs, lottery directors, curiosities which the peasants call "makers of see what." Dirty caravans with floating curtains, accompanied by a sad dog, going with lowered head between the wheels, had stopped one after the other in the plain of the mairie. Then a tent was hoisted before each ambulatory tenement, and in these tents could be seen through holes in the canvas brilliant sights which overexcited the imaginations and curiosities of the youngsters.

Since early morning of the feast, all barracks had opened spreading their splendor of glass or porcelain; and the peasants in going to Mass, looked already with a satisfied and open eye [at the] simple shops which they saw nevertheless each year.

From the beginning of the afternoon, there was a crowd in the place. From all the neighboring villages the farmers arrived, with their wives and children, in two-wheel carts that rattled in, oscillating like barques at sea. They had unhitched at friends' homes, and the farmyards were full of strange carts, gray, thin, crooked like long-pawed animals of the sea.

And each family, the babies in front, the larger ones behind, were going to the assembly with quiet steps, smiling air, open hands, large red bony hands accustomed to work and which seemed to be lost in response.

A juggler played upon the clarionettes—the barbarous organ of the wooden horns let fall upon the air its doleful, jumping notes. The wheel of the lottery scraped like stuff that is torn. The shots of the carbines sounded at every second. And the slow crowd (mollement) passed before the barracks like a running paste, with the movements of droves of animals, the awkwardness of beasts who have strayed out by accident.

The girls holding arms in lines of six and eight kept singing songs; the boys followed them vigilantly with caps on their ears, and blouses, stiffened by [starch], swelled like blue balloons.

All the country was there, masters, valets, and servants.

Father Amable, himself, decked in his old green [frock coat] wanted to see the assembly; for he never missed it.

He looked at the lotteries, stopped before the [galleries] to judge the shots, interested himself [specially] in a simple game which consisted in throwing a large ball of wood into the open mouth of a fellow painted on a board.

Someone tapped him on the shoulders. It was father Malivoire who cried out: "Hé père Amable, I invite you to drink a dram." And they seated themselves before the table of an [inn] installed in the open air. He took a glass, two glasses, three glasses, and father Amable started to wander through the assembly. His ideas became a little confused. He smiled without knowing why; he [seated himself] before the lotteries, before the wooden horses, and chiefly before the games of massacre. He stayed long, vanished when an amateur beat up the gendarme or the curé, two authorities which he instinctively mistrusted. Then he returned and seated himself at the [inn] and drank a glass of cider to refresh himself. It was late, night was approaching. A neighbor warned him: "You will get in after the *fricot*, father."

Then as he started toward the farm a soft shadow, the mild darkness of spring nights tread softly upon the earth.

When he was before his door, he thought he saw two persons through the lighted window. He stopped, surprised, then he entered and perceived Victor Lecoq seated before the table, in front of a plate full of potatoes, and who supped just in his son's place. Suddenly he turned as if to go away. The night was now dark. Céleste had arisen and called to him: "Come quick, father, here is some good ragout, to celebrate the assembly." Then he obeyed through inertia, and seating himself looked absently at the man, the woman, and the child, and he began to eat slowly as he did every day.

Victor Lecoq seemed to be at home, chatted from time to time with Céleste, took the child on his knees, and kissed it. And Céleste served him anew, refilled his glass, seemed pleased in talking to him. Father Amable followed them with a fixed glance, without hearing what they said. When he had finished supper (and he had hardly eaten, he felt so bothered) he arose, and instead of climbing to the loft as he did every night, he opened the yard door and went out into the country. When he had gone, Céleste, a little weary, asked: "What is he doing?" Victor, indifferent, answered, "Don't bother yourself, he'll come in when he gets tired." So she straightened up, washed the dishes, wiped the table, while the man tranquilly undressed himself. And he slipped into the deep, [hollow] niche where she had slept with Césaire.

The yard door opened. Father Amable reappeared. As soon as he entered he looked on all sides with the appearance of an old dog that scents. He was searching for Victor Lecoq. As he did not see him, he took the candle from the table and approached the somber window where his son had died. In the depths he perceived the man stretched beneath the sheets already asleep. Then the deaf man turned softly, replaced the candle, and went out again in the yard.

Céleste had finished her work, had put her child to bed, straightened everything, and she [waited] for her father-in-law to enter before she went to bed. She stayed seated in a chair, with hands inert, the glance vague. As he did not enter, she murmured with annoyance: "He will make us burn four sous of candle the old fool for nothing!'' Victor replied from the depths: ''He has been out there an hour, you had better see if he is asleep in the bush before the door.'' She said, ''I'll go,'' arose, took the light and went out, making a [shade] of her hands to distinguish in the dark.

She saw nothing before the door, nothing in the bush, not in the pile of manure, where the old man sometimes sat in the warmth. But as she was about to enter, she accidentally raised her eyes toward the big apple tree which [sheltered] the entrance to the farm, and she found suddenly two feet, two man's feet which hung the height of the face.

She uttered fearful cries, ''Victor, Victor, Victor.''

He ran out in his shirt: she could not talk, and holding her hand so as not to see, she pointed to the tree with her extended arm. Not understanding, he took the candle to look, and found in the midst of the leaves lighted far below, father Amable, hanging very high by the neck by means of a [halter] of the stable. A ladder stayed leaning against the trunk of the apple tree.

Victor ran and got a [hook], climbed into the tree, and cut the rope. But the old man was dead, cold. And he stuck out his tongue horribly, with a frightening grimace.

Period Maps

Northern Louisiana 1892. Louisiana Collection, Tulane University Library, New
Orleans, Louisiana 70118.

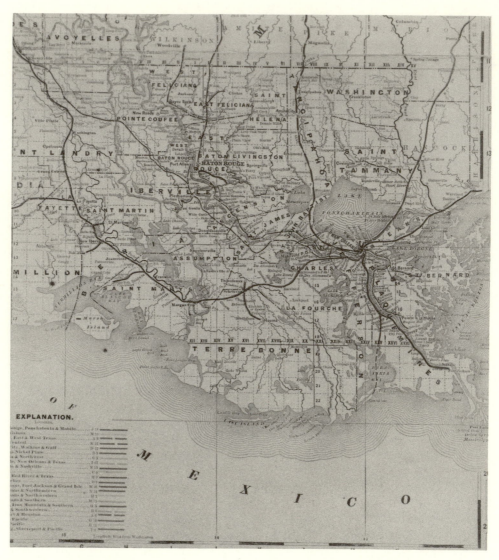

Southern Louisiana 1892. Louisiana Collection, Tulane University Library, New Orleans, Louisiana 70118.

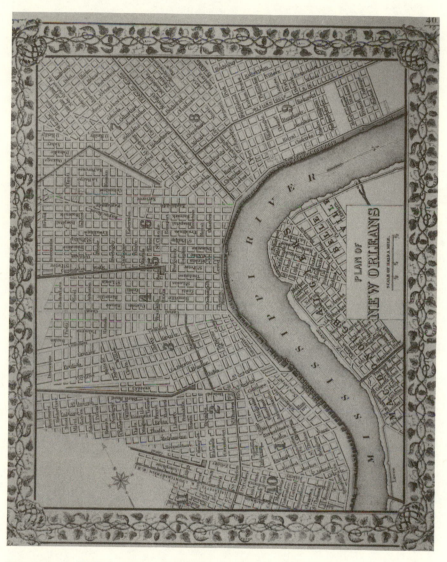

New Orleans 1872. Louisiana Collection, Tulane University Library, New Orleans, Louisiana 70118.

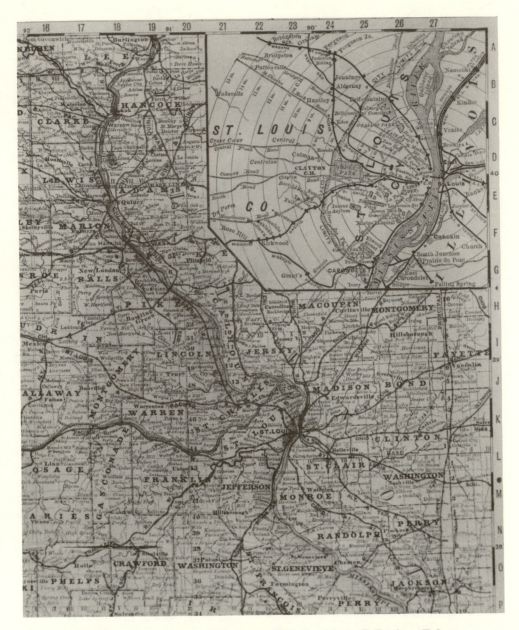

Eastern Missouri with an Inset of St. Louis 1881. Louisiana Collection, Tulane University Library, New Orleans, Louisiana 70118.

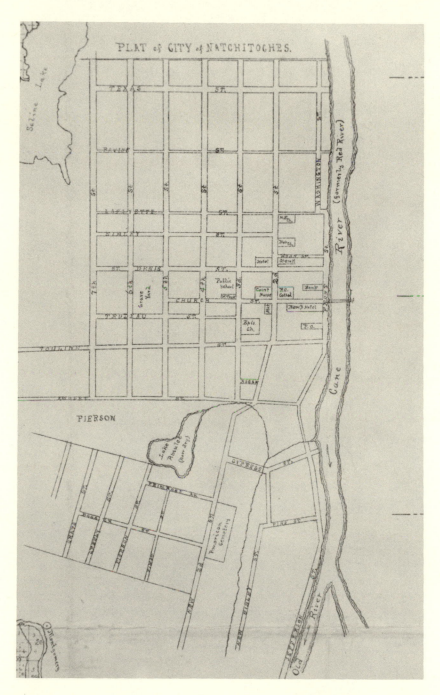

Plat of City of Natchitoches by Charles E. Everett 1902. Published by Florien Giauque. Louisiana Collection, Tulane University Library, New Orleans, Louisiana 70118.

Bibliographic Essay: A Guide to the Literary Works by and about Kate Chopin

᠊᠊

We seem to be between "definitive" book-length bibliographies of Chopin's works and essays about her life and work. Marlene Springer's *Kate Chopin and Edith Wharton: An Annotated Bibliographical Guide to Secondary Materials* (Boston: G. K. Hall, 1976), authoritative for work published between 1890 and 1973, includes scholarly articles, books, reviews and other commentary. A supplement appears in "Kate Chopin: A Reference Guide Updated" (*Resources for American Literary Study*, Autumn 1981). Another brief addition is Barbara C. Gannon's "Kate Chopin, A Secondary Bibliography" (*American Literary Realism*, Spring 1984). The most comprehensive bibliographical listing of primary and secondary sources with annotations can be found in the two bibliographies by Emily Toth in Per Seyersted and her edition of *A Kate Chopin Miscellany* (Natchitoches and Oslo: Northwestern State University Press, 1979), pp. 201–61. The only full, evaluative essay solely devoted to Chopin bibliography is Tonette Bond Inge's "Kate Chopin," in Maurice Duke et al. eds., *American Women Writers: Bibliographical Essays* (Westport, Conn.: Greenwood Press, 1983) pp. 47–69; it is organized chronologically through 1980.

Other listings include the "Selected Bibliography" in Per Seyersted's *Kate Chopin: A Critical Biography* (Baton Rouge: Louisiana State University Press, 1969) pp. 230–37; Richard H. Potter's "Kate Chopin and Her Critics: An Annotated Checklist" (*Missouri Historical Society Bulletin* 26, 1970), which is nearly definitive through 1969; Thomas Bonner, Jr.'s "Kate Chopin: An Annotated Bibliography" (*Bulletin of Bibliography* 32, 1975), which extends and supplements Potter to 1975 and provides editions and reprints. Seyersted's "Kate Chopin (1851–1904)" (*American Literary Realism*, Summer 1970) has a brief

annotated list of primary and secondary sources, including manuscripts, as well
as suggestions for research. The most recent selective bibliography is in Barbara
C. Ewell's *Kate Chopin* (New York: Ungar, 1986); it includes primary and
secondary sources. Most standard reference and bibliographical works on American literature, nineteenth-century American literature, women's literature, and
southern literature include lists of works by and about Chopin. Many anthologies
of American literature, like the *Norton Anthology of American Literature* (New
York: Norton, 1985), also have introductory bibliographies and bibliographical
commentary.

EDITIONS

The two-volume *Complete Works of Kate Chopin*, edited by Per Seyersted
and published by the Louisiana State University Press in 1969, is the standard
collection containing the novels *At Fault, The Awakening*, nearly 100 short
stories, poetry, criticism, and other nonfiction prose. Within the genres the works
appear in the order of composition. The following texts serve as the basis for
The Complete Works: At Fault (St. Louis: Nixon-Jones, 1890); *Bayou Folk*
(Boston: Houghton, Mifflin, 1894); *A Night in Acadie* (Chicago: Way and Williams, 1897); *The Awakening* (Chicago: Herbert C. Stone, 1899); Daniel S.
Rankin, *Kate Chopin and Her Creole Stories* (Philadelphia: University of Penn-
sylvania Press, 1932); Per Seyersted, "Kate Chopin: An Important St. Louis
Writer Reconsidered" (*Missouri Historical Society Bulletin*, January 1963); other
journals and manuscripts. A four-volume collection, which includes *At Fault,
Bayou Folk, A Night in Acadie*, and *The Awakening*, has been published by
Somerset.

Anthologies of selected Chopin works have been proliferating since Louis
Leary's edition, *The Awakening and Other Stories* (New York: Holt, Rinehart
and Winston, 1970). *The Storm and Other Stories by Kate Chopin: with The
Awakening* (Old Westbury, N.Y.: The Feminist Press), edited by Per Seyersted,
followed in 1974. Since then, collections have been published by Signet (1976),
Modern Library (1981), Bantam (1981), Penguin (1984), and Random House
(1984); *The Awakening* is the central text in all of these.

The most important collection of writings by Chopin not included in *The
Complete Works* is *A Kate Chopin Miscellany*, edited by Per Seyersted and
Emily Toth (Natchitoches and Oslo: Northwestern State University Press,
1979). It includes authoritative texts of three stories, a fragment of fiction,
twenty-six poems, two diaries, and all available letters, inscriptions, and
statements as well as a musical composition. Chopin's translations of stories
by Adrien Vely and Guy de Maupassant, five of which have never been
published before, are collected for the first time in *The Kate Chopin Companion*, this volume.

Reprints of Chopin's novels are readily available. Most often reprinted is *The
Awakening*, which had its initial republication by Duffield in 1906. Cyrille

Arnavon's translation *Edna* (Paris: Club Bibliophile de France) in 1953 and Kenneth Eble's Capricorn reprint in 1964 led the rise in attention to this novel in the second half of the twentieth century: Garrett (1970), Avon (1972), Gordon (1974), Norton (with selected criticism, 1977). These separate editions and those collections with *The Awakening* cited above indicate the extraordinary intensity of interest in the novel.

The collection of 23 stories, *Bayou Folk*, was principally responsible for Chopin's literary reputation from its publication in 1894 through much of the third quarter of the twentieth century. Reprints have come from these presses: Gregg (1967), Garrett (1970), and Gordon (1974). *A Night in Acadie*, a collection of 21 stories, was reprinted by Garrett Press (1968), Gordon (1974), and Irvington (1972). Chopin's publication least in demand seems to have been her first novel and first book *At Fault*, which originally was privately printed in 1890. The only reprint (separate and not part of a collection) is a paper one by the Green Street Press (1986).

MANUSCRIPTS AND LETTERS

The Missouri Historical Society in St. Louis is the most important repository of manuscripts, diaries, letters, and other documents written by Kate Chopin. Manuscripts of all fiction published to date and many of the letters published in *A Kate Chopin Miscellany* (Natchitoches and Oslo: Northwestern State University Press, 1979) are part of the holdings which also include letters and statements about Chopin and her works. The following institutions have small numbers of Chopin letters in their collections: Manuscript Division, Library of Congress; the Newberry Library; New York Public Library; Houghton Library, Harvard University; American Antiquarian Society; Barrett Library, University of Virginia; and the West Virginia University Library. The Department of Archives and Manuscripts, Louisiana State University, has memorabilia and documents. For more details on the holdings of institutions and individuals, one should see Per Seyersted's comments on pp. xvii-xviii of the *Miscellany*. Included in the *Miscellany* are Chopin's "Common Place Book, 1867–1870" and "Impressions 1894"; over 25 of her letters; correspondence from family, friends, and publisher; and various personal statements.

BIOGRAPHY

Emily Toth's *Kate Chopin: A Solitary Soul* (New York: Atheneum, 1989) will become the standard biography. Besides more precisely calculated dates and more accurate data than previous biographies, it includes an enormous amount of information that has only recently become available. Since its publication in 1969, Per Seyersted's *Kate Chopin: A Critical Biography* (Baton Rouge: Louisiana State University Press) has offered the most reliable, up-to-date, and comprehensive treatment of the fiction writer's life. Nine photographs accompany the text. It has provided the basis for most of the biographical work since then. Daniel S. Rankin's *Kate Chopin and Her Creole Stories* (Philadelphia: University of Pennsylvania Press, 1932) was the pioneering biography and the only one until Seyersted's. He emphasizes the conventional and traditional aspects of Chopin's life as a bright child, a dutiful wife, a good mother, and a fine local-color writer, all of this in contrast to the emphases in Toth's and Seyersted's later studies showing the tensions between self and society in her life and writings. Rankin's volume with illustrations is still important because of its material based on interviews with those who knew Chopin.

The first really comprehensive and accurate chronology of Chopin opens Barbara C. Ewell's *Kate Chopin* (New York: Ungar, 1986 pp. xi-xvi). Its first chapter, "St. Louis Woman, Louisiana Writer" (pp. 5–27), offers the best brief biography to date, as she draws much of her material from Rankin, Seyersted, and Toth. Biographical articles, several of which are cited in Ewell's book, appear in the *Kate Chopin Newsletter* (later *Regionalism and the Female Imagination*), edited by Toth. Jean Bardot's "Kate Chopin: Her Actual Birthdate" (*Xavier Review*, No. 1, 1987) is definitive.

The only near-contemporary "eyewitness" account of Chopin generally available is her son Felix Chopin's statement in Seyersted's *A Kate Chopin Miscellany* (Natchitoches and Oslo: Northwestern State University Press, 1979 pp. 166–68); the text is based on notes from an interview with him by Charles Van Ravenswaay in 1949. The *Miscellany* also includes 14 photographs and early accounts of Chopin by Sue V. Moore (1894), William Schuyler (1894), and Alexander N. DeMenil (1920, revised from a 1904 article).

Among the biographical reference books, Sara DeSaussure Davis's essay in the *Dictionary of American Literary Biography: American Realists and Naturalists*, Vol. 12 (1982), and Cynthia Griffin Wolff's essay in *American Writers: A Collection of Literary Biographies*, Supplement 1 (1979), offer the most complete commentaries on Chopin. Other books with essays on Chopin are *American Writers to 1900* (Chicago: St. James Press, 1983), *American Writers* (New York: Ungar, 1979), *Notable American Women 1607–1950: A Biographical Dictionary*, Volume 1 (Cambridge: Harvard University Press, Belknap Press, 1971), and *Southern Writers: A Biographical Dictionary* (Baton Rouge: Louisiana State University Press, 1979).

CRITICISM

General Estimates

The best and most comprehensive volume devoted to the fiction is Barbara C. Ewell's *Kate Chopin* (New York: Ungar, 1986). Her study focuses "on the work of Kate Chopin in its entirety, so that her famous novel [*The Awakening*] appears as an inescapable climax, but not the sum of her achievement as a writer." The essay in its organization observes the integrity of her two collections of stories, one planned collection, and two novels, with attention also being directed to the poems and fiction written shortly before Chopin's death. Robert Arner's book-length study "Kate Chopin," in *Louisiana Studies* (Spring 1975), has a similar organization; he focuses on her use of topography as imagery related to psychological themes as well as other devices associated with the symbolic romance. His study is marked by close and careful analyses of the texts—the only book-length study solely devoted to criticism of the text. Per Seyersted's *Kate Chopin: A Critical Biography* (Baton Rouge: Louisiana State University Press, 1969) has inspired much of the writing about Chopin over the last 18 years. It remains a key text in its survey of her writings in the context of a writer known for local realism who transcends its bonds and makes "female realism" a key element of her work. The earliest book to address Chopin's writings is Daniel S. Rankin's *Kate Chopin and Her Creole Stories* (Philadelphia: University of Pennsylvania Press, 1932), which limits Chopin's work to the classification of local color and fails to respond adequately to the artistry in *The Awakening*. Its criticism has been completely superceded by Ewell's, Arner's, and Seyersted's book-length studies and retains value mostly for its historical record. Another study has been published, Peggy Skaggs's *Kate Chopin* (Twayne United States Author Series). It has chapters introducing the collections of short fiction and the novels.

A number of essays in journals and books that address the canon continue to be helpful. Seyersted's "Kate Chopin: An Important St. Louis Writer Reconsidered" (*Missouri Historical Society Bulletin*, January 1963) emphasizes her exploration of women and passion; his introduction to *The Storm and Other Stories by Kate Chopin: with The Awakening* (Old Westbury, N.Y.: The Feminist Press, 1974) provides a fine overview of her writings and critical reputation. Anne Goodwyn Jones's *Tomorrow Is Another Day: The Woman Writer in the South, 1859–1936* (Baton Rouge: Louisiana State University Press, 1981) uses psychological, social and feminist approaches with selective attention to the stories and emphasis on *The Awakening*. Larzer Ziff in his *The American 1890s* (New York: Viking, 1966) traces Chopin's progress toward *The Awakening* and her development of the theme of female rebellion. Anne Rowe's essay on Chopin in *The History of Southern Literature* (Baton Rouge: Louisiana State University Press, 1985) offers a concise and competent estimate of her "small but vital legacy for twentieth-century literature." Barbara Solomon's introduction to *The Awakening and Selected Stories* (New York: Signet, 1976) links Chopin's stories and novels as she emphasizes her development as a writer. Thomas Bonner, Jr., calls attention to the modern temper of her works in "Kate Chopin: Tradition and the Moment," in *Southern Literature in Transition: Heritage and Promise*, ed. Phillip Castille and William Osborne (Memphis State University Press, 1983). Two essays are especially helpful in delineating the romantic and symbolic aspects: Winifred Fluck's "Tentative Transgressions: Kate Chopin's Fiction as a Mode of Symbolic Action" (*Studies in American Fiction*, Autumn 1982), and Patricia Hopkins Lattin's "The Search for Self in Kate Chopin's Fiction: Simple Versus Complex Vision" (*Southern Studies*, Summer 1982).

Special Topics and Themes

The most often cited aspect of critical interest in Chopin's fiction over the years has been in its use of and development of characters. Patricia Hopkins Lattin's "Kate Chopin's Repeating Characters" (*Mississippi Quarterly*, Winter 1979–80) helpfully charts and analyzes the reappearance of characters in the stories and novels, and Joyce Dyer in "Gouvernail, Kate Chopin's Sensitive Bachelor" (*Southern Literary Journal*, Fall 1981) focuses on this character who appears in "Athénaïse," "A Respectable Woman," and *The Awakening*. Chopin's female characters have been an important consideration, especially in their social roles as discussed in Marie Fletcher's "The Southern Woman in the Fiction of Kate Chopin" (*Louisiana History*, Spring 1976), but her characterization of men has also been noted in Dyer's "Kate Chopin's Sleeping Bruties" (*Markham Review*, Fall 1980-Winter 1981). Chopin's treatment of ethnic characters, especially Creoles and blacks is the subject of a section of Merrill Skagg's very sound *The Folk of Southern Fiction* (Athens: University of Georgia Press, 1972). Blacks also receive attention from Richard Potter in "Negroes in the Fiction of Kate Chopin" (*Louisiana History*, Winter 1971). Thomas Bonner, Jr., comments on the characterization of Texans in "Accommodations and Conflict: French Louisiana and Anglo-Saxon Texas in the Fiction of Kate Chopin." (*Louisiana Literature*, Spring 1984), as do J. C. Dyer and R. E. Monroe in "Texas and Texans in the Fiction of Kate Chopin" (*Western American Literature*, Spring 1985).

Feminist criticism has been integral to the rise in attention to Chopin's writings. While there are a number of approaches to specific works, there are four articles that place Chopin's fiction well within this context: Joan Zlotnick's "A Woman's Will: Kate Chopin on Selfhood, Wifehood, and Motherhood" (*Markham Review*, October 1968); Emily Toth's "The Independent Woman and 'Free' Love" (*Massachusetts Review*, Autumn 1975); Patricia Hopkins Lattin's "Childbirth and Motherhood in Kate Chopin's Fiction" (*Regionalism and the Female Imagination*, Spring 1978), and Gina M. Burchard's "Kate Chopin's Problematical Womanliness: The Frontier of American Feminism" *Journal of the American Studies Association of Texas*, 1984).

Religion with its spiritual, cultural, and societal effects forms a motif from Chopin's earliest to latest efforts. Elmo Howell's "Kate Chopin and the Pull of Faith: A Note on 'Lilacs' " (*Southern Studies*, Spring 1979) and Thomas Bonner, Jr.'s "Christianity and Catholicism in the Fiction of Kate Chopin" (*Southern Quarterly*, Winter 1982) offer insight into the tensions with spiritual and institutional bases that underlie the presence of disinterested points of view in moral questions as well as her use of liturgical imagery and the Christian tradition.

An area of increased interest is Chopin's use of humor. Thomas Bonner, Jr.'s essay on this subject in the supplement to the *Encyclopedia of American Humorists* (New York: Garland, 1988) surveys this element of her work.

At Fault

Aside from the relevant chapters in Barbara C. Ewell's *Kate Chopin* (New York: Ungar, 1986), Per Seyersted's *Kate Chopin: A Critical Biography* (Baton Rouge: Louisiana State University Press, 1969), and Robert Arner's essay (*Louisiana Studies*, Spring 1975), a useful overall discussion is Lewis Leary's "Kate Chopin's Other Novel" (*Southern Literary Journal*, August 1968), despite the detailed plot summary necessary for a then-obscure work. Donald A. Ringe's "Cane River World: Kate Chopin's *At Fault* and Related Stories" (*Studies in American Fiction*, Autumn 1975) establishes the historical setting and period with respect to the clash of agricultural and industrial cultures. Philip Tapley's "Kate Chopin's Sawmill: Technology and Change in *At Fault*," in *Proceedings of the 1985 Red River Symposium*, ed. Norman A. Dolch and Karen Douglas (Shreveport: Louisiana State University, 1986), extends the discussion. Emily Toth's "St. Louis and the Fiction of Kate Chopin" (*Missouri Historical Society Bulletin*, October 1975) elaborates on the role of Chopin's native city as an image of the modern urban world in *At Fault* (as well as in other stories set there). Robert Arner studies the Louisiana setting of the novel in "Landscape Symbolism in Kate Chopin's *At Fault*" (*Louisiana Studies*, Fall 1970); he observes the landscape as a place uniting two love stories and as the meeting ground for converging problems of North and South, past and present. Bernard J. Koloski's "The Structure of Kate Chopin's *At Fault*" (*Studies in American Fiction*, Autumn 1975) considers the strategy of narrative design to be a "skillfully contrived series of contrasts." Thomas Bonner, Jr.'s "Kate Chopin's *At Fault* and *The Awakening*: A Study in Structure" (*Markham Review*, Fall 1977) comments on the conventional narrative devices of *At Fault* and analyzes its resultant structure. William Warnken's "Fire, Light, and Darkness in Kate Chopin's *At Fault*" (*Kate Chopin Newsletter*, Fall 1975) establishes this pattern of imagery as a consistently unifying theme and structure. The earliest useful comment on *At Fault* was by an anonymous reviewer in *Fashion and Fancy* (December 1890) who admired the realism of setting and character, the latter with some qualification, but who recognized "unmistakable indications of strength" in the narrative.

The Awakening

In contrast to its original reception and the low critical opinion of it during the first 50 years of this century, *The Awakening* in recent years has been the subject of both lavish praise and close critical inquiry. Barbara C. Ewell's *Kate Chopin* (New York: Ungar, 1986), Per Seyersted's *Kate Chopin: A Critical Biography* (Baton Rouge: Louisiana State University Press, 1969), and Robert Arner's book-length study (*Louisiana Studies*, Spring 1975) have substantial chapters on the novel. Other comprehensive considerations include Kenneth Eble's "A Forgotten Novel: Kate Chopin's *The Awakening*" (*Western Humanities Review*, Summer

1956), which appears in slightly revised form as the introduction to the reprint of the novel by Capricorn in 1964. Still helpful is Robert Cantwell's *"The Awakening* by Kate Chopin" (*Georgia Review*, Winter 1956). George Arms offers a useful evaluation in "Kate Chopin's *The Awakening* in the Perspective of Her Literary Career," in *Essays in American Literature in Honor of J. B. Hubbell*, ed. Clarence Gohdes (Durham, N. C.: Duke University Press, 1967); he focuses on the novel's ironic method achieved through a pattern of oppositions. Jerome Klinkowitz's *The Practice of Fiction in American Writers from Hawthorne to the Present* (Ames: Iowa State University Press, 1980) places the novel in the American literary tradition. The most accessible source for a compendium of critical and contextual material on *The Awakening* is Margaret Culley's edition *Kate Chopin, The Awakening: An Authoritative Text, Contexts, Criticism* (New York: Norton, 1976); it includes comments on women's subjects contemporaneous with the novel, early reviews, and selections from previously published essays by Pollard, Rankin, Eble, Fletcher, Ziff, Arms, Seyersted, Spangler, May, Leary, Chametzky, Ringe, and Wolff; as well as fresh work by Culley, "Edna Pontellier: A Solitary Soul," and by Suzanne Wolkenfeld, "Edna's Suicide: The Problem of the One and the Many." An especially valuable work for teachers is Bernard Koloski's edition *Approaches to Teaching Kate Chopin's The Awakening* (New York: Modern Language Association, 1988); it places the novel in the context of American literature, southern literature, and women's studies; presents relevant cultural and biographical history; examines themes, language, style, and reader response; and provides a bibliography and materials list.

Several essays discuss *The Awakening* from the perspective of setting and cultural environment. John R. May's long and important "Local Color in *The Awakening*" (*Southern Review*, Autumn 1970) links the setting closely with the development of the protagonist. Joyce Coyne Dyer's "Lafcadio Hearn's *Chita* and Kate Chopin's *The Awakening*: Two Naturalistic Tales of the Gulf Islands" (*Southern Studies*, Winter 1984) explores Chopin's way of seeing the environment and its relation to the naturalistic elements in the fiction. Suzanne W. Jones in "Place, Perception, and Identity" (*Southern Quarterly*, Winter 1987) sees the urban and island settings as ways of viewing the Victorian woman in the face of change. Richard P. Adams addresses the cultural environment—Creole— in contrast with the Protestant character of other works in "Southern Literature in the 1890's (*Mississippi Quarterly*, Fall 1968). Lawrence Thornton in *"The Awakening*: A Political Romance" (*American Literature*, March 1980) studies Edna Pontellier's being affected by politics in the Creole society of Louisiana. Priscilla Leder's "An American Dilemma: Cultural Conflict in Kate Chopin's *The Awakening*" (*Southern Studies*, Spring 1983) compares Edna's relation to Creole society with Cooper's Natty Bumpo and the Indians and Melville's Tommo (*Typee*) and the Polynesians.

Studies of characters have concentrated on females. Peggy Skaggs's "Three Tragic Figures in Kate Chopin's *The Awakening*" (*Louisiana Studies*, Winter

1974) treats Edna Pontellier, Adèle Ratignolle, and Mademoiselle Reisz structurally and thematically. Kathleen Margaret Lant's "Siren of Grand Isle: Adèle's Role in *The Awakening*" (*Southern Studies*, Summer 1984) discusses her initiating Edna's quest for the self. Charles M. Mayer makes helpful distinctions between James's and Chopin's approaches to the role of choice and freedom in "Isabel Archer [*Portrait of a Lady*], Edna Pontellier, and the Romantic Self" (*Research Studies*, June 1979). An introductory view of Chopin's development of male characters can be found in Anna-Lise Paulsen's "The Masculine Dilemma in Kate Chopin's Fiction" (*Southern Studies*, Winter 1979).

A number of essays address narrative technique, structure, and composition. Ruth Sullivan and Stewart Smith's "Narrative Stance in Kate Chopin's *The Awakening*" (*Studies in American Fiction*, Spring 1973) emphasizes point of view as a strength; Jane P. Tompkin's "*The Awakening*: An Evaluation" (*Feminist Studies*, Spring-Summer 1976) sees Chopin's degree of distance as a weakness. Bernice Larson Webb charts the structure in "Four Points of Equilibrium in *The Awakening*" (*South Central Bulletin*, Winter 1982). Robert S. Levine comments on the function of sleep and daily activities in "Circadian Rhythms and Rebellion in Kate Chopin's *The Awakening*" (*Studies in American Fiction*, Spring 1982). The ending of the novel has been the subject of pointed discussion. George M. Spangler in "Kate Chopin's *The Awakening*: A Partial Dissent" (*Novel*, Spring 1970) sees the ending as contrived. However, Kenneth M. Rosen in "Kate Chopin's *The Awakening*: Ambiguity as Art" (*Journal of American Studies*, August 1971) sees the ambiguities of the close as consonant with the questions raised by the narrative. Marina L. Roscher views the suicide as appropriately poetic in "The Suicide of Edna Pontellier: The Ambiguous Ending?" (*Southern Studies*, Fall 1984). Paula Treichler's "The Construction of Ambiguity in *The Awakening*: A Linguistic Analysis," in *Women and Language in Literature and Society*, ed. Sally McConnel-Ginet et al. (New York: Praeger, 1980) poses some new questions about the relation of language and structure.

Some of the essays addressing *The Awakening* touch on the imagery as related to structure or theme more directly. Donald A. Ringe's "Romantic Imagery in Kate Chopin's *The Awakening*" (*American Literature*, January 1972) emphasizes the sleep-walking image in the context of Edna's self-discovery. Lewis Leary in "Kate Chopin and Walt Whitman" (*Walt Whitman Review*, December 1970) comments on the sea imagery; his introduction to *The Awakening and Other Stories* (New York: Holt, Rinehart and Winston, 1970) discusses the relation of the patterns of imagery to the narrative. Ottavio M. Casale's "Beyond Sex: The Dark Romanticism of Kate Chopin's *The Awakening*" (*Ball State University Forum*, Winter 1978) links the novel closer to Hawthorne and Melville. Robert White relates the indoors and outdoors to the theme of repression and freedom in "Inner and Outer Space in *The Awakening*" (*Mosaic*, Winter 1974). And Robert Collins observes both realism and romanticism through the images in "The Dismantling of Edna Pontellier: Garment Imagery in Chopin's *The Awakening*" (*Southern Studies*, Summer 1984).

Closely allied to the essays exploring images and romantic elements are those examining the theme of awakening itself. Nancy Walker's "Feminist or Naturalist: The Social Context of Kate Chopin's *The Awakening*" (*Southern Quarterly*, Winter 1979) focuses on Edna's growing awareness of the senses. Two essays place limitations on the theme of the expanding self: Otis B. Wheeler's "The Five Awakenings of Edna Pontellier" (*Southern Review*, January 1975) and James H. Justus's "The Unawakening of Edna Pontellier" (*Southern Literary Journal*, Spring 1978).

The most significant essay using psychological approaches is Cynthia G. Wolff's often-cited "Thanatos and Eros: Kate Chopin's *The Awakening*" (*American Quarterly*, October 1973), in which she sees the conflicts as being more internal than societal. Elizabeth Fox-Genovese in "Kate Chopin's Awakening" (*Southern Studies*, Fall 1979) uses a psychoanalytical method identifying Edna with the author herself. A portion of Cyrille Arnavon's introduction to *Edna* (Paris: Club Bibliophile de France, 1952) sees analogies between these figures as well. The translation appears in *A Kate Chopin Miscellany* (Natchitoches and Oslo: Northwestern State University Press, 1979).

Substantial mythic approaches have recently become available. Rosemary F. Franklin's "*The Awakening* and the Failure of Psyche" (*American Literature*, December 1984) draws a close parallel between Edna and Psyche in developing a theme of failure. Wayne Batten's "Illusion and Archetype: The Curious Story of Edna Pontellier" (*Southern Literary Journal*, Fall 1985) uses the same myth to suggest Edna's struggling through illusion. Sandra M. Gilbert's "The Second Coming of Aphrodite: Kate Chopin's Fantasy of Desire" (*Kenyon Review*, Summer 1983) presents Edna's desire for sexual independence in a classical context.

Feminist criticism has brought a whole new approach to the reading of *The Awakening*. Emily Toth's "*The Awakening* as Feminist Criticism" (*Louisiana Studies*, Fall 1976) places the novel in that literary tradition as a concrete and particular extension. In "The Domestic Orientation of American Novels, 1893–1918" (*American Literary Realism*, Spring 1980), Joseph L. Candela, Jr., places *The Awakening* in its contemporaneous social and political period with rewarding results. Patricia M. Spacks in *The Female Imagination* (New York: Knopf, 1975) addresses Edna's responsibility to sort out reality from fantasy. Gladys W. Milliner's "The Tragic Imperative: *The Awakening* and *The Bell Jar* [by Sylvia Plath]" (*Mary Wollstonecraft Newsletter*, December 1973) explores the biological and social entrapment affecting the principal characters and their authors. Toth's "Timely and Timeless: The Treatment of Time in *The Awakening* and *Sister Carrie* [by Theodore Dreiser]" (*Southern Studies*, Fall 1977) distinguishes between feminine and masculine senses of chronometry. Judith Fryer, in *The Faces of Eve: Women in the Nineteenth Century American Novel* (New York: Oxford University Press, 1976), focuses on Edna in the context of other American heroines and emphasizes her movement toward freedom. Priscilla Allen's "Old Critics and New: The Treatment of Chopin's *The Awakening*," in *The Authority of Experience: Essays in Feminist Criticism*, ed. Arlyn Diamond and Lee R.

Edwards (Amherst: University of Massachusetts Press, 1977), charges many critics with not seeing Edna as a whole person and simply being distracted by her sexual aspect.

Spiritual development and moral distinctions receive attention in these works: Carol P. Christ's *Diving Deep and Surfacing: Women Writers on Spiritual Quest* (Boston: Beacon Press, 1980) and Allen F. Stein's "Kate Chopin's *The Awakening* and the Limits of Moral Judgment," in *A Fair Day in the Affections: Literary Essays in Honor of Robert B. White, Jr.*, ed. Jack M. Durant and M. Thomas Inge (Raleigh, N.C.: Winston, 1980).

In the area of source studies, three essays examine French contributions. Elaine Jasenas's "The French Influence in Kate Chopin's *The Awakening*" (*Nineteenth Century Fiction Studies*, Spring 1976) makes connections with Mallarme, de Maupassant, Baudelaire, and Flaubert. An essay complementing this one is Pamela Gaude's "A Comparative Study of Kate Chopin's *The Awakening* and Guy de Maupassant's *Une Vie*" (*Revue de Louisiane / Louisiana Review*, Winter 1975). Nancy E. Roger's "Echoes of George Sand in Kate Chopin" (*Revue de Littérature Comparée*, January-March 1983) is helpful with this as well as with her other fiction. In addition to Leary's relating Chopin to Whitman (cited earlier) Candela does so in "Walt Whitman and Kate Chopin: A Further Connection" (*Walt Whitman Review*, December 1978). Bernard Koloski comments on the influence of "A Cameo" in "The Swinburne Lines in *The Awakening*" (*American Literature*, January 1974). William Warnken connects Edna's duty to herself with Nora in "Kate Chopin and Henrik Ibsen: A Study of *The Awakening* and *A Doll's House*" (*Massachusetts Studies in English*, Autumn 1974-Winter 1975).

Of interest are John R. May's "Louisiana Writers in Film" (*Southern Quarterly*, Fall 1984), which comments on recent productions of *The Awakening*; and Robert McIlvaine's "Two Awakenings: Edna Pontellier and Helena Ritchie" (*Regionalism and the Female Imagination*, Winter 1979), which suggests that Margaret Deland's novel *The Awakening of Helena Ritchie* (1906) is a response to Chopin's novel. Robert Stone's novel *Children of Light* (New York: Knopf, 1986) makes use of the filming of *The Awakening* as a structural and thematic element.

Among the reviews of the novel, most of which find fault with the work on an extratextual basis, C. L. Deyo's, in the May 20, 1899 edition of the St. Louis *Post-Dispatch* (reprinted in Culley) offered contemporary readers the best look at *The Awakening* during that time; the criticism is still viable and concludes with this sentence: "The integrity of its art is that of well-knit individuality at one with itself, with nothing superfluous to weaken the impression of a perfect whole."

The Stories

The major studies of the short fiction continue to be Barbara Ewell's *Kate Chopin* (New York: Ungar, 1986), Per Seyersted's *Kate Chopin: A Critical Biography*

(Baton Rouge: Louisiana State University Press, 1969), and Robert Arner's book-length study in the special issue of *Louisiana Studies* (Spring 1975). Ewell and Arner devote separate chapters to the published collections *Bayou Folk* (1894) and *A Night in Acadie* (1897) as well as to the proposed collection of "A Vocation and a Voice." Thomas Bonner Jr.'s "Bayou Folk Revisited" (*New Laurel Review*, Fall 1977) examines and surveys the fictional elements in the stories from this volume.

The setting and environment of the stories figure in several studies. Emily Toth's "St. Louis and the Fiction of Kate Chopin" (*Missouri Historical Society Bulletin*, October 1975) and Thomas Bonner, Jr.'s "Kate Chopin's European Consciousness" (*American Literary Realism*, Summer 1975) address the St. Louis and European settings respectively. Discussion of the Louisiana setting is available in Donald A. Ringe's "Cane River World: Kate Chopin's *At Fault* and Related Stories" (*Studies in American Fiction*, Autumn 1975) and Marcia Gaudet's "Kate Chopin and the Lore of Cane River's Creoles of Color." (*Xavier Review*, No. 1, 1986).

Joyce Coyne Dyer studies the male characters in "Azélie," "At Chênière Caminada," and "A Vocation and a Voice" in "Kate Chopin's Sleeping Bru-ties" (*Markham Review*, Fall 1980-Winter 1981) and in "The Restive Brute: the Symbolic Presentation of Repression and Sublimation in Kate Chopin's 'Fedora' " (*Studies in Short Fiction*, Summer 1981). Peggy Skaggs's "The Man-Instinct of Possession: A Persistent Theme in Kate Chopin's Stories" (*Lou-isiana Studies*, Fall 1975) explores the male role in women's development of their identities, and she comments on the male point of view in "The Boy's Quest in Kate Chopin's 'A Vocation and a Voice' " (*American Literature*, May 1979).

Narrative technique and its related elements have received most of the critical attention thus far. Bert Bender's "Kate Chopin's Lyrical Short Stories" (*Studies in Short Fiction*, Summer 1974) explores transcendent elements beyond local color in "A Vocation and a Voice," "An Idle Fellow," "Athénaïse," "The Story of An Hour," and "The Storm." James E. Rocks's "Kate Chopin's Ironic Vision" (*Revue de Louisiane / Louisiana Review*, Winter 1972) shows how Chopin achieves narrative objectivity. An extension and further elaboration are Joyce Coyne Dyer's "Techniques of Distancing in the Fiction of Kate Chopin" (*Southern Studies*, Spring 1985) and "Epiphanies Through Nature in the Stories of Kate Chopin" (*University of Dayton Review*, Winter 1983–1984). Dyer's "Night Images in the Work of Kate Chopin" (*American Literary Realism*, Autumn 1981) emphasizes romantic elements as agents of mystery and memory. Bernice Larson Webb's "The Circular Structure of Kate Chopin's Life and Writing" (*New Laurel Review*, Fall 1986) comments on "Charlie," "Athén-aïse," and "Nég Créol."

"Désirée's Baby," for years the most available of Chopin's stories, continues to merit attention, especially with regard to its craft. Robert Arner's "Pride and Prejudice: Kate Chopin's 'Désirée's Baby' " (*Mississippi Quarterly*, Spring

1972) focuses on image patterns supporting the ironic turn of events. Cynthia Griffin Wolff's "Kate Chopin and the Fiction of Limits: 'Désirée's Baby' " (*Southern Literary Journal*, Spring 1978) examines her use of physical boundaries to suggest psychological ones. And Emily Toth's "Kate Chopin and Literary Convention: 'Désirée's Baby' " (*Southern Studies*, Summer 1981) focuses on the use of the "Tragic Octaroon."

Susan Lohafer offers a substantial examination of "Athénaïse" in *Coming to Terms with the Short Story* (Baton Rouge: Louisiana State University Press, 1983). Robert Arner's "Kate Chopin's Realism: 'At the 'Cadian Ball' and 'The Storm' " (*Markham Review*, February 1970) traces her progress from local color to mainstream realism. And in "Characterization and the Colloquial Style in Kate Chopin's 'Vagabonds' " (*Markham Review*, May 1971), Arner studies her use of dialogue and voice in this narrative written between the previous two stories. Elaine Gardiner's " 'Ripe Figs': Kate Chopin in Miniature" (*Modern Fiction Studies*, Autumn 1982) comments on Chopin's use of contrasting patterns and nature imagery. Anne Rowe's "A Note on Kate Chopin's 'Beyond the Bayou' " (*Kate Chopin Newsletter*, Fall 1975) observes a symbolic use of setting. Coyne's "A Note on Kate Chopin's 'The White Eagle' " (*Arlington Quarterly*, Summer 1984) treats the symbolic use of the eagle. The spare story that inspired the film *The Joy That Kills* is the subject of Madonne M. Miner's "Veiled Hints: An Affective Stylist's Reading of Kate Chopin's 'Story of an Hour' " (*Markham Review*, Winter 1982).

Source studies include Pamela Gaude's "Kate Chopin's 'The Storm': A Story of Maupassant's Influence" (*Kate Chopin Newsletter*, Fall 1975), which links the story to "Marroca" and "Moonlight." In the same issue Emily Toth's "The Cult of Domesticity and 'A Sentimental Soul' " suggests a parallel to the "life-illusion" technique of Ibsen. Susan Wolstenhome makes concrete connections to Ibsen and Wagner in "Kate Chopin's Sources for 'Mrs. Mobry's Reason' " (*American Literature*, January 1980).

Two reviews of Chopin's short-story collections remain helpful. Sue V. Moore (probable author) reviewed *Bayou Folk* in *St. Louis Life* (June 9, 1894; reprinted in *A Kate Chopin Miscellany*); she included selected items from other reviews. The commentary on *A Night in Acadie*, which appeared in the *St. Louis Mirror* (November 25, 1897), is especially interesting for its observations about "Athénaïse."

About the Author

THOMAS BONNER, JR., Professor of English at Xavier University of Louisiana, has written *William Faulkner: The William B. Wisdom Collection*. He has contributed essays to *Teaching Chopin's The Awakening, The History of Southern Literature, Southern Writers: A Biographical Dictionary*, and other books on Southern literature and culture. His essays on Kate Chopin have appeared in journals such as *American Literary Realism* since 1975.